Bilingual
VISUAL
dictionary

Bilingual VISUAL dictionary

Penguin
Random
House

DK LONDON
Senior Editor Angela Wilkes
Editors Hazel Eriksson, Stuart Neilson
Designers Renata Latipova, Stephen Bere
Project Manager Christine Stroyan
Jacket Editor Claire Gell
Jacket Design Development Manager Sophia MTT
Preproduction Producer Andy Hillard
Senior Producer Alex Bell
Managing Art Editor Christine Keilty
Art Director Karen Self
Associate Publisher Liz Wheeler
Publishing Director Jonathan Metcalf

DK INDIA
Editor Arpita Dasgupta
Assistant Editor Priyanjali Narain
Art Editor Yashashvi Choudhary
DTP Designers Jaypal Chauhan Singh, Anita Yadav
Jacket Designer Tanya Mehrotra
Jackets Editorial Coordinator Priyanka Sharma
Preproduction Manager Balwant Singh
Production Manager Pankaj Sharma

Designed for Dorling Kindersley by WaltonCreative.com
Art Editor Colin Walton, assisted by Tracy Musson
Designers Peter Radcliffe, Earl Neish, Ann Cannings
Picture Research Marissa Keating

Language content for Dorling Kindersley by
First Edition Translations Ltd, Cambridge, UK
Translators: Elena Edwards, Milana Michalevic
and Tatsiana Artsiusheuskaya

This American Edition, 2019
First American Edition, 2016
Published in the United States by DK Publishing
1745 Broadway, 20th Floor, New York, NY 10019

A catalog record for this book is available from the
Library of Congress.
ISBN: 978-1-4654-6917-5

DK books are available at special discounts when purchased in bulk
for sales promotions, premiums, fund-raising, or educational use.
For details, contact: DK Publishing Special Markets,
1745 Broadway, 20th Floor, New York, NY 10019
SpecialSales@dk.com

Printed and bound in China

For the curious
www.dk.com

содержание
soderzhaniye
contents

42

146

252

9

о словаре
o slovare
about the dictionary

9

как пользоваться
словарем
kak pol'zovatsa
slovaryom
how to use this book

10

люди
lyudi
people

28

внешность
vneshnost'
appearance

56

дом
dom
home

92

службы
sluzhby
services

102

покупки
pokupki
shopping

116

продукты питания
produkti pitaniya
food

160

учёба
uchyoba
study

170

работа
rabota
work

192

транспорт
transport
transportation

218

спорт
sport
sports

278

окружающая среда
okruzhayushchaya
sreda
environment

302

справка
spravka
reference

324

указатель
ukazatel'
indexes

360

благодарности
blagodarnosti
acknowledgments

СОДЕРЖАНИЕ SODERZHANIYE • CONTENTS

русский ruskiy • english

о словаре

Доказано, что использование изображений способствует пониманию и запоминанию информации. Данный принцип был положен в основу создания этого красочно иллюстрированного англо-русского словаря, представляющего широкий спектр полезной актуальной лексики.

В словаре подробно отражено большинство аспектов повседневной жизни, от ресторана до спортзала, от дома до работы, от космоса до животного мира. Вы также найдете дополнительные слова и выражения для использования в беседе и расширения своего словарного запаса.

Некоторые замечания
Русская лексика в словаре представлена в кириллическом написании и сопровождается системой упрощенной транслитерации. При чтении транслитерации ставьте ударение на подчеркнутые гласные буквы в словах. Записи представлены в одном и том же порядке—на русском, транслитерация, английский эквивалент:

лук	**дети**
luk	deti
onion	**children**

У глаголов после английского слова в скобках указано **(v)**, например: **тренироваться** trenirovat'sya | **train (v)**

Для каждого из языков в конце книги приводится алфавитный указатель. Вы можете найти там слово на английском или русском языках и узнать номер(а) страниц(ы), на которой или на которых имеется данное слово. Род обозначен следую-щими сокращениями:

m = мужской
f = женский
n = средний

как пользоваться словарем

Для каких целей вы бы ни изучали язык – для бизнес-контактов, удовольствия или при подготовке к отпуску за рубежом, данный словарь станет ценным инструментом обучения, которым вы можете пользоваться различными способами.

Активные методы обучения
Находясь дома, на работе или в университете, просмотрите страницы словаря, относящиеся к соответствующей обстановке. Затем закройте книгу, оглянитесь вокруг и проверьте, сколько предметов или деталей обстановки вы можете назвать.
• Изготовьте флеш-карточки с английским текстом с одной стороны и русским переводом с другой. Носите их с собой ипроверяйте свои знания, тасуя карточки перед каждой проверкой.
• Напишите рассказ или диалог, используя как можно больше слов и выражений с определенной страницы. Это поможет вам сохранить словарный запас и запомнить правильное написание. Хотите усовершенствовать свои знания и перейти к созданию более длинных текстов? Начинайте с предложений из 2-3 слов.
• Если у вас хорошая зрительная память, попробуйте нарисовать изображения предметов из книги на листе бумаги, а затем подпишите картинки по памяти.
• Набравшись уверенности, перейдите к работе с указателем. Выберите из него слова и проверьте, знаете ли вы их значение, перед тем как обратиться к соответствующей странице и проверить себя.

Бесплатное аудиоприложение

это Аудио-приложение содержит все слова и фразы из книги, которые используются в русском и английском языках, что увеличить ваш словарные запаз и поможет улучшить произношение.

Как пользоваться аудиоприложением

• Найдите «DK Visual Dictionary» и загрузите бесплатное приложение на свой смартфон или планшет из выбранного магазина приложений.
• Откройте приложение и сканируйте штрих-код (или введите ISBN), чтобы разблокировать визуальный словарь в библиотеке.
• Загрузите аудиофайлы для вашей книги.
• Введите номер страницы, затем прокрутите вверх и вниз по списку, чтобы найти слово или фразу. Слова можно заказать по алфавитному порядку, на русском или английском.
• Нажмите на слово чтобы услышать произношение.
• Проведите пальцем по экрану влево или вправо, чтобы посмотреть предыдущую или следующую страницу.
• Добавьте слова к вашей страничке "Избранное".

русский ru<u>s</u>kiy • **english**

about the dictionary

Using pictures is proven to aid understanding and the retention of information. Working on this principle, this highly-illustrated English–Russian bilingual dictionary presents a large range of useful current vocabulary.

The dictionary covers most aspects of the everyday world in detail, from the restaurant to the gym, the home to the workplace, outer space to the animal kingdom. You will also find additional words and phrases for conversational use and for extending your vocabulary.

This is an essential reference tool for anyone interested in languages—practical, stimulating, and easy-to-use.

A few things to note
The Russian in the dictionary is in the Cyrillic alphabet.

The pronunciation for the Russian words follows a systematic coding of transliterations that English speakers should find easy to follow. When reading the transliteration, stress the vowel that is underlined. The entries are always given in the same order—Russian, transliteration, then English—for example:

лук	дети
luk	deti
onion	**children**

Verbs are indicated by a **(v)** after the English, for example:
тренироваться trenirovat'sya | **train (v)**

Each language also has its own index at the back of the book. Here you can look up a word in either English or Russian and be referred to the page number(s) where it appears. The gender is shown using the following abbreviations: .

m = masculine
f = feminine
n = neuter

how to use this book

Whether you are learning a new language for business, pleasure, or in preparation for an overseas vacation, or are hoping to extend your vocabulary in an already familiar language, this dictionary is a valuable learning tool that you can use in a number of different ways.

Practical learning activities
• As you move around your home, workplace, or school, try looking at the pages that cover that setting. You could then close the book, look around you, and see how many of the objects and features you can name.
• Make flashcards for yourself with English on one side and Russian on the other side. Carry the cards with you and test yourself frequently, making sure you shuffle them between each test.
• Challenge yourself to write a story, letter, or dialogue using as many of the terms on a particular page as possible. This will help you retain the vocabulary and remember the spelling. If you want to build up to writing a longer text, start with sentences incorporating two to three words.
• If you have a very visual memory, try drawing or tracing items from the book onto a piece of paper, then close the book and see if you can fill in the words below the picture.
• Once you are more confident, pick out words in the foreign language index and see if you know what they mean before turning to the relevant page to check if you were right.

free audio app

The audio app contains all the words and phrases in the book, spoken by native speakers in both Russian and English, making it easier to learn important vocabulary and improve your pronunciation.

how to use the audio app

• Search for "DK Visual Dictionary" and download the free app on your smartphone or tablet from your chosen app store.
• Open the app and scan the barcode (or enter the ISBN) to unlock your Visual Dictionary in the Library.
• Download the audio files for your book.
• Enter a page number, then scroll up and down through the list to find a word or phrase. Words can be ordered alphabetically in Russian or English.
• Tap a word to hear it.
• Swipe left or right to view the previous or next page.
• Add words to your Favorites.

люди lyudi
people

тело telo • body

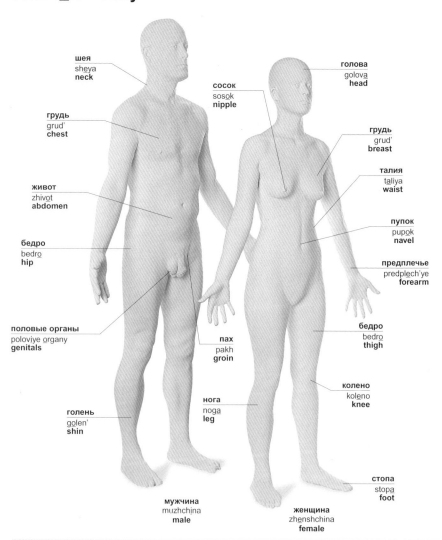

шея
sheya
neck

грудь
grud'
chest

живот
zhivot
abdomen

бедро
bedro
hip

половые органы
poloviye organy
genitals

голень
golen'
shin

сосок
sosok
nipple

голова
golova
head

грудь
grud'
breast

талия
taliya
waist

пупок
pupok
navel

предплечье
predplech'ye
forearm

бедро
bedro
thigh

колено
koleno
knee

стопа
stopa
foot

пах
pakh
groin

нога
noga
leg

мужчина
muzhchina
male

женщина
zhenshchina
female

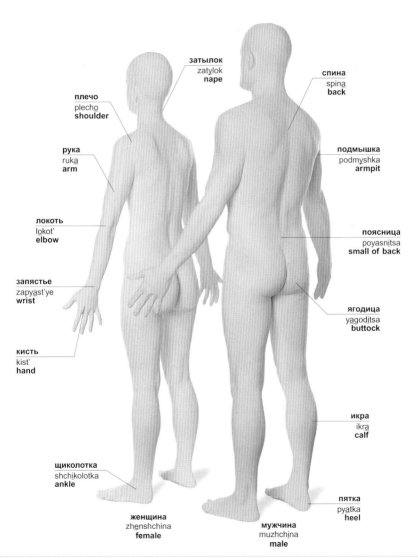

затылок
zatylok
nape

спина
spina
back

плечо
plecho
shoulder

подмышка
podmyshka
armpit

рука
ruka
arm

локоть
lokot'
elbow

поясница
poyasnitsa
small of back

запястье
zapyast'ye
wrist

ягодица
yagoditsa
buttock

кисть
kist'
hand

икра
ikra
calf

щиколотка
shchikolotka
ankle

пятка
pyatka
heel

женщина
zhenshchina
female

мужчина
muzhchina
male

лицо litso • face

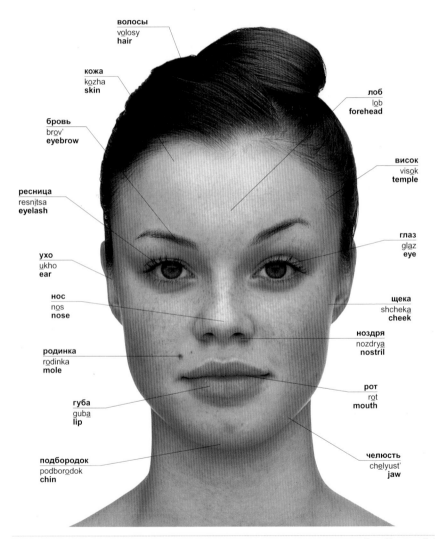

волосы
volosy
hair

кожа
kozha
skin

лоб
lob
forehead

бровь
brov'
eyebrow

висок
visok
temple

ресница
resnitsa
eyelash

глаз
glaz
eye

ухо
ukho
ear

нос
nos
nose

щека
shcheka
cheek

ноздря
nozdrya
nostril

родинка
rodinka
mole

рот
rot
mouth

губа
guba
lip

подбородок
podborodok
chin

челюсть
chelyust'
jaw

морщина
morshchina
wrinkle

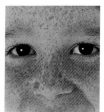

веснушка
vesnushka
freckle

пора
pora
pore

ямочка
yamochka
dimple

кисть kist' • hand

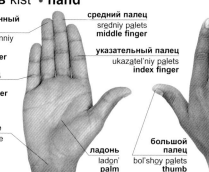
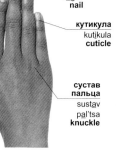

безымянный палец
bezymyanniy palets
ring finger

средний палец
sredniy palets
middle finger

указательный палец
ukazatel'niy palets
index finger

ноготь
nogot'
nail

кутикула
kutikula
cuticle

мизинец
mizinets
little finger

сустав пальца
sustav pal'tsa
knuckle

запястье
zapyast'ye
wrist

ладонь
ladon'
palm

большой палец
bol'shoy palets
thumb

кулак
kulak
fist

стопа stopa • foot

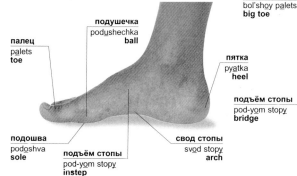

подушечка
podushechka
ball

большой палец
bol'shoy palets
big toe

ноготь на пальце ноги
nogot' na pal'tse nogi
toenail

палец
palets
toe

пятка
pyatka
heel

мизинец
mizinets
little toe

подъём стопы
pod-yom stopy
bridge

подошва
podoshva
sole

подъём стопы
pod-yom stopy
instep

свод стопы
svod stopy
arch

щиколотка
shchikolotka
ankle

мышцы myshtsy • muscles

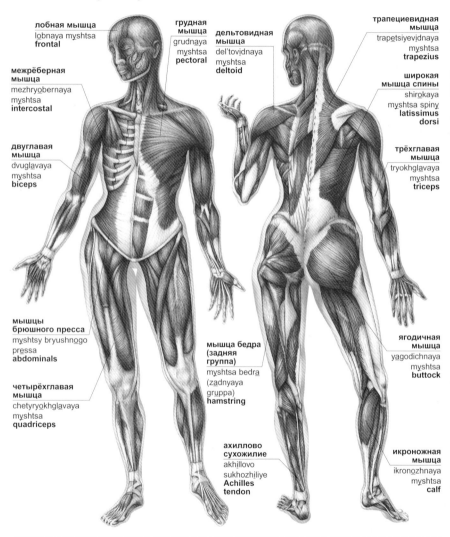

лобная мышца
lobnaya myshtsa
frontal

грудная мышца
grudnaya myshtsa
pectoral

дельтовидная мышца
del'tovidnaya myshtsa
deltoid

трапециевидная мышца
trapetsiyevidnaya myshtsa
trapezius

межрёберная мышца
mezhryobernaya myshtsa
intercostal

широкая мышца спины
shirokaya myshtsa spiny
latissimus dorsi

двуглавая мышца
dvuglavaya myshtsa
biceps

трёхглавая мышца
tryokhglavaya myshtsa
triceps

мышцы брюшного пресса
myshtsy bryushnogo pressa
abdominals

мышца бедра (задняя группа)
myshtsa bedra (zadnyaya gruppa)
hamstring

ягодичная мышца
yagodichnaya myshtsa
buttock

четырёхглавая мышца
chetyryokhglavaya myshtsa
quadriceps

ахиллово сухожилие
akhillovo sukhozhiliye
Achilles tendon

икроножная мышца
ikronozhnaya myshtsa
calf

скелет skelet • skeleton

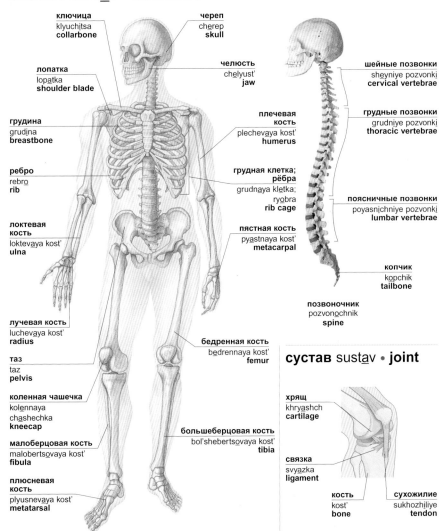

ключица
klyuchitsa
collarbone

череп
cherep
skull

челюсть
chelyust'
jaw

лопатка
lopatka
shoulder blade

грудина
grudina
breastbone

плечевая кость
plechevaya kost'
humerus

ребро
rebro
rib

грудная клетка; рёбра
grudnaya kletka; ryobra
rib cage

локтевая кость
loktevaya kost'
ulna

пястная кость
pyastnaya kost'
metacarpal

лучевая кость
luchevaya kost'
radius

таз
taz
pelvis

бедренная кость
bedrennaya kost'
femur

коленная чашечка
kolennaya chashechka
kneecap

малоберцовая кость
malobertsovaya kost'
fibula

большеберцовая кость
bol'shebertsovaya kost'
tibia

плюсневая кость
plyusnevaya kost'
metatarsal

шейные позвонки
sheyniye pozvonki
cervical vertebrae

грудные позвонки
grudniye pozvonki
thoracic vertebrae

поясничные позвонки
poyasnichniye pozvonki
lumbar vertebrae

копчик
kopchik
tailbone

позвоночник
pozvonochnik
spine

сустав sustav • joint

хрящ
khryashch
cartilage

связка
svyazka
ligament

кость
kost'
bone

сухожилие
sukhozhiliye
tendon

внутренние органы vnutrenniye organy • internal organs

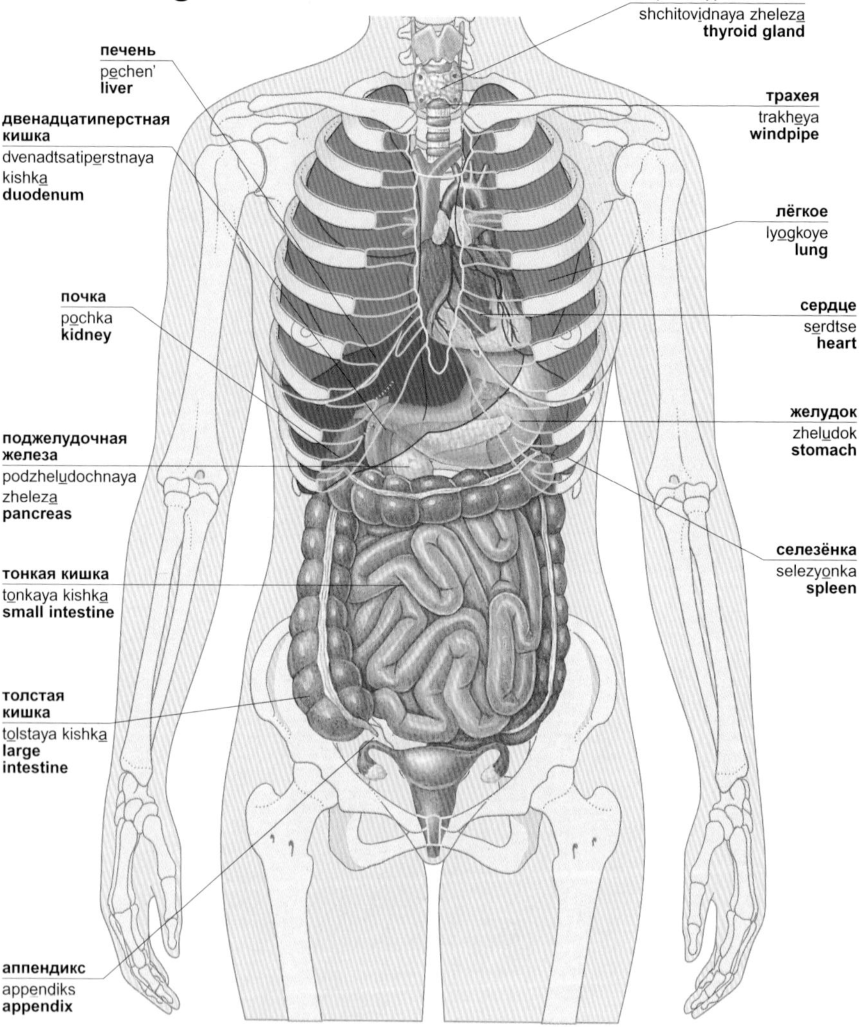

щитовидная железа
shchitovidnaya zheleza
thyroid gland

печень
pechen'
liver

трахея
trakheya
windpipe

двенадцатиперстная
кишка
dvenadtsatiperstnaya
kishka
duodenum

лёгкое
lyogkoye
lung

почка
pochka
kidney

сердце
serdtse
heart

желудок
zheludok
stomach

поджелудочная
железа
podzheludochnaya
zheleza
pancreas

селезёнка
selezyonka
spleen

тонкая кишка
tonkaya kishka
small intestine

толстая
кишка
tolstaya kishka
**large
intestine**

аппендикс
appendiks
appendix

голова golova • head

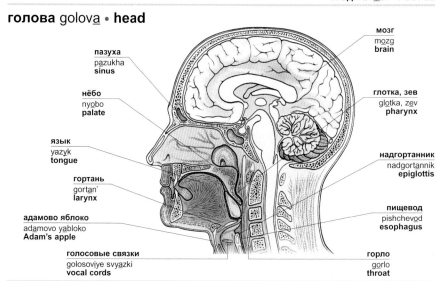

пазуха
pazukha
sinus

нёбо
nyobo
palate

язык
yazyk
tongue

гортань
gortan'
larynx

адамово яблоко
adamovo yabloko
Adam's apple

голосовые связки
golosoviye svyazki
vocal cords

мозг
mozg
brain

глотка, зев
glotka, zev
pharynx

надгортанник
nadgortannik
epiglottis

пищевод
pishchevod
esophagus

горло
gorlo
throat

системы организма sistemy organizma • body systems

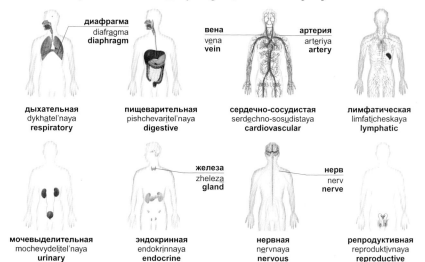

диафрагма
diafragma
diaphragm

дыхательная
dykhatel'naya
respiratory

пищеварительная
pishchevaritel'naya
digestive

вена
vena
vein

артерия
arteriya
artery

сердечно-сосудистая
serdechno-sosudistaya
cardiovascular

лимфатическая
limfaticheskaya
lymphatic

мочевыделительная
mochevydelitel'naya
urinary

железа
zheleza
gland

эндокринная
endokrinnaya
endocrine

нервная
nervnaya
nervous

нерв
nerv
nerve

репродуктивная
reproduktivnaya
reproductive

половые органы poloviye organy • reproductive organs

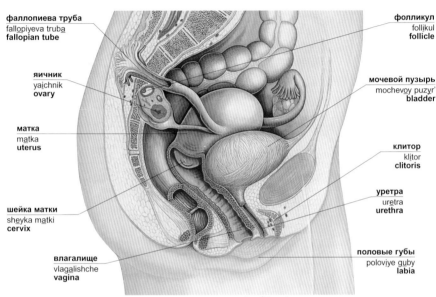

фаллопиева труба
fallopiyeva truba
fallopian tube

яичник
yaichnik
ovary

матка
matka
uterus

шейка матки
sheyka matki
cervix

влагалище
vlagalishche
vagina

фолликул
follikul
follicle

мочевой пузырь
mochevoy puzyr'
bladder

клитор
klitor
clitoris

уретра
uretra
urethra

половые губы
poloviye guby
labia

женские zhenskiye | female

размножение
razmnozheniye •
reproduction

сперма
sperma
sperm

яйцеклетка
yaytsekletka
egg

оплодотворение oplodotvoreniye
fertilization

словарь slovar' • vocabulary

гормон gormon **hormone**	**импотент** impotent **impotent**	**способный к деторождению** sposobniy k detorozhdeniyu **fertile**
овуляция ovulyatsiya **ovulation**	**зачать** zachat' **conceive**	**менструация** menstruatsiya **menstruation**
бесплодный besplodniy **infertile**	**половой акт** polovoy akt **intercourse**	**венерическая болезнь** venericheskaya bolezn' **sexually transmitted disease**

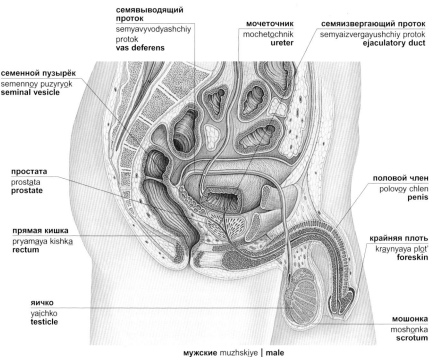

семявыводящий проток
semyavyvodyashchiy protok
vas deferens

мочеточник
mochetochnik
ureter

семяизвергающий проток
semyaizvergayushchiy protok
ejaculatory duct

семенной пузырёк
semennoy puzyryok
seminal vesicle

простата
prostata
prostate

половой член
polovoy chlen
penis

прямая кишка
pryamaya kishka
rectum

крайняя плоть
kraynyaya plot'
foreskin

яичко
yaichko
testicle

мошонка
moshonka
scrotum

мужские muzhskiye | male

контрацепция kontratseptsiya • contraception

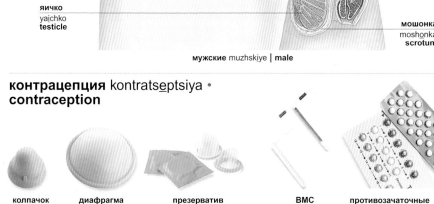

колпачок
kolpachok
cervical cap

диафрагма
diafragma
diaphragm

презерватив
prezervativ
condom

ВМС
ve-em-es
IUD

противозачаточные таблетки
protivozachatochniye tabletki
pill

семья sem'ya · family

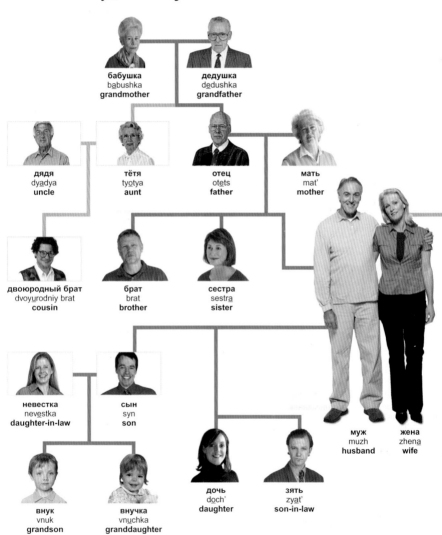

бабушка
babushka
grandmother

дедушка
dedushka
grandfather

дядя
dyadya
uncle

тётя
tyotya
aunt

отец
otets
father

мать
mat'
mother

двоюродный брат
dvoyurodniy brat
cousin

брат
brat
brother

сестра
sestra
sister

муж
muzh
husband

жена
zhena
wife

невестка
nevestka
daughter-in-law

сын
syn
son

дочь
doch'
daughter

зять
zyat'
son-in-law

внук
vnuk
grandson

внучка
vnuchka
granddaughter

словарь slovar' • vocabulary

родственники rodstvenniki **relatives**	**родители** roditeli **parents**	**внуки** vnuki **grandchildren**	**мачеха** machekha **stepmother**	**пасынок** pasynok **stepson**	**партнёр** partnyor **partner**
поколение pokoleniye **generation**	**дети** deti **children**	**бабушка и дедушка** babushka i dedushka **grandparents**	**отчим** otchim **stepfather**	**падчерица** padcheritsa **stepdaughter**	**близнецы** bliznetsy **twins**

этапы etapy • stages

тёща tyoshcha **mother-in-law**

тесть test' **father-in-law**

младенец mladenets **baby**

ребёнок rebyonok **child**

шурин shurin **brother-in-law**

свояченица svoyachenitsa **sister-in-law**

мальчик mal'chik **boy**

девочка devochka **girl**

племянница plemyannitsa **niece**

племянник plemyannik **nephew**

госпожа gospozha **Mrs**

подросток podrostok **teenager**

взрослый vzrosliy **adult**

обращения
obrashcheniya • **titles**

господин gospodin **Mr**

девушка devochka **Miss/Ms.**

мужчина muzhchina **man**

женщина zhenshchina **woman**

ОТНОШЕНИЯ otnosheniya • relationships

ассистент
assistent
assistant

менеджер
menedzher
manager

деловой партнёр
delovoy partnyor
business partner

работодатель
rabotodatel'
employer

подчинённый
podchinyonniy
employee

коллега
kollega
colleague

офис ofis | office

сосед/соседка
sosed/sosedka
neighbor

друг/подруга
drug/podruga
friend

знакомый/знакомая
znakomiy/znakomaya
acquaintance

друг по переписке
drug po perepiske
pen pal

**(любимый)
парень**
(lyubimiy) paryen'
boyfriend

**(любимая)
девушка**
(lyubimaya)
devushka
girlfriend

жених
zhenikh
fiancé

невеста
nevesta
fiancée

пара para | couple

помолвленная пара pomolvlennaya para | engaged couple

эмоции emotsii • emotions

улыбка
ulybka
smile

радостный
radostniy
happy

грустный
grustniy
sad

возбуждённый
vozbuzhdyonniy
excited

скучающий
skuchayushchiy
bored

удивлённый
udivlyonniy
surprised

испуганный
ispuganniy
scared

хмурый
взгляд
khmuriy
vzglyad
frown

сердитый
serditiy
angry

сбитый с толку
sbitiy s tolku
confused

взволнованный
vzvolnovanniy
worried

нервный
nervniy
nervous

гордый
gordiy
proud

уверенный
uverenniy
confident

смущённый
smushchyonniy
embarrassed

застенчивый
zastenchiviy
shy

словарь slovar' • vocabulary

расстроенный rasstroyenniy **upset**	**смеяться** smeyat'sya **laugh (v)**	**вздыхать** vzdykhat' **sigh (v)**	**кричать** krichat' **shout (v)**
поражённый porazhonniy **shocked**	**плакать** plakat' **cry (v)**	**падать в обморок** padat' v obmorok **faint (v)**	**зевать** zevat' **yawn (v)**

события в жизни sobytiya v zhizni • life events

родиться
rodit'sya
be born (v)

пойти в школу
poyti v shkolu
start school (v)

подружиться
podruzhit'sya
make friends (v)

окончить университет
okonchit' universitet
graduate (v)

получить работу
poluchit' rabotu
get a job (v)

влюбиться
vlyubit'sya
fall in love (v)

жениться/выйти замуж
zhenit'sya/viyti zamuzh
get married (v)

родить ребёнка
rodit' rebyonka
have a baby (v)

свадьба svad'ba | **wedding**

словарь slovar' • vocabulary

крещение
kreshcheniye
christening

юбилей
yubiley
anniversary

эмигрировать
emigrirovat'
emigrate (v)

выйти на пенсию
viyti na pensiyu
retire (v)

умереть
umeret'
die (v)

составить завещание
sostavit' zaveshchaniye
make a will (v)

свидетельство о рождении
svidetel'stvo o rozhdenii
birth certificate

свадебный приём
svadebniy priyom
wedding reception

медовый месяц
medoviy mesyats
honeymoon

бар-мицва
barmitsva
bar mitzvah

развод
razvod
divorce

похороны
pokhorony
funeral

праздники prazdniki • celebrations

праздники prazdniki • festivals

вечеринка в честь дня рождения
vecherinka v chest' dnya rozhdeniya
birthday party

день рождения
den' rozhdeniya
birthday

открытка
otkrytka
card

подарок
podarok
present

Рождество
rozhdestvo
Christmas

Пасха
Paskha
Passover

Новый год
noviy god
New Year

карнавал
karnaval
carnival

процессия
protsessiya
procession

Рамадан
ramadan
Ramadan

лента
lenta
ribbon

День Благодарения
den' blagodareniya
Thanksgiving

Пасха
paskha
Easter

Хеллоуин
khellouin
Halloween

Дивали (Праздник огней)
divali (prazdnik ogney)
Diwali

внешность vneshnost'
appearance

детская одежда d<u>e</u>tskaya odezhda • children's clothing

младенец mlad<u>e</u>nets • baby

зимний комбинезон
zimniy kombinez<u>o</u>n
snowsuit

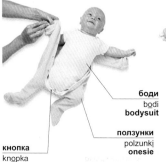

боди
b<u>o</u>di
bodysuit

ползунки
polzunk<u>i</u>
onesie

кнопка
kn<u>o</u>pka
snap

комбинезон для сна
kombinez<u>o</u>n dlya sn<u>a</u>
sleeper

ромпер
r<u>o</u>mper
romper

нагрудник
nagr<u>u</u>dnik
bib

рукавички
rukav<u>i</u>chki
mittens

пинетки
pin<u>e</u>tki
booties

подгузник
podg<u>u</u>znik
cloth diaper

**одноразовый
подгузник**
odnor<u>a</u>zoviy podg<u>u</u>znik
disposable diaper

**непромокаемые
трусы**
nepromok<u>a</u>yemiye
trusy
plastic pants

малыш mal<u>y</u>sh • toddler

панама
pan<u>a</u>ma
sun hat

комбинезон
kombinez<u>o</u>n
overalls

футболка
futb<u>o</u>lka
T-shirt

шорты
sh<u>o</u>rty
shorts

юбка
y<u>u</u>bka
skirt

фартук
f<u>a</u>rtuk
apron

ребёнок rebyonok • child

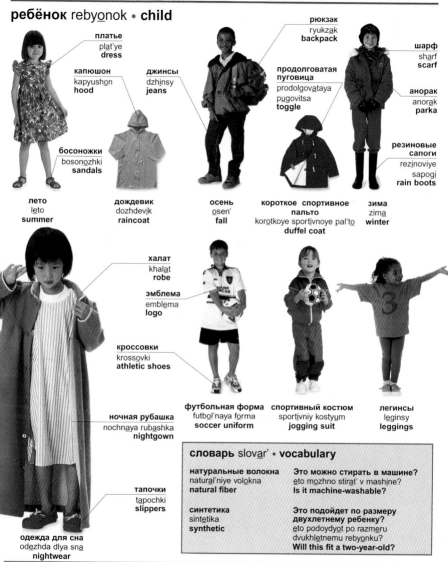

платье
plat'ye
dress

капюшон
kapyushon
hood

джинсы
dzhinsy
jeans

рюкзак
ryukzak
backpack

шарф
sharf
scarf

продолговатая пуговица
prodolgovataya pugovitsa
toggle

анорак
anorak
parka

босоножки
bosonozhki
sandals

резиновые сапоги
rezinoviye sapogi
rain boots

лето
leto
summer

дождевик
dozhdevik
raincoat

осень
osen'
fall

короткое спортивное пальто
korotkoye sportivnoye pal'to
duffel coat

зима
zima
winter

халат
khalat
robe

эмблема
emblema
logo

кроссовки
krossovki
athletic shoes

ночная рубашка
nochnaya rubashka
nightgown

тапочки
tapochki
slippers

одежда для сна
odezhda dlya sna
nightwear

футбольная форма
futbol'naya forma
soccer uniform

спортивный костюм
sportivniy kostyum
jogging suit

легинсы
leginsy
leggings

словарь slovar' • vocabulary

натуральные волокна
natural'niye volokna
natural fiber

синтетика
sintetika
synthetic

Это можно стирать в машине?
eto mozhno stirat' v mashine?
Is it machine-washable?

Это подойдет по размеру двухлетнему ребенку?
eto podoydyot po razmeru dvukhletnemu rebyonku?
Will this fit a two-year-old?

мужская одежда muzhsk<u>a</u>ya od<u>e</u>zhda • **men's clothing**

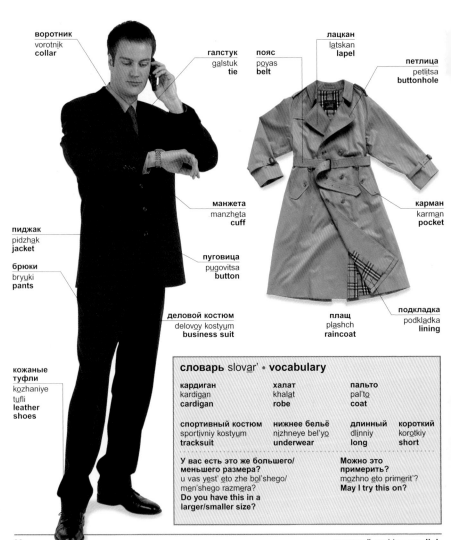

воротник
vorotn<u>i</u>k
collar

галстук
g<u>a</u>lstuk
tie

пояс
p<u>o</u>yas
belt

лацкан
l<u>a</u>tskan
lapel

петлица
petl<u>i</u>tsa
buttonhole

манжета
manzh<u>e</u>ta
cuff

карман
karm<u>a</u>n
pocket

пиджак
pidzh<u>a</u>k
jacket

брюки
br<u>yu</u>ki
pants

пуговица
p<u>u</u>govitsa
button

деловой костюм
delov<u>o</u>y kost<u>yu</u>m
business suit

плащ
pl<u>a</u>shch
raincoat

подкладка
podkl<u>a</u>dka
lining

кожаные
туфли
k<u>o</u>zhaniye
t<u>u</u>fli
**leather
shoes**

словарь slov<u>ar</u>' • **vocabulary**

кардиган	халат	пальто	
kardig<u>a</u>n	khal<u>a</u>t	pal't<u>o</u>	
cardigan	**robe**	**coat**	
спортивный костюм	нижнее бельё	длинный	короткий
sport<u>i</u>vniy kost<u>yu</u>m	n<u>i</u>zhneye bel'y<u>o</u>	dl<u>i</u>nniy	kor<u>o</u>tkiy
tracksuit	**underwear**	**long**	**short**

У вас есть это же большего/
меньшего размера?
u vas y<u>e</u>st' <u>e</u>to zhe bol'sh<u>e</u>go/
men'sh<u>e</u>go razm<u>e</u>ra?
**Do you have this in a
larger/smaller size?**

Можно это
примерить?
m<u>o</u>zhno <u>e</u>to primer<u>i</u>t'?
May I try this on?

блейзер
bl**e**yzer
blazer

спортивный пиджак
sport**i**vniy pidzh**a**k
sport coat

жилет
zhil**e**t
vest

треугольный вырез
treugol'niy vyrez
V-neck

круглый вырез
kr**u**gliy
v**y**rez
crew neck

футболка
futb**o**lka
T-shirt

анорак
anor**a**k
parka

толстовка
tolst**o**vka
sweatshirt

рубашка
rub**a**shka
shirt

джинсы
dzh**i**nsy
jeans

свитер
sv**i**ter
sweater

пижама
pizh**a**ma
pajamas

майка
m**a**yka
undershirt

повседневная одежда
povsedn**e**vnaya od**e**zhda
casual wear

длинные трусы, шорты
dl**i**nniye trus**y**, sh**o**rty
shorts

трусы-плавки, брифы
trusy-pl**a**vki, br**i**fy
briefs

трусы-боксёры
trusy-boks**yo**ry
boxer shorts

носки
nosk**i**
socks

женская одежда zhenskaya odezhda • women's clothing

жакет
zhaket
jacket

шов
shov
seam

рукав
rukav
sleeve

до пола
do pola
ankle length

юбка
yubka
skirt

подол
podol
hem

по колено
po koleno
knee length

туфли
tufli
shoes

деловой
(костюм)
delovoy (kostyum)
formal

без
бретелек
bez bretelek
strapless

без рукавов
bez rukavov
sleeveless

вечернее платье
vecherneye plat'ye
evening dress

платье
plat'ye
dress

блузка
bluzka
blouse

брюки
bryuki
pants

повседневный
povsednevniy
casual

нижнее бельё nizhneye bel'yo • lingerie

бретелька
bretel'ka
strap

халат
khalat
robe

комбинация
kombinatsiya
slip

топик
topik
camisole

подвязки
podvyazki
garter straps

майка-корсет
mayka-korset
bustier

чулок
chulok
stocking

колготки
kolgotki
panty hose

бюстгальтер
byustgal'ter
bra

трусы
trusy
panties

ночная рубашка
nochnaya rubashka
nightgown

свадьба svad'ba • wedding

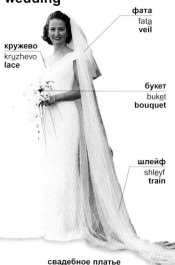

фата
fata
veil

кружево
kruzhevo
lace

букет
buket
bouquet

шлейф
shleyf
train

свадебное платье
svadebnoye plat'ye
wedding dress

словарь slovar' • vocabulary

корсет
korset
corset

подвязка
podvyazka
garter

подплечник
podplechnik
shoulder pad

пояс
poyas
waistband

сшитый на заказ
sshitiy na zakaz
tailored

воротник хомутиком (на открытом платье)
vorotnik khomutikom (na otkrytom plat'ye)
halter neck

на косточках
na kostochkakh
underwire

спортивный бюстгальтер
sportivniy byustgal'ter
sports bra

аксессуары aksessuary • accessories

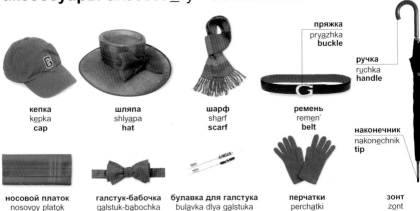

пряжка
pryazhka
buckle

ручка
ruchka
handle

кепка
kepka
cap

шляпа
shlyapa
hat

шарф
sharf
scarf

ремень
remen'
belt

наконечник
nakonechnik
tip

носовой платок
nosovoy platok
handkerchief

галстук-бабочка
galstuk-babochka
bow tie

булавка для галстука
bulavka dlya galstuka
tiepin

перчатки
perchatki
gloves

зонт
zont
umbrella

ювелирные изделия yuvelirniye izdeliya • jewelry

кулон
kulon
pendant

брошь
brosh
brooch

запонка
zaponka
cuff links

жемчужное ожерелье
zhemchuzhnoye ozherel'ye
strand of pearls

звено
zveno
link

застёжка
zastyozhka
clasp

серьги
ser'gi
earrings

кольцо
kol'tso
ring

камень
kamen'
stone

ожерелье
ozherel'ye
necklace

браслет
braslet
bracelet

цепочка
tsepochka
chain

наручные часы
naruchniye chasy
watch

ювелирная шкатулка yuvelirnaya shkatulka
jewelry box

сумки sumki • bags

бумажник
bumazhnik
wallet

кошелёк
koshelyok
change purse

застёжка
zastyozhka
clasp

сумка через плечо
sumka cherez plecho
shoulder bag

лямка
lyamka
shoulder strap

ручки
ruchki
handles

дорожная сумка
dorozhnaya sumka
duffel bag

портфель
portfel'
briefcase

сумочка
sumochka
handbag

рюкзак
ryukzak
backpack

обувь obuv' • shoes

отверстие для шнурка
otverstiye dlya shnurka
eyelet

шнурок
shnurok
lace

подошва
podoshva
sole

язычок
yazychok
tongue

ботинок со шнурками
botinok so shnurkami
lace-up

каблук
kabluk
heel

сапоги
sapogi
boot

туристический ботинок
turisticheskiy botinok
hiking boot

кроссовок
krosovok
sneaker

вьетнамка
v'yetnamka
flip-flop

**броги,
полуботинки**
brogi, polubotinki
dress shoe

туфля на каблуке
tuflya na kabluke
high-heeled shoe

танкетка
tanketka
wedge

босоножка
bosonozhka
sandal

мокасин
mokasin
slip-on

балетка
baletka
pump

волосы volosy • hair

расчёска
raschoska
comb

расчёсывать
raschosyvat'
comb (v)

щётка
shchotka
brush

причёсывать щёткой
prichesivat' shchotkoy
brush (v)

ополаскивать
opolaskivat'
rinse (v)

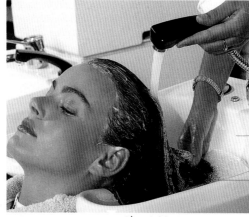

парикмахер
parikmakher
hairdresser

раковина
rakovina
sink

клиент/клиентка
kliyent / kliyentka
client

мыть myt' | **wash (v)**

накидка
nakidka
robe

стричь
strich'
cut (v)

сушить феном
sushit' fenom
blow-dry (v)

делать укладку
delat' ukladku
set (v)

аксессуары aksesuary • accessories

фен
fen
blow-dryer

шампунь
shampun'
shampoo

кондиционер
konditsioner
conditioner

гель
gel'
gel

лак для волос
lak dlya volos
hairspray

плойка
ployka
curling iron

ножницы
nozhnitsy
scissors

ободок для волос
obodok dlya volos
headband

выпрямитель для волос
vypryamitel' dlya volos
hair straightener

невидимка
nevidimka
bobby pins

причёски prichoski • styles

конский хвост
konskiy khvost
ponytail

коса
kosa
braid

французский узел
frantsuzkij uzel
French twist

пучок
puchok
bun

хвостики
khvostiki
pigtails

стрижка каре
strizhka kare
bob

короткая стрижка
korotkaya strizhka
crop

кудрявые
kudryaviye
curly

химическая завивка
khimicheskaya zavivka
perm

прямые
pryamiye
straight

корни
korni
roots

мелирование
melirovaniye
highlights

лысый
lysiy
bald

парик
parik
wig

словарь slovar' • vocabulary

подровнять podrovnyat' **trim (v)**	**жирный** zhirniy **greasy**
выпрямить vypryamit' **straighten (v)**	**сухой** sukhoy **dry**
мужской парикмахер muzhskoy parikmakher **barber**	**нормальный** normal'niy **normal**
перхоть perkhot' **dandruff**	**кожа головы** kozha golovy **scalp**
секущиеся кончики sekushchiyesya konchiki **split ends**	**ободок для волос** obodok dlya volos **hairband**
борода boroda **beard**	**усы** usy **mustache**

цвета tsveta • colors

блонд
blond
blonde

тёмно-каштановый
tyomno-kashtanoviy
brunette

тёмно-рыжий
tyomno-ryzhiy
auburn

рыжий
ryzhiy
red

чёрный
chorniy
black

седой
sedoy
gray

белый
beliy
white

крашеный
krasheniy
dyed

красота krasot<u>a</u> • **beauty**

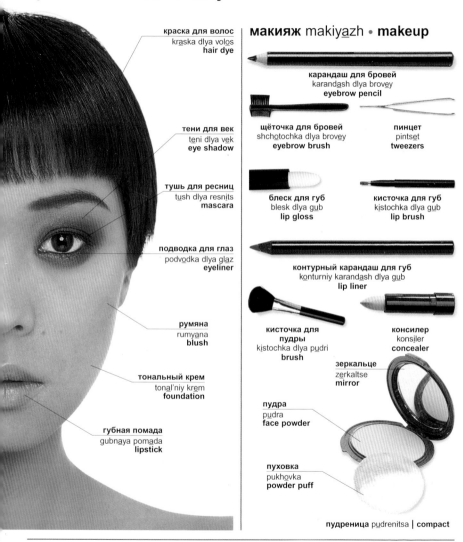

краска для волос
kr<u>a</u>ska dlya vol<u>o</u>s
hair dye

тени для век
t<u>e</u>ni dlya v<u>e</u>k
eye shadow

тушь для ресниц
t<u>u</u>sh dlya resn<u>i</u>ts
mascara

подводка для глаз
podv<u>o</u>dka dlya gl<u>a</u>z
eyeliner

румяна
rumy<u>a</u>na
blush

тональный крем
ton<u>a</u>l'niy kr<u>e</u>m
foundation

губная помада
gubn<u>a</u>ya pom<u>a</u>da
lipstick

макияж makiy<u>a</u>zh • **makeup**

карандаш для бровей
karand<u>a</u>sh dlya brov<u>e</u>y
eyebrow pencil

щёточка для бровей
shch<u>o</u>tochka dlya brov<u>e</u>y
eyebrow brush

пинцет
pints<u>e</u>t
tweezers

блеск для губ
bl<u>e</u>sk dlya g<u>u</u>b
lip gloss

кисточка для губ
k<u>i</u>stochka dlya g<u>u</u>b
lip brush

контурный карандаш для губ
k<u>o</u>nturniy karand<u>a</u>sh dlya g<u>u</u>b
lip liner

кисточка для пудры
k<u>i</u>stochka dlya p<u>u</u>dri
brush

консилер
kons<u>i</u>ler
concealer

зеркальце
z<u>e</u>rkaltse
mirror

пудра
p<u>u</u>dra
face powder

пуховка
pukh<u>o</u>vka
powder puff

пудреница p<u>u</u>drenitsa | **compact**

косметические процедуры
kosmeticheskiye protsedury •
beauty treatments

маска для лица
maska dlya litsa
face mask

солярий
solyariy
sunbed

уход за кожей лица
ukhod za kozhey litsa
facial

отшелушивать
otshelushivat'
exfoliate (v)

эпиляция воском
epilyatsiya voskom
wax

педикюр
pedikyur
pedicure

маникюр manikyur • manicure

жидкость для снятия лака
zhidkost' dlya snyatiya laka
nail polish remover

пилка для ногтей
pilka dlya nogtey
nail file

лак для ногтей
lak dlya nogtey
nail polish

маникюрные ножницы
manikyurniye nozhnitsy
nail scissors

щипчики для ногтеи
shipchiki dlya nogtey
nail clippers

гигиеническая косметика
gigienicheskaya kosmetika •
toiletries

очищающее средство
ochishchayushcheye sredstvo
cleanser

тоник
tonik
toner

увлажняющий крем
uvlazhnyayushchiy krem
moisturizer

крем-автозагар
krem-avtozagar
self-tanning lotion

духи
dukhi
perfume

туалетная вода
tualetnaya voda
eau de toilette

словарь slovar' • vocabulary

цвет лица tsvet litsa **complexion**	**жирная** zhirnaya **oily**	**загар** zagar **tan**
светлыи svetlij **fair**	**чувствительная** chuvstvitel'naya **sensitive**	**татуировка** tatuirovka **tattoo**
тёмная tyomnaya **dark**	**гипоаллергенный** gipoallergenniy **hypoallergenic**	**против морщин** protiv morshchin **antiwrinkle**
сухая sukhaya **dry**	**тональность** tonalnost' **shade**	**ватные шарики** vatniye shariki **cotton balls**

здоровье zdor<u>o</u>v'ye
health

болезнь bolezn' • illness

головная боль
golovnaya bol'
headache

носовое кровотечение
nosovoye krovotecheniye
nosebleed

кашель
kashel'
cough

жар zhar | **fever**

чихание
chikhaniye
sneeze

простуда
prostuda
cold

грипп
grip
flu

ингалятор
ingalyator
inhaler

астма
astma
asthma

спазмы
spasmi
cramps

тошнота
toshnota
nausea

ветряная оспа
vetryanaya ospa
chicken pox

сыпь
syp'
rash

словарь slovar' • vocabulary

инсульт insul't **stroke**	**диабет** diabet **diabetes**	**экзема** ekzema **eczema**	**озноб** oznob **chill**	**страдать** **рвотой** stradat' rvotoi **vomit (v)**	**понос** ponos **diarrhea**
кровяное **давление** krovyanoe davlenie **blood pressure**	**аллергия** allergiya **allergy**	**инфекция** infektsiya **infection**	**боль в** **животе** bol' v zhivote **stomachache**	**эпилепсия** epilepsiya **epilepsy**	**корь** kor' **measles**
инфаркт infarkt **heart attack**	**сенная** **лихорадка** sennaya likhoradka **hay fever**	**вирус** virus **virus**	**потерять** **сознание** poteryat' soznanie **faint (v)**	**мигрень** migren' **migraine**	**свинка** svinka **mumps**

врач vrach • doctor
консультация konsul'tatsiya • consultation

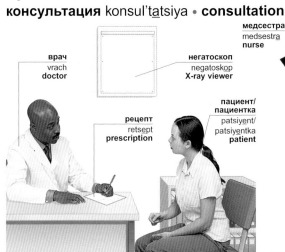

врач
vrach
doctor

негатоскоп
negatoskop
X-ray viewer

медсестра
medsestra
nurse

рецепт
retsept
prescription

пациент/
пациентка
patsiyent/
patsiyentka
patient

весы
vesy
scale

манжета
manzheta
cuff

электронный тонометр
elektronniy tonometr
electric blood
pressure monitor

словарь slovar' • vocabulary

запись на
приём
zapis' na priyom
appointment

прививка
privivka
vaccination

кабинет врача
kabinet vracha
doctor's office

градусник
gradusnik
thermometer

приёмная
priyomnaya
waiting room

медицинский
осмотр
meditsinskiy
osmotr
medical
examination

Мне нужен врач.
mne nuzhen vrach
I need to see a doctor.

Здесь болит.
zdes' bolit
It hurts here.

травма travma • injury

косыночная
повязка
kosynochnaya
povyazka
sling

шейный
ортез
sheyniy
ortez
neck brace

растяжение связок rastyazheniye svyazok | **sprain**

перелом
perelom
fracture

травма шеи
travma shei
whiplash

порез
porez
cut

ссадина
ssadina
graze

синяк
sinyak
bruise

заноза
zanoza
splinter

солнечный ожог
solnechniy ozhog
sunburn

ожог
ozhog
burn

укус
ukus
bite

укус насекомого
ukus nasekomogo
sting

словарь slovar' • vocabulary

несчастный
случай
neschasniy sluchay
accident

неотложная
помощь
neotlozhnaya
pomoshch
emergency

рана
rana
wound

кровотечение
krovotechenie
hemorrhage

волдырь
voldyr'
blister

сотрясение мозга
sotryaseniye mozga
concussion

отравление
otravleniye
poisoning

поражение
электрическим током
porazheniye elektricheskim
tokom
electric shock

травма головы
travma golovy
head injury

С ним/ней всё будет хорошо?
s nim/ney vsyo budet khorosho?
Will he/she be all right?

Где у вас болит?
Gde u vas bolit?
Where does it hurt?

Пожалуйста, вызовите
скорую помощь.
pozhalusta, vyzovite skoruyu
pomoshch'
Please call an ambulance.

первая помощь pervaya pomoshch' • first aid

мазь
maz'
ointment

пластырь
plastyr'
adhesive bandage

булавка
bulavka
safety pin

бинт
bint
bandage

обезболивающие
obezbolivayushchiye
painkillers

антибактериальная салфетка
antibakterial'naya salfetka
antiseptic wipe

пинцет
pintset
tweezers

ножницы
nozhnitsy
scissors

антисептик
antiseptik
antiseptic

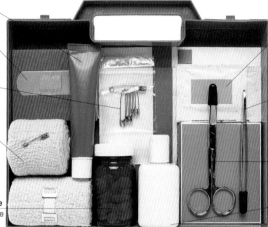

аптечка aptechka | first-aid kit

марля/ бинт
marlya/bint
gauze

повязка
povyazka
dressing

шина shina | splint

лейкопластырь
leykoplastyr'
adhesive tape

реанимация
reanimatsiya
resuscitation

словарь slovar' • vocabulary

шок shok **shock**	**пульс** pul's **pulse**	**задыхаться / подавиться** zadykhatsa / podavitsa **choke (v)**	**Вы можете помочь?** vy mozhete pomoch'? **Can you help?**
без сознания bez soznaniya **unconscious**	**дыхание** dykhaniye **breathing**	**стерильный** steril'niy **sterile**	**Вы умеете оказывать первую помощь?** vy umeyete okazyvat' pervuyu pomoshch'? **Do you know first aid?**

больница bol'nitsa • hospital

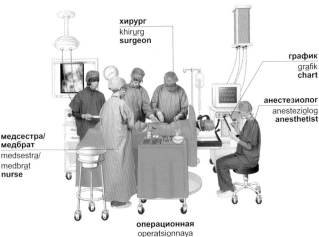

хирург
khirurg
surgeon

график
grafik
chart

анестезиолог
anesteziolog
anesthetist

медсестра/ медбрат
medsestra/ medbrat
nurse

операционная
operatsionnaya
operating room

анализ крови
analiz krovi
blood test

инъекция
inyektsiya
injection

рентген
rentgen
X-ray

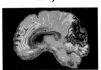

томограмма
tomogramma
scan

каталка
katalka
gurney

кнопка вызова персонала
knopka vyzova personala
call button

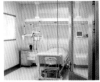

приёмный покой неотложной помощи
priyemnyy pokoy neotlozhnoy pomoshchi
emergency room

палата
palata
ward

кресло-каталка
kreslo-katalka
wheelchair

словарь slovar' • vocabulary

операция operatsiya **operation**	**выписан** vypisan **discharged**	**время посещений** vremya poseshcheniy **visiting hours**	**детское отделение** detskoye otdeleniye **children's ward**	**отделение реанимации и интенсивной терапии** otdeleniye reanimatsii i intensivnoy terapii **intensive care unit**
поступил postupil **admitted**	**клиника** klinika **clinic**	**родильное отделение** rodil'noye otdeleniye **maternity ward**	**отдельная палата** otdel'naya palata **private room**	**амбулаторный пациент** ambulatorniy patsiyent **outpatient**

отделения otdeleniya • departments

ЛОР-отделение
lor-otdelenie
ENT

кардиология
kardiologiya
cardiology

ортопедия
ortopediya
orthopedics

гинекология
ginekologiya
gynecology

физиотерапия
fizioterapiya
physiotherapy

дерматология
dermatologiya
dermatology

педиатрия
pediatriya
pediatrics

рентгенология
rentgenologiya
radiology

хирургия
khirurgiya
surgery

родильное отделение
rodilnoye otdeleniye
maternity

психиатрия
psikhiatriya
psychiatry

офтальмология
oftal'mologiya
ophthalmology

словарь slovar' • vocabulary

неврология nevrologiya **neurology**	**урология** urologiya **urology**	**эндокринология** endokrinologiya **endocrinology**	**патология** patologiya **pathology**	**результат** rezul'tat **result**
онкология onkologiya **oncology**	**пластическая** **хирургия** plasticheskaya khirurgiya **plastic surgery**	**направление к** **специалисту** napravleniye k spetsialistu **referral**	**анализ** analiz **test**	**консультирующий** **специалист** konsultiruyushchiy spetsialist **specialist**

зубной врач zubnoy vrach • dentist

зуб zub • tooth

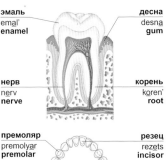

эмаль
emal'
enamel

десна
desna
gum

нерв
nerv
nerve

корень
koren'
root

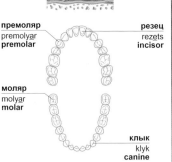

премоляр
premolyar
premolar

резец
rezets
incisor

моляр
molyar
molar

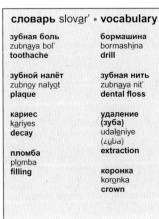

клык
klyk
canine

осмотр osmotr • checkup

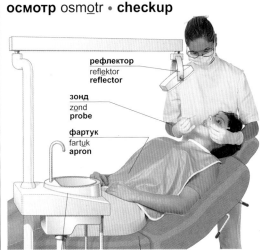

рефлектор
reflektor
reflector

зонд
zond
probe

фартук
fartuk
apron

раковина
rakovina
sink

стоматологическое кресло
stomatologicheskoye kreslo
dentist's chair

словарь slovar' • vocabulary

зубная боль zubnaya bol' **toothache**	бормашина bormashina **drill**
зубной налёт zubnoy nalyot **plaque**	зубная нить zubnaya nit' **dental floss**
кариес kariyes **decay**	удаление (зуба) udaleniye (zuba) **extraction**
пломба plomba **filling**	коронка koronka **crown**

чистить зубной
нитью
chistit' zubnoy nit'yu
floss (v)

чистить зубы
chistit' zubi
brush (v)

брекеты
brekety
braces

рентгеновский
снимок зуба
rentgenovskiy snimok
zuba
dental X-ray

рентгеновская
плёнка
rentgenovskaya
plyonka
X-ray film

зубные протезы
zubniye protezy
dentures

оптик optik • optometrist

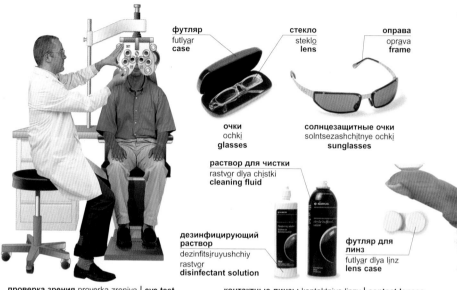

футляр
futlyar
case

стекло
steklo
lens

оправа
oprava
frame

очки
ochki
glasses

солнцезащитные очки
solntsezashchitnye ochki
sunglasses

раствор для чистки
rastvor dlya chistki
cleaning fluid

дезинфицирующий раствор
dezinfitsiruyushchiy rastvor
disinfectant solution

футляр для линз
futlyar dlya linz
lens case

проверка зрения proverka zreniya | **eye test**

контактные линзы kontaktniye linzy | **contact lenses**

глаз glaz • eye

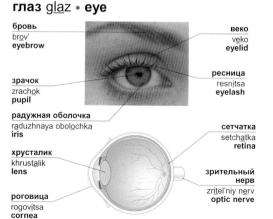

бровь
brov'
eyebrow

веко
veko
eyelid

ресница
resnitsa
eyelash

зрачок
zrachok
pupil

радужная оболочка
raduzhnaya obolochka
iris

сетчатка
setchatka
retina

хрусталик
khrustalik
lens

зрительный нерв
zritel'niy nerv
optic nerve

роговица
rogovitsa
cornea

словарь slovar' • vocabulary

зрение zreniye **vision**	**астигматизм** astigmatizm **astigmatism**
диоптрия dioptriya **diopter**	**дальнозоркость** dal'nozorkost' **farsighted**
слеза sleza **tear**	**близорукость** blizorukost' **nearsighted**
катаракта katarakta **cataract**	**бифокальный** bifokal'niy **bifocal**

беременность ber**e**mennost' • **pregnancy**

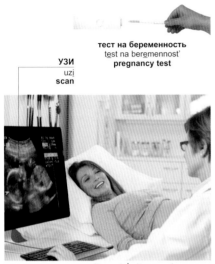

УЗИ
uzi
scan

тест на беременность
test na ber**e**mennost'
pregnancy test

ультразвук ul'trazv**u**k | **ultrasound**

пуповина
pupovina
umbilical cord

плацента
plats**e**nta
placenta

шейка матки
sh**e**yka m**a**tki
cervix

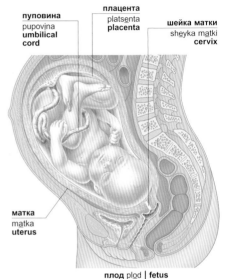

матка
m**a**tka
uterus

плод pl**o**d | **fetus**

словарь slov**a**r' • **vocabulary**

овуляция ovul**ya**tsiya **ovulation**	**пренатальный** prenat**a**l'niy **prenatal**	**схватка** skhv**a**tka **contraction**	**раскрытие** raskr**y**tiye **dilation**	**роды** r**o**dy **delivery**	**роды при тазовом предлежании** r**o**dy pri t**a**zovom predlezh**a**nii **breech birth**
зачатие zach**a**tiye **conception**	**эмбрион** embri**o**n **embryo**	**отходят воды** otkh**o**dyat v**o**dy **break water (v)**	**эпидуральная анестезия** epidur**a**l'naya anest**e**ziya **epidural**	**рождение** rozhd**e**niye **birth**	**преждевременные (роды)** prezhdevr**e**menniye (r**o**dy) **premature**
беременная ber**e**mennaya **pregnant**	**матка** m**a**tka **womb**	**околоплодные воды** okolopl**o**dniye v**o**dy **amniotic fluid**	**эпизиотомия** epizi**o**tomiya **episiotomy**	**выкидыш** v**y**kidysh **miscarriage**	**гинеколог** gine**ko**log **gynecologist**
готовящаяся стать матерью got**o**vyashchayasya stat' m**a**ter'yu **expecting**	**триместр** trim**e**str **trimester**	**амниоцентез** amniots**e**ntez **amniocentesis**	**кесарево сечение** kes**a**revo sech**e**niye **cesarean section**	**швы** shvy **stitches**	**акушер** akush**e**r **obstetrician**

роды rody • childbirth

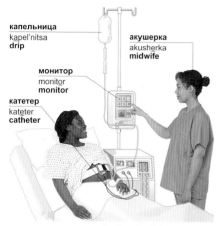

капельница
kapel'nitsa
drip

акушерка
akusherka
midwife

монитор
monitor
monitor

катетер
kateter
catheter

стимулировать роды stimulirovat' rody | **induce labor (v)**

инкубатор inkubator | **incubator**

вес при рождении ves pri rozhdeniyi
birth weight

акушерские щипцы
akusherskiye shchiptsy
forceps

вакуум-экстрактор
vakuum-ekstraktor
suction cup

родовспоможение
rodovspomozheniye
assisted delivery

бирка с именем
birka s imenem
identity tag

новорождённый novorozhdyonniy | **newborn baby**

кормление грудью kormleniye grudyu • nursing

молокоотсос
molokootsos
breast pump

бюстгальтер для кормящих
byustgal'ter dlya kormyashchikh
nursing bra

кормить грудью
kormit' grud'yu
breastfeed (v)

прокладки
prokladki
nursing pads

нетрадиционная медицина netraditsi<u>o</u>nnaya medits<u>i</u>na • alternative therapy

позы йоги
poza i<u>o</u>gi
yoga pose

коврик
k<u>o</u>vrik
mat

йога y<u>o</u>ga | **yoga**

массаж
mass<u>a</u>zh
massage

шиацу
shiats<u>u</u>
shiatsu

хиропрактика
khiropr<u>a</u>ktika
chiropractic

остеопатия
osteop<u>a</u>tiya
osteopathy

рефлексология
refleksol<u>o</u>giya
reflexology

медитация
medit<u>a</u>tsiya
meditation

психолог-консультант
psikholog-konsul'tant
counselor

рейки
reyki
reiki

иглоукалывание
igloukalyvaniye
acupuncture

групповая терапия
gruppovaya terapiya
group therapy

аюрведа
ayurveda
ayurveda

гипнотерапия
gipnoterapiya
hypnotherapy

эфирные масла
efirniye masla
essential oils

фитотерапия
fitoterapiya
herbalism

ароматерапия
aromaterapiya
aromatherapy

гомеопатия
gomeopatiya
homeopathy

акупрессура
akupressura
acupressure

психотерапевт
psikhoterapevt
therapist

психотерапия
psikhoterapiya
psychotherapy

словарь slovar' • vocabulary

(пищевая) добавка (pishchevaya) dobavka **supplement**	**натуропатия** naturopatiya **naturopathy**	**релаксация** relaksatsiya **relaxation**	**лекарственное растение** lekarstvennoye rasteniye **herb**
водолечение vodolecheniye **hydrotherapy**	**фэншуй** fenshuy **feng shui**	**стресс** stress **stress**	**кристаллотерапия** kristalloterapiya **crystal healing**

дом d<u>o</u>m
home

дом dom • house

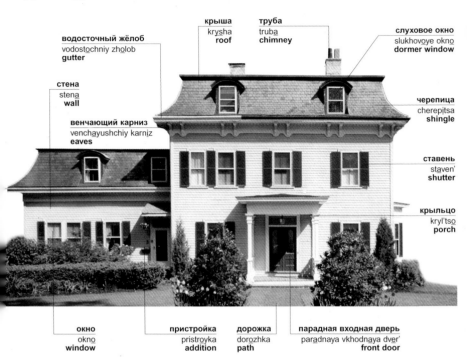

крыша
krysha
roof

труба
truba
chimney

слуховое окно
slukhovoye okno
dormer window

водосточный жёлоб
vodostochniy zholob
gutter

стена
stena
wall

венчающий карниз
venchayushchiy karniz
eaves

черепица
cherepitsa
shingle

ставень
staven'
shutter

крыльцо
kryl'tso
porch

окно
okno
window

пристройка
pristroyka
addition

дорожка
dorozhka
path

парадная входная дверь
paradnaya vkhodnaya dver'
front door

словарь slovar' • vocabulary

коттедж
cottedzh
single-family

двухквартирный дом
dvukhkvartirnyy dom
duplex

таунхаус
taunkhaus
townhouse

дом блокированной застройки
dom blokirovannoy zastroyki
row house

бунгало
bungalo
bungalow

подвал
podval
basement

гараж
garazh
garage

чердак
cherdak
attic

комната
komnata
room

почтовый ящик
pochtoviy yashchik
mailbox

наниматель, жилец
nanimatel', zhilets
tenant

арендодатель
arendodatel'
landlord

охранная сигнализация
okhrannaya signalizatsiya
burglar alarm

двор
dvor
courtyard

этаж
etazh
floor

снимать
snimat'
rent (v)

арендная плата
arendnaya plata
rent

фонарь над крыльцом
fonar' nad kryl'tsom
porch light

вход vkh<u>o</u>d • entrance

квартира
kvart<u>i</u>ra •
apartment

поручень
por<u>u</u>chen'
hand rail

лестница
l<u>e</u>snitsa
staircase

**лестничная
площадка**
l<u>e</u>snichnaya
ploshch<u>a</u>dka
landing

перила
per<u>i</u>la
banister

прихожая
prikh<u>o</u>zhaya
foyer

балкон
balk<u>o</u>n
balcony

многоквартирный дом
mnogokv<u>a</u>rtirniy dom
apartment building

домофон
domof<u>o</u>n
intercom

дверной звонок
dvern<u>o</u>y zvon<u>o</u>k
doorbell

коврик
k<u>o</u>vrik
doormat

дверной молоток
dvern<u>o</u>y molot<u>o</u>k
door knocker

ключ
kly<u>u</u>ch
key

дверная цепочка
dvern<u>a</u>ya tsep<u>o</u>chka
door chain

замок
zam<u>o</u>k
lock

задвижка
zadv<u>i</u>zhka
bolt

лифт
lift
elevator

инженерные коммуникации inzhenernye kommunikatsii • internal systems

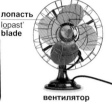

лопасть
lopast'
blade

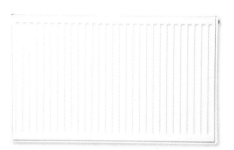 

вентилятор
ventilyator
fan

батарея
batareya
radiator

обогреватель
obogrevatel'
space heater

конвектор
konvektor
convector heater

электричество elektrichestvo • electricity

заземление
zazemleniye
ground

нулевой провод
nulevoy provod
neutral

штекер
shteker
pin

энергосберегающая лампа
energosberegayushchaya lampa
energy-saving bulb

под напряжением
pod napryazheniyem
live

штепсельная вилка
shtepsel'naya vilka | **plug**

проводка provodka | **wires**

словарь slovar' • vocabulary

напряжение napryazheniye **voltage**	**предохранитель** predokhranitel' **fuse**	**розетка** rozetka **outlet**	**постоянный ток** postoyanny tok **direct current**	**отключение электроэнергии** otklyucheniye elektroenergii **power outage**
ампер amper **amp**	**блок плавких предохранителей** blok plavkikh predokhraniteley **fuse box**	**выключатель** vyklyuchatel' **switch**	**трансформатор** transformator **transformer**	**электрическая сеть** elektricheskaya set' **household current**
электроэнергия elektroenergiya **power**	**генератор** generator **generator**	**переменный ток** peremenniy tok **alternating current**	**электросчётчик** elektroschotchik **electric meter**	

водопровод vodoprovod • plumbing

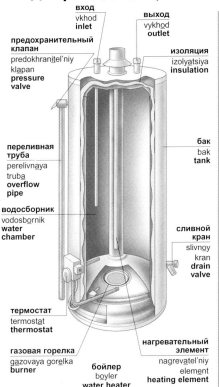

вход
vkhod
inlet

выход
vykhod
outlet

предохранительный клапан
predokhranitel'niy klapan
pressure valve

изоляция
izolyatsiya
insulation

переливная труба
perelivnaya truba
overflow pipe

бак
bak
tank

водосборник
vodosbornik
water chamber

сливной кран
slivnoy kran
drain valve

термостат
termostat
thermostat

газовая горелка
gazovaya gorelka
burner

бойлер
boyler
water heater

нагревательный элемент
nagrevatel'niy element
heating element

раковина rakovina • sink

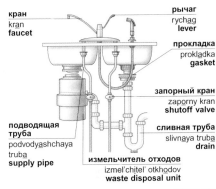

кран
kran
faucet

рычаг
rychag
lever

прокладка
prokladka
gasket

запорный кран
zaporny kran
shutoff valve

подводящая труба
podvodyashchaya truba
supply pipe

сливная труба
slivnaya truba
drain

измельчитель отходов
izmel'chitel' otkhodov
waste disposal unit

туалет tualet • toilet

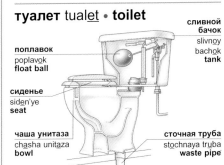

сливной бачок
slivnoy bachok
tank

поплавок
poplavok
float ball

сиденье
siden'ye
seat

чаша унитаза
chasha unitaza
bowl

сточная труба
stochnaya truba
waste pipe

утилизация мусора utilizatsiya musora • waste disposal

бутылка
butylka
bottle

крышка
kryshka
lid

педаль
pedal'
pedal

контейнер для мусора
konteyner dlya musora
recycling bin

ведро для мусора
vedro dlya musora
trash can

сортировочный ящик
sortirovochniy yashchik
sorting unit

органические отходы
organicheskiye otkhody
organic waste

гостиная gostinaya • **living room**

бра
bra
wall light

камин
kamin
fireplace

потолок
potolok
ceiling

ваза
vaza
vase

**диванная
подушка**
divannaya
podushka
pillow

лампа
lampa
lamp

**журнальный
столик**
zhurnal'niy
stolik
coffee table

диван
divan
sofa

пол
pol
floor

рама
r<u>a</u>ma
frame

картина
kart<u>i</u>na
painting

штора
sht<u>o</u>ra
curtain

занавеска
zanav<u>e</u>ska
sheer curtain

жалюзи
zhaly<u>u</u>zi
Venetian blind

рулонная штора
rul<u>o</u>nnaya sht<u>o</u>ra
roller shade

лепной карниз
lepn<u>o</u>y karn<u>i</u>z
molding

кресло
kr<u>e</u>slo
armchair

книжная полка
kn<u>i</u>zhnaya p<u>o</u>lka
bookshelf

диван-кровать
div<u>a</u>n-krov<u>a</u>t'
sofa bed

ковёр
kovy<u>o</u>r
rug

кабинет kabin<u>e</u>t | **study**

столовая stolovaya • dining room

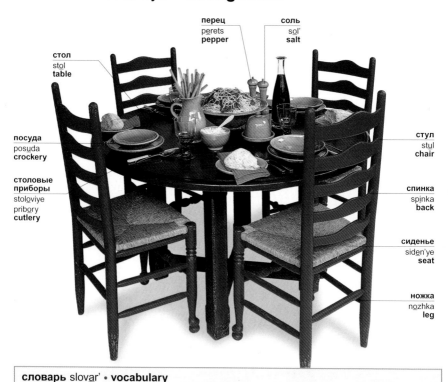

перец
perets
pepper

соль
sol'
salt

стол
stol
table

посуда
posuda
crockery

столовые приборы
stoloviye
pribory
cutlery

стул
stul
chair

спинка
spinka
back

сиденье
siden'ye
seat

ножка
nozhka
leg

словарь slovar' • vocabulary

накрывать на стол nakryvat' na stol **set the table (v)**	**голодный** golodniy **hungry**	**обед** obed **lunch**	**сыт(ый)** syt(iy) **full**	**хозяин** khozyain **host**	**Можно мне добавки?** mozhno mne dobavki? **Can I have some more, please?**
подавать podavat' **serve (v)**	**скатерть** skatert' **tablecloth**	**ужин** uzhin **dinner**	**порция** portsiya **portion**	**хозяйка** khozyayka **hostess**	**Нет, спасибо, я сыт/сыта.** net, spasibo, ya syt/syta **I've had enough, thank you.**
есть yest' **eat (v)**	**завтрак** zavtrak **breakfast**	**сервировочная салфетка** servirovochnaya salfetka **placemat**	**прием пищи** priyom pishchi **meal**	**гость** gost' **guest**	**Это было очень вкусно.** eto bylo ochen' vkusno **That was delicious.**

посуда и столовые приборы posuda i stoloviye pribory · crockery and cutlery

чайная ложечка
chaynaya lozhechka
teaspoon

кружка
kruzhka
mug

кофейная чашка
kofeynaya
chashka
coffee cup

чайная чашка
chaynaya chashka
teacup

тарелка
tarelka
plate

миска
miska
bowl

бокал
bokal
wine glass

стакан
stakan
tumbler

кофейный пресс
kofeyny press
French press

заварочный чайник
zavarochniy chaynik
teapot

кувшин
kuvshin
pitcher

подставка для яиц
podstavka dlya yayts
eggcup

стеклянная посуда
steklyannaya posuda
glassware

кольцо для салфетки
kol'tso dlya
salfetki
napkin ring

тарелочка для хлеба
tarelochka
dlya khleba
side plate

мелкая тарелка
melkaya
tarelka
dinner plate

суповая тарелка
supovaya tarelka
soup bowl

суповая ложка
supovaya lozhka
soup spoon

салфетка
salfetka
napkin

вилка
vilka
fork

сервировка на одну персону
servirovka na odnu personu
place setting

ложка
lozhka
spoon

нож
nozh
knife

кухня kukhnya • kitchen

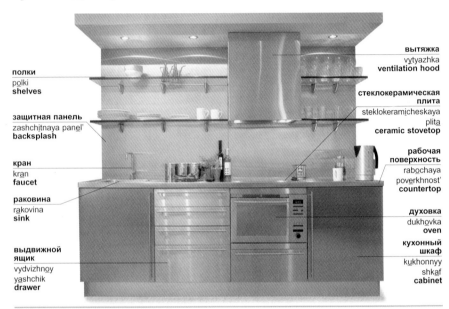

полки
polki
shelves

защитная панель
zashchitnaya panel'
backsplash

кран
kran
faucet

раковина
rakovina
sink

выдвижной ящик
vydvizhnoy yashchik
drawer

вытяжка
vytyazhka
ventilation hood

стеклокерамическая плита
steklokeramicheskaya plita
ceramic stovetop

рабочая поверхность
rabochaya poverkhnost'
countertop

духовка
dukhovka
oven

кухонный шкаф
kukhonnyy shkaf
cabinet

бытовые приборы bytoviye pribory • appliances

чаша для смешивания
chasha dlya smeshivaniya
mixing bowl

крышка
kryshka
lid

нож
nozh
blade

микроволновая печь
mikrovolnovaya pech'
microwave oven

чайник
chaynik
electric kettle

тостер
toster
toaster

кухонный комбайн
kukhonniy kombayn
food processor

блендер
blender
blender

посудомоечная машина
posudomoyechnaya mashina
dishwasher

льдогенератор
l'dogenerator
ice maker

холодильник
kholodil'nik
refrigerator

полка
polka
shelf

морозильник
morozil'nik
freezer

отделение для овощей и фруктов
otdeleniye dlya ovoshchey i fruktov
crisper

холодильник с морозильным отделением
kholodilnik s morozilnym otdeleniyem
side-by-side refrigerator

словарь slovar' •
vocabulary

подставка для сушки
podstavka dlya sushki
draining board

конфорка газовой плиты
konforka gazovoy plity
burner

конфорка плиты
konforka plity
stovetop

мусорное ведро
musornoe vedro
garbage can

замораживать
zamorazhivat'
freeze (v)

размораживать
razmorazhivat'
defrost (v)

готовить на пару
gotovit' na paru
steam (v)

пассеровать
passerovat'
sauté (v)

приготовление пищи prigotovleniye pishchi • cooking

 чистить chistit' **peel (v)**

 нарезать narezat' **slice (v)**

 натирать natirat' **grate (v)**

 наливать nalivat' **pour (v)**

 смешивать smeshivat' **mix (v)**

 взбивать vzbivat' **whisk (v)**

 варить varit' **boil (v)**

 жарить zharit' **fry (v)**

 раскатывать raskatyvat' **roll (v)**

 помешивать pomeshivat' **stir (v)**

 готовить на медленном огне gotovit' na medlennom ogne | **simmer (v)**

 варить, не доводя до кипения varit', ne dovodya do kipeniya | **poach (v)**

 печь pech' **bake (v)**

 жарить, запекать zharit', zapekat' **roast (v)**

 жарить на гриле zharit' na grile **broil (v)**

кухонная утварь kukhonnaya utvar' • kitchenware

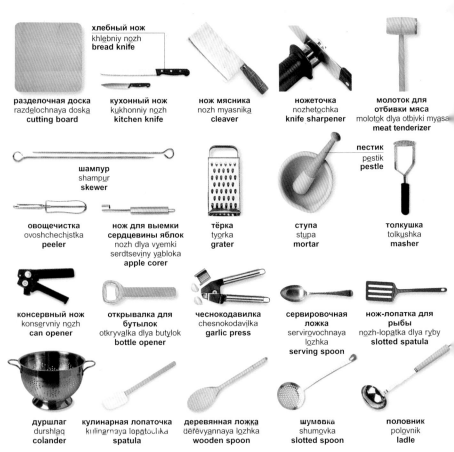

хлебный нож
khlebniy nozh
bread knife

разделочная доска
razdelochnaya doska
cutting board

кухонный нож
kukhonniy nozh
kitchen knife

нож мясника
nozh myasnika
cleaver

ножеточка
nozhetochka
knife sharpener

**молоток для
отбивки мяса**
molotok dlya otbivki myasa
meat tenderizer

шампур
shampur
skewer

пестик
pestik
pestle

овощечистка
ovoshchechistka
peeler

**нож для выемки
сердцевины яблок**
nozh dlya vyemki
serdtseviny yabloka
apple corer

тёрка
tyorka
grater

ступа
stupa
mortar

толкушка
tolkushka
masher

консервный нож
konservniy nozh
can opener

**открывалка для
бутылок**
otkryvalka dlya butylok
bottle opener

чеснокодавилка
chesnokodavilka
garlic press

**сервировочная
ложка**
servirovochnaya
lozhka
serving spoon

**нож-лопатка для
рыбы**
nozh-lopatka dlya ryby
slotted spatula

дуршлаг
durshlag
colander

кулинарная лопаточка
kulinarnaya lopatochka
spatula

деревянная ложка
derevyannaya lozhka
wooden spoon

шумовка
shumovka
slotted spoon

половник
polovnik
ladle

разделочная вилка
razdelochnaya vilka
carving fork

ложка для мороженого
lozhka dlya morozhenogo
ice-cream scoop

венчик
venchik
whisk

ситечко
sitechko
sieve

крышка
kryshka
lid

антипригарный
antiprigarniy
nonstick

сковорода
skovoroda
frying pan

кастрюля
kastryulya
saucepan

сковорода-гриль
skovoroda-gril'
grill pan

вок
vok
wok

керамическая
кастрюля
keramicheskaya kastryulya
earthenware dish

стекло
Steklo
glass

жаропрочный
zharoprochniy
ovenproof

миска
miska
mixing bowl

форма для суфле
forma dlya sufle
soufflé dish

форма для запеканки
forma dlya zapekanki
gratin dish

рамекин
ramekin
ramekin

кастрюля-
кассероль
kastryulya-kasserol'
casserole dish

выпечка vypechka • baking cakes

весы
vesy
scale

мерная емкость
mernaya emkost'
measuring cup

форма для торта
forma dlya torta
cake pan

форма для пирога
с начинкой
forma dlya piroga s
nachinkoy
pie pan

форма для флана
forma dlya flana
quiche pan

кондитерская кисть
konditerskaya kist'
pastry brush

скалка skalka | **rolling pin**

кондитерский мешок
konditerskiy meshok | **piping bag**

форма для
маффинов
forma dlya mafinov
muffin pan

противень
protiven'
cookie sheet

решётка (для
охлаждения)
reshotka (dlya
okhlazhdeniya)
cooling rack

рукавица-
прихватка
rukavitsa-prikhvatka
oven mitt

передник
perednik
apron

спальня sp<u>a</u>l'nya · **bedroom**

платяной шкаф
platyan<u>o</u>y shk<u>a</u>f
wardrobe

ночник
nochn<u>i</u>k
bedside lamp

изголовье
izgol<u>o</u>v'ye
headboard

тумбочка
t<u>u</u>mbochka
nightstand

комод
kom<u>o</u>d
chest of drawers

выдвижной ящик	**кровать**	**матрас**	**покрывало**	**подушка**
vydvizhn<u>o</u>y y<u>a</u>shchik	krov<u>a</u>t'	matr<u>a</u>s	pokryv<u>a</u>lo	pod<u>u</u>shka
drawer	**bed**	**mattress**	**bedspread**	**pillow**

грелка
gr<u>e</u>lka
hot-water bottle

часы-радио
chasy-r<u>a</u>dio
clock radio

будильник
bud<u>i</u>l'nik
alarm clock

**пачка бумажных
салфеток**
p<u>a</u>chka bumazhnykh
salf<u>e</u>tok
box of tissues

вешалка
v<u>e</u>shalka
coat hanger

постельное бельё postel'noye bel'yo • bed linen

наволочка
navolochka
pillowcase

простыня
prostynya
sheet

подзор
podzor
dust ruffle

зеркало
zerkalo
mirror

туалетный столик
tualetniy stolik
dressing table

пуховое одеяло
pukhovoye odeyalo
comforter

стёганое одеяло
steganoye odeyalo
quilt

шерстяное одеяло
sherstyanoye odeyalo
blanket

пол
pol
floor

словарь slovar' • vocabulary

односпальная кровать odnospal'naya krovat' **twin bed**	**изножье** iznozh'ye **footboard**	**бессонница** bessonnitsa **insomnia**	**проснуться** prosnut'sya **wake up (v)**	**ставить будильник** stavit' budil'nik **set the alarm (v)**
двуспальная кровать dvuspal'naya krovat' **full bed**	**пружина** pruzhina **bedspring**	**идти спать** idti spat' **go to bed (v)**	**вставать** vstavat' **get up (v)**	**храпеть** khrapet' **snore (v)**
электроодеяло elektroodeyalo **electric blanket**	**ковёр** kovyor **carpet**	**заснуть** zasnut' **go to sleep (v)**	**заправлять постель** zapravlyat' postel' **make the bed (v)**	**встроенный шкаф** vstroyenniy shkaf **closet**

ванная комната v<u>a</u>nnaya k<u>o</u>mnata • **bathroom**

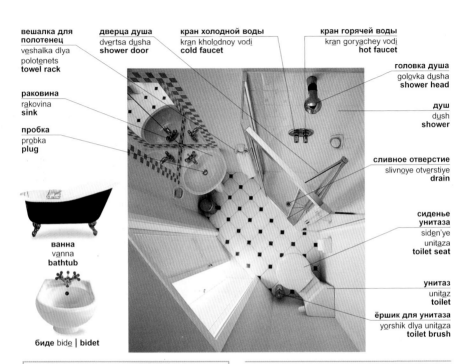

вешалка для полотенец
v<u>e</u>shalka dlya pol<u>o</u>tenets
towel rack

дверца душа
dv<u>e</u>rtsa d<u>u</u>sha
shower door

кран холодной воды
kr<u>a</u>n khol<u>o</u>dnoy vodi
cold faucet

кран горячей воды
kr<u>a</u>n gory<u>a</u>chey vodi
hot faucet

головка душа
gol<u>o</u>vka d<u>u</u>sha
shower head

раковина
r<u>a</u>kovina
sink

душ
d<u>u</u>sh
shower

пробка
pr<u>o</u>bka
plug

сливное отверстие
slivn<u>o</u>ye otv<u>e</u>rstiye
drain

сиденье унитаза
sid<u>e</u>n'ye unit<u>a</u>za
toilet seat

ванна
v<u>a</u>nna
bathtub

унитаз
unit<u>a</u>z
toilet

ёршик для унитаза
y<u>o</u>rshik dlya unit<u>a</u>za
toilet brush

биде bid<u>e</u> | **bidet**

словарь slov<u>a</u>r' • **vocabulary**

аптечка
apt<u>e</u>chka
medicine cabinet

коврик для ванной
k<u>o</u>vrik dlya v<u>a</u>nnoy
bath mat

рулон туалетной бумаги
rul<u>o</u>n tual<u>e</u>tnoy bum<u>a</u>gi
toilet paper

занавеска для душа
zanav<u>e</u>ska dlya d<u>u</u>sha
shower curtain

принимать душ
prinim<u>a</u>t' d<u>u</u>sh
take a shower (v)

принимать ванну
prinim<u>a</u>t' v<u>a</u>nnu
take a bath (v)

гигиена полости рта gigiy<u>e</u>na p<u>o</u>losti rt<u>a</u> • **dental hygiene**

зубная щётка
zubn<u>a</u>ya shch<u>o</u>tka
toothbrush

зубная нить
zubn<u>a</u>ya nit'
dental floss

зубная паста
zubn<u>a</u>ya p<u>a</u>sta
toothpaste

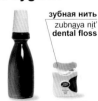

ополаскиватель для рта
opol<u>a</u>skivatel' dlya rt<u>a</u>
mouthwash

губка
gubka
sponge

пемза
pemza
pumice stone

щётка для спины
shchotka dlya spiny
back brush

дезодорант
dezodorant
deodorant

мыльница
milnitsa
soap dish

гель для душа
gel' dlya dusha
shower gel

мыло
mylo
soap

крем для лица
krem dlya litsa
face cream

пена для ванны
pena dlya vanni
bubble bath

**полотенце
для рук**
polotentse dlya ruk
hand towel

**банное
полотенце**
bannoye
polotentse
bath towel

полотенца
polotentsa
towels

молочко для тела
molochko dlya tela
body lotion

тальк
tal'k
talcum powder

банный халат
banniy khalat
bathrobe

бритьё brit'yo • shaving

электробритва
elektrobritva
electric razor

пена для бритья
pena dlya brit'ya
shaving foam

**одноразовый станок для
бритья**
odnorazoviy stanok dlya brit'ya
disposable razor

лезвие
lezviye
razor blade

лосьон после бритья
los'yon posle brit'ya
aftershave

детская комната d<u>e</u>tskaya k<u>o</u>mnata • **nursery**

уход за младенцем ukh<u>o</u>d za mlad<u>e</u>ntsem • **baby care**

губка
g<u>u</u>bka
sponge

крем от опрелостей
kr<u>e</u>m ot opr<u>e</u>lostey
diaper rash cream

влажная салфетка
vl<u>a</u>zhnaya
salf<u>e</u>tka
wet wipe

ванночка
v<u>a</u>nnochka
baby bath

горшок
gorsh<u>o</u>k
potty

пеленальный коврик
pelen<u>a</u>l'niy k<u>o</u>vrik
changing mat

сон s<u>o</u>n • **sleeping**

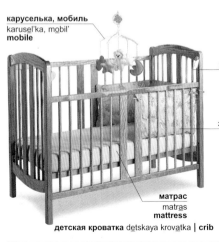

каруселька, мобиль
karus<u>e</u>l'ka, m<u>o</u>bil'
mobile

простыня
prost<u>y</u>nya
sheet

одеяльце
odey<u>a</u>l'tse
blanket

прутья решётки
pr<u>u</u>tia
resh<u>e</u>tki
bars

ворсистое покрывало
vors<u>i</u>stoe
pokriv<u>a</u>lo
fleece

постельное бельё
post<u>e</u>l'noe bel'<u>e</u>
bedding

защитный бампер
zashch<u>i</u>tny b<u>a</u>mper
bumper

матрас
matr<u>a</u>s
mattress

детская кроватка d<u>e</u>tskaya krov<u>a</u>tka | **crib**

погремушка
pogrem<u>u</u>shka
rattle

колыбелька с ручками
kolyb<u>e</u>l'ka s r<u>u</u>chkami
bassinet

игры igry • playing

кукла
kukla
doll

мягкая игрушка
myakhkaya igrushka
stuffed toy

кукольный домик
kukol'niy domik
dollhouse

домик для игр
domik dlya igr
playhouse

плюшевый мишка
plusheviy mishka
teddy bear

игрушка
igrushka
toy

корзина для игрушек
korzina dlya igrushek
toy basket

мячик
myachik
ball

манеж
manezh
playpen

безопасность
bezopasnost' •
safety

блокиратор от детей
blokirator ot detey
child lock

радионяня
radionyanya
baby monitor

воротца
vorottsa
stair gate

еда yeda • eating

детский стульчик
detskiy stulchik
high chair

соска
soska
nipple

поильник
poil'nik
drinking cup

бутылочка
butylochka
bottle

прогулка progulka • going out

капюшон
kapyushon
hood

прогулочная коляска
progulochnaya kolyaska
stroller

коляска с люлькой
kolyaska s lyul'koy
baby carriage

переносная люлька
perenosnaya lyul'ka
carrier

подгузник
podguznik
diaper

сумка для смены подгузника
sumka dlya smeny podguznika
diaper bag

сумка-кенгуру
sumka-kenguru
baby sling

подсобное помещение podsobnoye pomescheniye • utility room

стирка stirka • laundry

чистая одежда
chistaya
odezhda
clean clothes

грязное бельё
gryaznoye
bel'yo
dirty laundry

корзина для
белья
korzina dlya bel'ya
laundry basket

стиральная
машина
stiral'naya mashina
washing machine

стиральная
машина с сушкой
stiral'naya
mashina s sushkoy
washer-dryer

сушилка
sushilka
tumble dryer

верёвка для белья
veryovka dlya bel'ya
clothesline

утюг
utyug
iron

прищепка
prishchepka
clothespin

сушить
sushit'
dry (v)

гладильная доска gladil'naya doska | **ironing board**

словарь slovar' • vocabulary

загружать zagruzhat' **load (v)**	отжимать (в центрифуге) otzhimat' (v tsentrifuge) **spin (v)**	гладить gladit' **iron (v)**	Как пользоваться этой стиральной машиной? kak pol'zovat'sya etoy stiral'noy mashinoy? **How do I operate the washing machine?**
полоскать poloskat' **rinse (v)**	центрифуга tsentrifuga **spin dryer**	кондиционер для белья konditsioner dlya bel'ya **fabric softener**	Какая программа предназначен для цветного/белого белья? kakaya programma prednaznachen dlya tsvetnova/belova bel'ya?? **What is the setting for colors/whites?**

оборудование для уборки oborudovaniye dlya uborki •
cleaning equipment

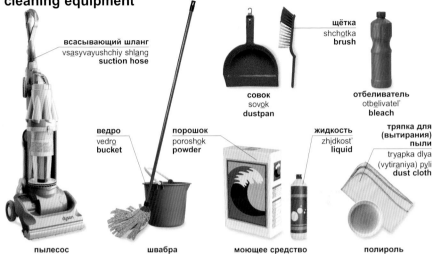

всасывающий шланг
vsasyvayushchiy shlang
suction hose

щётка
shchotka
brush

совок
sovok
dustpan

отбеливатель
otbelivatel'
bleach

ведро
vedro
bucket

порошок
poroshok
powder

жидкость
zhidkost'
liquid

**тряпка для
(вытирания)
пыли**
tryapka dlya
(vytiraniya) pyli
dust cloth

пылесос
pylesos
vacuum cleaner

швабра
shvabra
mop

моющее средство
moyushcheye sredstvo
detergent

полироль
polirol'
polish

действия deystviya • activities

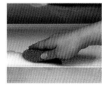

протирать, очищать
protirat', ochishchat'
clean (v)

мыть
myt'
wash (v)

вытирать
vytirat'
wipe (v)

тереть
teret'
scrub (v)

скрести
skresti
scrape (v)

щётка
schyotka
broom

подметать
podmetat'
sweep (v)

вытирать пыль
vytirat' pyl'
dust (v)

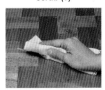

полировать, натирать
polirovat', natirat'
polish (v)

мастерская masterskaya • **workshop**

патрон
patron
chuck

сверло
sverlo
drill bit

аккумулятор
akumulyator
battery pack

электрический лобзик
elektricheskiy lobzik
jigsaw

аккумуляторная дрель
akumulyatornaya drel'
cordless drill

электродрель
elektrodrel'
electric drill

клеевой пистолет
kleyevoy pistolet
glue gun

струбцина
strubtsina
clamp

диск пилы
disk pily
blade

тиски
tiski
vise

шлифовальная машинка
shlifoval'naya mashinka
sander

циркулярная пила
tsirkulyarnaya pila
circular saw

верстак
verstak
workbench

клей для дерева
kley dlya dereva
wood glue

стеллаж для инструментов
stellazh dlya instrumentov
tool rack

фрезер
frezer
router

коловорот
kolovorot
bit brace

древесная стружка
drevesnaya struzhka
wood shavings

удлинитель
udlinitel'
extension cord

виды обработки vidy obrabotki • techniques

резать
rezat'
cut (v)

пилить
pilit'
saw (v)

сверлить
sverlit
drill (v)

прибивать
pribivat'
hammer (v)

строгать strogat'
plane (v)

точить tochit' | **turn (v)**

припой
pripoy
solder

вырезать vyrezat'
carve (v)

паять payat' | **solder (v)**

материалы materialy • materials

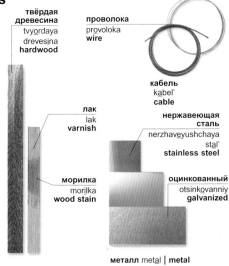

МДФ
em-de-ef
MDF

фанера
fanera
plywood

ДСП (древесно-стружечная плита)
de es pe (drevesno-struzhechnaya plita)
particle board

ДВП (древесно-волокнистая плита)
de ve pe (drevesno-voloknlstaya plita)
hardboard

мягкая древесина
myagkaya drevesina
softwood

твёрдая древесина
tvyordaya drevesina
hardwood

лак
lak
varnish

морилка
morilka
wood stain

дерево derevo | **wood**

проволока
provoloka
wire

кабель
kabel'
cable

нержавеющая сталь
nerzhaveyushchaya stal'
stainless steel

оцинкованный
otsinkovanniy
galvanized

металл metal | **metal**

инструментальный ящик instrumentalnyj yashik • toolbox

гаечный ключ
gayechniy
klyuch
wrench

разводной ключ
razvodnoy klyuch
adjustable wrench

молоток
molotok
hammer

плоскогубцы
ploskogubtsy
needle-nose pliers

торцовый гаечный ключ
tortsoviy gayechniy klyuch
socket wrench

насадки для отвёртки
nasadki dlya otvyortki
screwdriver bits

спиртовой уровень
spirtovoy uroven'
level

шайба
shayba
washer

отвёртка
otvyortka
screwdriver

гайка
gayka
nut

рулетка
ruletka
tape measure

макетный нож
maketniy nozh
utility knife

пассатижи
passatizhi
bull-nose pliers

насадка для гаечного ключа
nasadka dlya gayechnogo klyucha
socket

ключ-шестигранник
klyuch-shestigrannik
Allen wrench

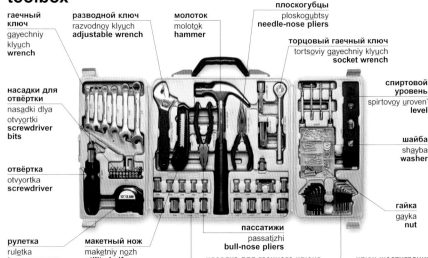

свёрла sverla • drill bits

сверло по металлу
sverlo po metallu
metal bit

плоское (перовое) сверло по дереву
ploskoye (perovoye) sverlo po derevu
flat wood bit

крестовая отвёртка
krestovaya otvertka
Phillips screwdriver

развёртка
razvyortka
reamer

шляпка
shlyapka
head

столярные свёрла
stolyarniye svyorla
carpentry bits

безопасное сверло
bezopasnoye sverlo
security bit

гвоздь
gvozd'
nail

сверло по камню
sverlo po kamnu
masonry bit

винт
vint
screw

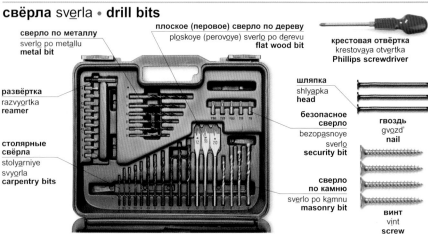

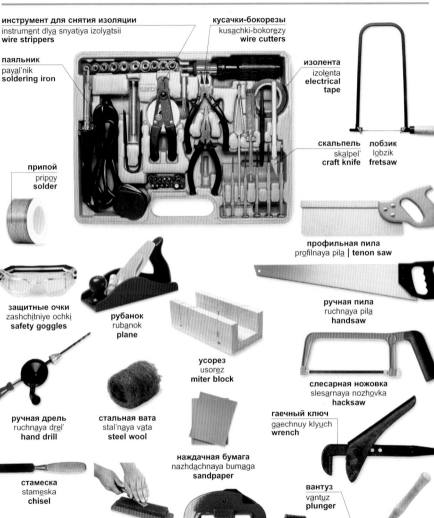

инструмент для снятия изоляции
instrument dlya snyatiya izolyatsii
wire strippers

кусачки-бокорезы
kusachki-bokorezy
wire cutters

паяльник
payal'nik
soldering iron

изолента
izolenta
electrical tape

припой
pripoy
solder

скальпель
skalpel'
craft knife

лобзик
lobzik
fretset

профильная пила
profilnaya pila | **tenon saw**

защитные очки
zashchitniye ochki
safety goggles

рубанок
rubanok
plane

усорез
usorez
miter block

ручная пила
ruchnaya pila
handsaw

ручная дрель
ruchnaya drel'
hand drill

стальная вата
stal'naya vata
steel wool

слесарная ножовка
slesarnaya nozhovka
hacksaw

гаечный ключ
gaechnuy klyuch
wrench

наждачная бумага
nazhdachnaya bumaga
sandpaper

стамеска
stameska
chisel

вантуз
vantuz
plunger

напильник
napil'nik
file

оселок
oselok
whetstone

труборез truborez | **pipe cutter**

отделочные работы otdelochniye raboty • decorating

ножницы
nozhnitsy
scissors

макетный нож
maketniy nozh
utility knife

отвес
otves
plumb line

шпатель
shpatel'
scraper

обойщик
oboyshik
decorator

обои
oboi
wallpaper

стремянка
stremyanka
stepladder

щётка для обоев
shchotka dlya
oboyev
wallpaper brush

рабочий стол
rabochiy stol
pasting table

кисть для клея
kist' dlya kleya
pasting brush

обойный клей
oboynyy kley
wallpaper paste

ведро
vedro
bucket

наклеивать обои nakleivat' oboi | **wallpaper (v)**

сдирать sdirat' | **strip (v)**

шпаклевать shpaklevat' | **fill (v)**

шлифовать shlifovat'
sand (v)

штукатурить shtukaturit'
plaster (v)

оклеивать (обоями)
okleivat' (oboyami) | **hang (v)**

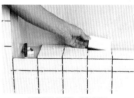

укладывать плитку
ukladivat' plitku | **tile (v)**

красить krasit' | **paint (v)**

валик
valik
roller

лоток для краски
lotok dlya kraski
paint tray

краска
kraska
paint

кисть
kist'
brush

банка с
краской
banka s
kraskoy
paint can

губка
gubka
sponge

малярная лента
malyarnaya lenta
masking tape

наждачная
бумага
nazhdachnaya
bumaga
sandpaper

рабочий
комбинезон
rabochiy
kombinezon
coveralls

защитное
покрытие от
пыли
zashchitnoye
pokrytiye ot pyli
drop cloth

скипидар
skipidar
turpentine

шпаклёвка
shpaklyovka
filler

уайт-спирит
uayt-spirit
paint thinner

словарь slovar' · vocabulary

штукатурка
shtukaturka
plaster

лак
lak
varnish

эмульсия
emul'siya
latex paint

глянцевый
glyantseviy
gloss

матовый
matoviy
matte

трафарет
trafaret
stencil

тиснёные обои
tisnyoniye oboi
embossed paper

оклеечная
бумага
okleyechnaya
bumaga
lining paper

грунтовка
gruntovka
primer

нижний слой
покрытия
nizhniy sloy pokrytiya
undercoat

верхний слой
покрытия
verkhniy sloy pokrytiya
topcoat

защитная пропитка
zashchitnaya propitka
preservative

герметик
germetik
sealant

растворитель
rastvoritel'
solvent

жидкий
строительный
раствор / затирка
zhidkiy stroitel'niy
rastvor / zatirka
grout

сад s<u>a</u>d • garden

садовые стили sad<u>o</u>viye st<u>i</u>li • garden styles

патио p<u>a</u>tio | patio garden

сад на крыше
s<u>a</u>d na kr<u>y</u>she
roof garden

подвесное кашпо
podvesn<u>o</u>ye kashp<u>o</u>
hanging basket

английский сад angl<u>i</u>yskiy sad | formal garden

сад камней
s<u>a</u>d kamn<u>e</u>y
rock garden

трельяжная опора
trel'y<u>a</u>zhnaya op<u>o</u>ra | **trellis**

двор dv<u>o</u>r | courtyard

сельский сад
s<u>e</u>lskiy sad
cottage garden

сад пряных трав
s<u>a</u>d pry<u>a</u>nykh tr<u>a</u>v
herb garden

водный сад
v<u>o</u>dniy s<u>a</u>d
water garden

пергола
p<u>e</u>rgola
arbor

почва
p_ochva • **soil**

мощёное покрытие
moshch_onoye pokr_ytiye
paving

дорожка
dor_ozhka
path

компостная куча
komp_ostnaya k_ucha
compost pile

калитка
kal_itka
gate

клумба
kl_umba
flowerbed

сарай
sar_ay
shed

теплица
tepl_itsa
greenhouse

газон
gaz_on
lawn

пруд
pr_ud
pond

забор
zab_or
fence

живая
изгородь
zhiv_aya
_izgorod'
hedge

арка
_arka
arch

огород
ogor_od
vegetable garden

цветочный бордюр
tsvet_ochniy bordyur
herbaceous border

верхний слой
почвы
verkhniy sl_oy p_ochvy
topsoil

песок
pes_ok
sand

известь
_izvest'
chalk

илистый грунт
_ilistiy gr_unt
silt

глина
gl_ina
clay

настил
nast_il
deck

фонтан font_an | **fountain**

садовые растения sad<u>o</u>vie rast<u>e</u>niya • **garden plants**

виды растений v<u>i</u>dy rast<u>e</u>niy • **types of plants**

однолетнее
odnol<u>e</u>tnee
annual

двулетнее
dvul<u>e</u>tnee
biennial

многолетнее
mnogol<u>e</u>tnee
perennial

лук
luk
bulb

папоротник
pap<u>o</u>rotnik
fern

камыш
kam<u>y</u>sh
cattail

бамбук
bamb<u>u</u>k
bamboo

сорняки
sornyak<u>i</u>
weeds

травянистое растение
travyan<u>i</u>stoye rast<u>e</u>nie
herb

водное растение
v<u>o</u>dnoye rast<u>e</u>niye
water plant

дерево
d<u>e</u>revo
tree

пальма
pal'ma
palm

хвойное растение
khv<u>o</u>ynoye rast<u>e</u>niye
conifer

вечнозелёное растение
vechnozely<u>o</u>noye
rast<u>e</u>niye
evergreen

лиственное дерево
l<u>i</u>stvennoye d<u>e</u>revo
deciduous

**фигурная стрижка,
топиарий**
figurnaya strizhka, topiariy
topiary

альпийское растение
al'piyskoye rasteniye
alpine

суккулент
sukkulent
succulent

кактус
kaktus
cactus

горшочное растение
gorshochnoe rastenie
potted plant

тенелюбивое растение
tenelyubivoye rasteniye
shade plant

**вьющееся
растение**
v'yushcheyesya
rasteniye
climber

**цветущий
кустарник**
tsvetushchiy
kustarnik
flowering shrub

**почвопокровное
растение**
pochvopokrovnoye
rasteniye
ground cover

ползучее растение
polzucheye rasteniye
creeper

декоративное (растение)
dekorativnoye (rasteniye)
ornamental

трава
trava
grass

садовые инструменты sad<u>o</u>viye instrum<u>e</u>nty • **garden tools**

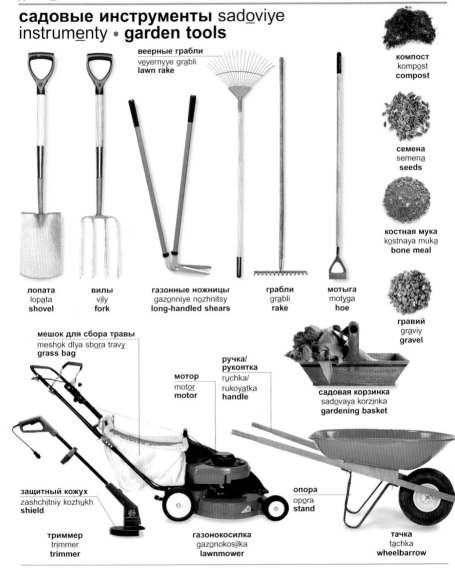

веерные грабли
veyernyye gr<u>a</u>bli
lawn rake

компост
komp<u>o</u>st
compost

семена
sem<u>e</u>na
seeds

костная мука
k<u>o</u>stnaya muk<u>a</u>
bone meal

лопата
lop<u>a</u>ta
shovel

вилы
v<u>i</u>ly
fork

газонные ножницы
gaz<u>o</u>nniye n<u>o</u>zhnitsy
long-handled shears

грабли
gr<u>a</u>bli
rake

мотыга
mot<u>y</u>ga
hoe

гравий
gr<u>a</u>viy
gravel

мешок для сбора травы
mesh<u>o</u>k dlya sb<u>o</u>ra trav<u>y</u>
grass bag

**ручка/
рукоятка**
r<u>u</u>chka/
ruko<u>ya</u>tka
handle

мотор
mot<u>o</u>r
motor

садовая корзинка
sad<u>o</u>vaya korz<u>i</u>nka
gardening basket

защитный кожух
zashch<u>i</u>tniy kozh<u>u</u>kh
shield

опора
op<u>o</u>ra
stand

триммер
tr<u>i</u>mmer
trimmer

газонокосилка
gaz<u>o</u>nok<u>o</u>silka
lawnmower

тачка
t<u>a</u>chka
wheelbarrow

садовая вилка
sadovaya vilka
hand fork

садовый совок
sadoviy sovok
trowel

лезвие
lezviye
blade

садовые ножницы
sadoviye nozhnitsy
shears

ручная пила
ruchnaya pila
handsaw

секатор
sekator
pruners

ящик для рассады
yashchik dlya rassady
seed tray

пестицид
pestitsid
pesticide

садовые перчатки
sadoviye perchatki
gardening gloves

бечёвка
bechovka
twine

бирки
birki
labels

проволочки для подвязки растений
provolochki dlya podvyazki rasteniy
twist ties

кольца для подвязки растений
kol'tsa dlya podvyazki rasteniy
ring ties

опоры для подвязывания
opory dlya podvyazyvaniya
canes

сито
sito
sieve

цветочный горшок
tsvetochniy gorshok
plant pot

резиновые сапоги
rezinoviye sapogi
rubber boots

полив poliv • watering

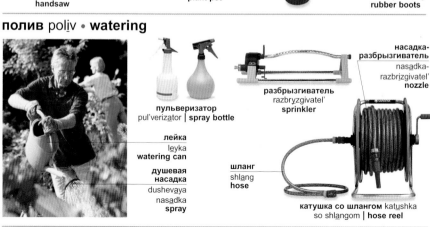

пульверизатор
pul'verizator | **spray bottle**

лейка
leyka
watering can

душевая насадка
dushevaya nasadka
spray

разбрызгиватель
razbryzgivatel'
sprinkler

насадка-разбрызгиватель
nasadka-razbrizgivatel'
nozzle

шланг
shlang
hose

катушка со шлангом katushka
so shlangom | **hose reel**

садовые работы sadovie raboti • gardening

газон, лужайка
gazon, luzhayka
lawn

живая изгородь
zhivaya izgorod'
hedge

цветочная клумба
tsvetochnaya klumba
flowerbed

колышек
kolyshek
stake

газонокосилка
gazonokosilka
lawnmower

стричь газон strich' gazon | mow (v)

укладывать дёрн
ukladivat' dern'
sod (v)

прокалывать
prokalyvat'
spike (v)

сгребать
sgrebat'
rake (v)

стричь
strich
trim (v)

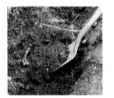

копать
kopat'
dig (v)

сеять
seyat'
sow (v)

подкармливать
podkarmlivat'
top-dress (v)

поливать
polivat'
water (v)

колышек
kolyshek
cane

направлять рост
napravlyat' rost
train (v)

обрывать увядшие соцветия
obryvat' uvyadshiye sotsvetiya
deadhead (v)

опрыскивать
opryskivat'
spray (v)

прививать
privivat'
graft (v)

черенок
cherenok
cutting

разводить черенкованием
razvodit' cherenkovaniyem
propagate (v)

обрезать
obrezat'
prune (v)

подвязывать
podvyazyvat'
stake (v)

пересаживать
peresazhivat'
transplant (v)

полоть
polot'
weed (v)

мульчировать
mul'chirovat'
mulch (v)

собирать урожай
sobirat' urozhay
harvest (v)

словарь slovar' • vocabulary

выращивать vyrashchivat' **cultivate (v)**	**благоустраивать (участок)** blagoustraivat' (uchastok) **landscape (v)**	**удобрять** udobryat' **fertilize (v)**	**просеивать** proseivat' **sift (v)**	**органический** organicheskiy **organic**	**рассада** rassada **seedling**	**подпочва** podpochva **subsoil**
ухаживать ukhazhivat' **tend (v)**	**сажать в горшок** sazhat' v gorshok **pot (v)**	**собирать** sobirat' **pick (v)**	**рыхлить** rikhlit' **aerate (v)**	**дренаж** drenazh **drainage**	**удобрение** udobreniye **fertilizer**	**гербицид** gerbitsid **weedkiller**

службы sluzhby
services

экстренные службы ekstrenniye sluzhby • emergency services

скорая помощь skoraya pomoshch' • ambulance

носилки
nosilki
stretcher

машина скорой помощи
mashina skoroy pomoshchi | **ambulance**

парамедик paramedik | **paramedic**

полиция politsiya • police

жетон (нагрудный знак)
zheton (nagrudniy znak)
badge

форма
forma
uniform

сирена
sirena
siren

проблесковый маячок
probleskoviy mayachok
lights

дубинка
dubinka
nightstick

полицейский автомобиль
politseyskiy avtomobil'
police car

полицейский участок
politseyskiy uchastok
police station

пистолет
pistolet
gun

наручники
naruchniki
handcuffs

полицейский politseyskiy | **police officer**

словарь slovar' • vocabulary

инспектор inspektor **captain**	**подозреваемый** podozrevayemiy **suspect**	**заявление** zayavlenie **complaint**	**задержание** zaderzhanie **arrest**
преступление prestuplenie **crime**	**нападение** napadenie **assault**	**расследование** rassledovaniye **investigation**	**камера** kamera **cell**
сотрудник уголовного розыска sotrudnik ugolovnogo rozyska **detective**	**отпечаток пальца** otpechatok pal'tsa **fingerprint**	**кража со взломом** krazha so vzlomom **burglary**	**обвинение** obvineniye **charge**

пожарная бригада pozharnaya brigada • fire department

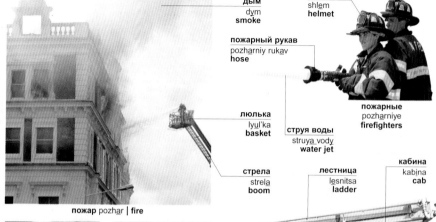

дым
dym
smoke

шлем
shlem
helmet

пожарный рукав
pozharniy rukav
hose

люлька
lyul'ka
basket

струя воды
struya vody
water jet

пожарные
pozharniye
firefighters

стрела
strela
boom

лестница
lesnitsa
ladder

кабина
kabina
cab

пожар pozhar | fire

пожарная часть
pozharnaya chast'
fire station

пожарный выход, пожарная лестница
pozharniy vykhod, pozharnaya lesnitsa
fire escape

пожарная машина
pozharnaya mashina
fire engine

дымовой извещатель
dymovoy izveshchatel'
smoke alarm

пожарная сигнализация
pozharnaya signalizatsiya
fire alarm

топор
topor
ax

огнетушитель
ognetushitel'
fire extinguisher

гидрант
gidrant
hydrant

мне нужна полиция/пожарная бригада/скорая помощь.
mne nuzhna politsiya/pozharnaya brigada/skoraya pomoshch'
I need the police/fire department/ambulance.

Пожар по адресу...
pozhar po adresu...
There's a fire at...

Произошёл несчастный случай.
proizoshol neschasniy sluchay
There's been an accident.

Вызовите полицию!
vyzovite politsiyu!
Call the police!

банк b<u>a</u>nk • **bank**

клиент
kliy<u>e</u>nt
customer

окно
okno
window

кассир
kassir
teller

рекламные листовки
reklamniye listovki
brochures

стойка
st<u>o</u>yka
counter

бланки квитанций о внесении на счёт
bl<u>a</u>nki kvit<u>a</u>ntsiy o vnes<u>e</u>niyi na shch<u>o</u>t
deposit slips

дебетовая карточка
debet<u>o</u>vaya k<u>a</u>rtochka
debit card

корешок
koresh<u>o</u>k
stub

номер счёта
n<u>o</u>mer shch<u>o</u>ta
account number

подпись
p<u>o</u>dpis'
signature

сумма
s<u>u</u>mma
amount

менеджер банка
m<u>e</u>nedzher b<u>a</u>nka
branch manager

кредитная карточка
kred<u>i</u>tnaya k<u>a</u>rtochka
credit card

чековая книжка
ch<u>e</u>kovaya kn<u>i</u>zhka
checkbook

чек
chek
check

словарь slov<u>a</u>r' • **vocabulary**

сбережения sberezh<u>e</u>niya **savings**	ипотека ip<u>o</u>teka **mortgage**	платёж plat<u>yo</u>zh **payment**	вносить vnos<u>i</u>t' **deposit (v)**	текущий счёт tek<u>u</u>shchiy shch<u>o</u>t **checking account**
налог nal<u>o</u>g **tax**	овердрафт overdr<u>a</u>ft **overdraft**	прямое дебетование pryam<u>o</u>ye debetov<u>a</u>niye **bank transfer**	банковская комиссия b<u>a</u>nkovskaya kom<u>i</u>ssiya **bank charge**	сберегательный счёт sberег<u>a</u>tel'niy shch<u>o</u>t **savings account**
заём za<u>yo</u>m **loan**	процентная ставка prots<u>e</u>ntnaya st<u>a</u>vka **interest rate**	квитанция о снятии денег с депозита kvit<u>a</u>ntsiya o sny<u>a</u>tiyi d<u>e</u>neg s depoz<u>i</u>ta **withdrawal slip**	банковский перевод b<u>a</u>nkovskiy perev<u>o</u>d **automatic payment**	ПИН-код pin-kod **PIN**

монета
moneta
coin

банкнота
banknota
bill

деньги den'gi | **money**

экран
ekran
screen

клавиатура
klaviatura
keypad

**щель
считывающего
устройства**
shchel
schityvayushchego
ustroystva
card reader

банкомат bankomat | **ATM**

иностранная валюта inostrannaya valyuta • foreign currency

обменный пункт
obmenniy punkt
currency exchange

дорожный чек
dorozhnyj chek
traveler's check

обменный курс
obmenniy kurs
exchange rate

финансы finansy • finance

финансовый консультант
finansoviy konsul'tant
financial advisor

курс акций
kurs aktsiy
share price

брокер
broker
stockbroker

фондовая биржа fondovaya
birzha | **stock exchange**

словарь slovar' • vocabulary

обналичить
obnalichit'
cash (v)

**номинальная
стоимость**
nominalnaya
stoimost'
denomination

комиссия
komissiya
commission

инвестиция
investitsiya
investment

ценные бумаги
tsenniye bumagi
stocks

акции
aktsii
shares

дивиденды
dividendy
dividends

бухгалтер
bukhgalter
accountant

**портфель (ценных
бумаг)**
portfel' (tsennykh
bumag)
portfolio

**собственный
капитал**
sobstvenniy kapital
equity

Могу я это обменять?
mogu ya eto obmenyat'?
Can I change this, please?

Какой сегодня курс обмена?
kakoy sevodnya kurs obmena?
What's today's exchange rate?

связь svyaz' • communications

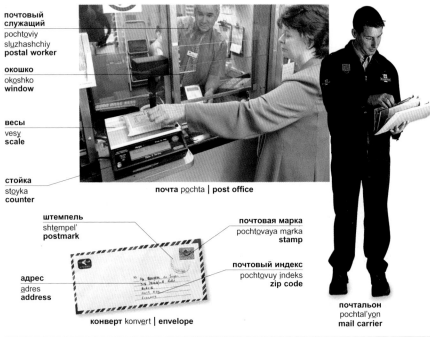

почтовый служащий
pochtoviy sluzhashchiy
postal worker

окошко
okoshko
window

весы
vesy
scale

стойка
stoyka
counter

почта pochta | post office

штемпель
shtempel'
postmark

почтовая марка
pochtovaya marka
stamp

адрес
adres
address

почтовый индекс
pochtovuy indeks
zip code

конверт konvert | envelope

почтальон
pochtal'yon
mail carrier

словарь slovar' • vocabulary

письмо
pis'mo
letter

обратный адрес
obratniy adres
return address

доставка
dostavka
delivery

хрупкое/ «осторожно!»
khrupkoye/ «ostorozhno!»
fragile

не сгибать
ne sgibat'
do not bend (v)

авиа
avia
by airmail

подпись
podpis'
signature

почтовый перевод
pochtoviy perevod
money order

верх
verkh
this way up

сумка почтальона
sumka pochtal'yona
mailbag

заказная почта
zakaznaya pochta
registered mail

выемка
vyemka
pickup

почтовый сбор
pochtoviy sbor
postage

телеграмма
telegramma
telegram

почтовый ящик
pochtoviy yashchik
mailbox

почтовый ящик (для писем)
pochtoviy yashchik (dlya pisem)
letter slot

посылка
posylka
package

курьер
kur'yer
courier

телефон telefon • telephone

телефонная трубка
telefonnaya trubka
handset

база
baza
base station

автоответчик
avtootvetchik
answering machine

беспроводной телефон
besprovodnoy telefon
cordless phone

телефонная будка
telefonnaya budka
phone booth

трубка
trubka
receiver

возврат монет
vozvrat monet
coin return

смартфон
smartfon
smartphone

мобильный телефон
mobil'niy telefon
cell phone

клавиатура
klaviatura
keypad

таксофон
taksofon
payphone

словарь slovar' • vocabulary

справочное бюро
spravochnoye byuro
directory assistance

приложение
prilozheniye
app

отвечать
otvechat'
answer (v)

обратный звонок
obratn'ye zvonok'
collect call

сообщение (СМС)
soobshcheniye (esemes)
text (SMS)

голосовое сообщение
golosovoye soobshcheniye
voice message

код доступа
kod dostupa
passcode

оператор
operator
operator

набирать номер
nabirat' nomer
dial (v)

занято
zanyato
busy

(разговор) прерван
(razgovor) prervan
disconnected

Можете дать мне номер ...?
mozhete dat' mne nomer ...?
Can you give me the number for ...?

Какой телефонный код у ...?
kakoy telefonnyy kod u ...?
What is the area code for ...?

Пришлите мне СМС!
prishlite mne esemes!
Text me!

гостиница gostinitsa • hotel
фойе foye • lobby

гость
gost'
guest

ключ от номера
klyuch ot nomera
room key

сообщения
soobshcheniya
messages

ячейка для
писем
yacheyka dlya
pisem
pigeonhole

администратор
administrator
receptionist

журнал
регистрации
zhurnal registratsii
register

стойка
stoyka
counter

стойка администратора stoyka administratora | **reception**

багаж
bagazh
luggage

тележка
telezhka
cart

швейцар shveytsar | **porter**

лифт lift | **elevator**

номер комнаты
nomer komnaty
room number

номера nomera • rooms

одноместный номер
odnomesniy nomer
single room

**двухместный номер
(номер на двоих)**
dvukhmesniy nomer
(nomer na dvoikh)
double room

**номер с двумя
односпальными
кроватями** nomer s
dvumya odnospalnymi
krovatyami | **twin room**

отдельная ванная
otdel'naya vannaya
private bathroom

услуги uslugi • services

поднос с завтраком
podnos s zavtrakom
breakfast tray

уборка номера
uborka nomera
maid service

услуги прачечной
uslugi prachechnoy
laundry service

обслуживание в номере obsluzhivanie v nomere
room service

мини-бар
mini-bar
minibar

ресторан
restoran
restaurant

тренажёрный зал
trenazhorniy zal
gym

бассейн
basseyn
swimming pool

словарь slovar' • vocabulary

ночлег с завтраком
nochleg s zavtrakom
bed and breakfast

пансион
pansion
all meals included

полупансион
polupansion
some meals included

**У вас есть свободный
номер?**
u vas yest' svobodniy nomer?
Do you have any vacancies?

**Для меня забронирован
номер.**
dlya menya zabronirovan nomer.
I have a reservation.

**Мне нужен одноместный
номер.**
mne nuzhen odnomestnuy
nomer.
I'd like a single room.

Мне нужен номер на трое суток.
mne nuzhen nomer na troye sutok.
I'd like a room for three nights.

Сколько стоит номер на сутки?
skolko stoit nomer na sutki?
What is the charge per night?

**Когда я должен/должна
освободить номер?**
kogda ya dolzhen/dolzhna
osvobodit' nomer?
When do I have to check out?

покупки pokupki
shopping

торговый центр torgoviy tsentr • shopping center

атриум
atrium
atrium

третий этаж
tretiy etazh
third floor

вывеска
vyveska
sign

второй этаж
vtoroy etazh
second floor

эскалатор
eskalator
escalator

лифт
lift
elevator

первый этаж
perviy etazh
ground floor

посетитель,
покупатель
posetitel',
pokupatel'
customer

словарь slovar' • vocabulary

отдел товаров для
детей
otdel tovarov dlya detey
children's department

камера хранения
kamera khraneniya
luggage department

обувной отдел
obuvnoy otdel
shoe department

панель информации
panel' informatsii
store directory

продавец-
консультант
prodavets-konsul'tant
salesclerk

отдел по работе
с клиентами
otdel po rabote
s kliyentami
customer services

примерочные
primerochniye
fitting rooms

комната матери
и ребёнка
komnata materi i rebyonka
baby changing room

туалеты
tualety
restroom

Сколько это стоит?
skol'ko eto stoit?
How much is this?

Можно это заменить?
mozhno eto zamenit'?
May I exchange this?

универмаг univermag • department store

мужская одежда
muzhskaya odezhda
menswear

женская одежда
zhenskaya odezhda
womenswear

женское бельё
zhenskoye bel'yo
lingerie

парфюмерия
parfyumeriya
perfumes

косметика
kosmetika
cosmetics

постельное и столовое бельё
postel'noye i stolovoye bel'yo
linens

товары для дома
tovary dlya doma
home furnishings

галантерея
galantereya
notions

кухонные принадлежности и посуда
kukhonnyye prinadlezhnosti i posuda
kitchenware

фарфор
farfor
china

электротовары
elektrotovary
electronics

светильники
svetil'niki
lighting

спортивные товары
sportivnye tovari
sportswear

игрушки
igrushki
toys

канцтовары
kantstovary
stationery

продовольственный отдел prodovolstvennyj otdel | **groceries**

супермаркет supermarket • supermarket

проход
prokhod
aisle

полка
polka
shelf

конвейерная лента
konveiyernaya lenta
conveyor belt

кассир
kassir
checker

**предложения/
акции**
predlozheniya/
aktsii
specials

касса kassa | checkout

покупатель
pokupatel'
customer

**кассовый
аппарат**
kassoviy apparat
cash register

**хозяйственная
сумка**
khozyaystvennaya
sumka
shopping bag

продукты (питания)
produkty (pitaniya)
groceries

ручка
ruchka
handle

780863 185779

штрихкод
shtrikhkod
bar code

тележка telezhka | grocery cart

корзинка korzinka | basket

сканер skaner | scanner

ыпечка, хлебобулочные изделия
ypechka, khlebobulochniye izdeliya
bakery

молочные продукты
molochniye produkty
dairy

хлопья для завтрака
khlop'ya dlya zavtraka
breakfast cereals

консервы
konservy
canned food

кондитерские изделия
konditerskiye izdeliya
candy

овощи
ovoshchi
vegetables

фрукты
frukty
fruit

мясо и птица
myaso i ptitsa
meat and poultry

рыба
ryba
fish

деликатесы
delikatesy
deli

замороженные продукты
zamorozhenniye produkty
frozen food

полуфабрикаты
polufabrikaty
prepared food

напитки
napitki
drinks

хозяйственные товары
khozyaystvenniye tovary
household products

гигиенические товары gigienicheskeie
tovary | **toiletries**

товары для детей
tovary dlya detey
baby products

электротовары
elektrotovary
electrical goods

корм для животных
korm dlya zhivotnykh
pet food

журналы zhurnaly | **magazines**

аптека apteka • drugstore

уход за зубами
ukhod za zubami
dental care

женская
гигиена
zhenskaya
gigiyena
**feminine
hygiene**

дезодоранты
dezodoranty
deodorants

витамины
vitaminy
vitamins

отдел отпуска по рецептам,
рецептурный отдел
otdel otpuska po retseptam,
retsepturniy otdel
pharmacy

фармацевт
farmatsevt
pharmacist

лекарство от кашля
lekarstvo ot kashlya
cough medicine

растительные
лекарственные
средства
rastitel'niye
lekarstvenniye
sredstva
herbal remedies

уход за кожей
ukhod za kozhey
skin care

средство
после загара
sredstvo posle
zagara
**aftersun
lotion**

солнцезащитный крем
sontsezashchitniy krem
sunscreen

крем-блок от загара
krem-blok ot zagara
sunblock

репеллент
repellent
insect repellent

влажная салфетка
vlazhnaya salfetka
wet wipe

бумажная салфетка
bumazhnaya salfetka
tissue

гигиеническая прокладка
gigiyenicheskaya prokladka
sanitary napkin

тампон
tampon
tampon

прокладка на каждый день
prokladka na kazhdiy den'
panty liner

капсула
kapsula
capsule

таблетка
tabletka
pill

мерная ложка
mernaya lozhka
measuring spoon

сироп
sirop
syrup

инструкция
instruktsiya
instructions

ингалятор
ingalyator
inhaler

крем
krem
cream

мазь
maz'
ointment

гель
gel'
gel

свеча, суппозиторий
svecha, suppozitoriy
suppository

пипетка
pipetka
dropper

капли
kapli
drops

игла
igla
needle

шприц
shprits
syringe

спрей
sprey
spray

порошок
poroshok
powder

словарь slovar' • vocabulary

железо zhelezo **iron**	инсулин insulin **insulin**	одноразовый odnorazoviy **disposable**	лекарство lekarstvo **medicine**	обезболивающее obezbolivayushcheye **painkiller**
кальций kal'tsiy **calcium**	побочные действия pobochniye deystviya **side effects**	растворимый rastvorimiy **soluble**	слабительное slabitel'noye **laxative**	успокоительное uspokoitel'noye **sedative**
магний magniy **magnesium**	дата окончания срока годности data okonchaniya sroka godnosti **expiration date**	доза doza **dosage**	диарея; понос diareya; ponos **diarrhea**	противовоспалительное protivovospalitel'noye **anti-inflammatory**
мультивитамины mul'tivitaminy **multivitamins**	таблетки от укачивания tabletki ot ukachivaniya **travel-sickness pills**	медикаментозное лечение medikamentoznoye lecheniye **medication**	снотворное snotvornoye **sleeping pill**	пастилки от кашля или боли в горле pastilki ot kashlya ili boli v gorle **throat lozenge**

цветочный магазин tsvetochniy magazin • florist

цветы
tsvety
flowers

лилия
liliya
lily

акация
akatsiya
acacia

гвоздика
gvozdika
carnation

**горшочное
растение**
gorshochnoye
rasteniye
potted plant

гладиолус
gladiolus
gladiolus

ирис
iris
iris

маргаритка
margaritka
daisy

хризантема
khrizantema
chrysanthemum

гипсофила
gipsofila
gypsophila

левкой	**гербера**	**листья**	**роза**	**фрезия**
levkoy	gerbera	listya	roza	freziya
stocks	**gerbera**	**foliage**	**rose**	**freesia**

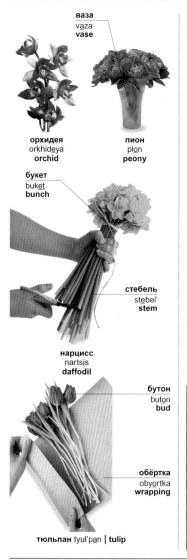

ваза
vaza
vase

орхидея
orkhideya
orchid

пион
pion
peony

букет
buket
bunch

стебель
stebel'
stem

нарцисс
nartsis
daffodil

бутон
buton
bud

обёртка
obyortka
wrapping

тюльпан tyul'pan | **tulip**

композиции kompozitsiyi • arrangements

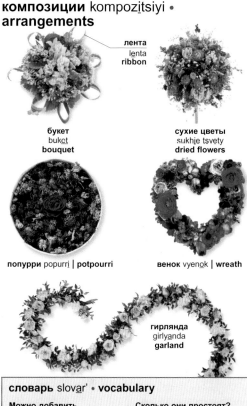

лента
lenta
ribbon

букет
buket
bouquet

сухие цветы
sukhie tsvety
dried flowers

попурри popurri | **potpourri**

венок vyenok | **wreath**

гирлянда
girlyanda
garland

словарь slovar' • vocabulary

Можно добавить записку?
mozhno dobavit' zapisku?
Can I attach a message?

Можно их завернуть?
mozhno ikh zavernut'?
Can I have them wrapped?

Можно отправить их по адресу...?
mozhno otpravit' ikh po adresu...?
Can you send them to ...?

Сколько они простоят?
skol'ko oni prostoyat?
How long will these last?

Они пахнут?
oni pakhnut?
Are they fragrant?

Можно мне букет из ...?
mozhno mne buket iz...?
Can I have a bunch of ... please?

продавец газет prodavets gaz<u>e</u>t • **newsstand**

сигареты
sigar<u>e</u>ty
cigarettes

пачка сигарет
p<u>a</u>chka sigar<u>e</u>t
pack of cigarettes

марки
m<u>a</u>rki
stamps

открытка
otkr<u>y</u>tka
postcard

комикс
k<u>o</u>miks
comic book

журнал
zhurn<u>a</u>l
magazine

газета
gaz<u>e</u>ta
newspaper

курение kur<u>e</u>niye • **smoking**

табак
tab<u>a</u>k
tobacco

зажигалка
zazhig<u>a</u>lka
lighter

мундштук
mundsht<u>u</u>k
stem

чаша
ch<u>a</u>sha
bowl

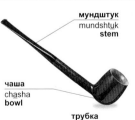

трубка
tr<u>u</u>bka
pipe

сигара
sig<u>a</u>ra
cigar

кондитер konditer · candy store

коробка шоколадных конфет
korobka shokoladnykh konfet
box of chocolates

энергетический батончик
energeticheskiy batonchik
snack bar

чипсы
chipsy
potato chips

кондитер konditer | candy store

словарь slovar' · vocabulary

молочный шоколад
molochniy shokolad
milk chocolate

карамель
karamel'
caramel

тёмный шоколад
tyomniy shokolad
dark chocolate

трюфель
tryufel'
truffle

белый шоколад
beliy shokolad
white chocolate

печенье
pechen'ye
cookie

выбор сладостей на развес
vybor sladostey na razves
pick and mix

сладости sladosti · confectionery

шоколад
shokolad
chocolate

плитка шоколада
plitka shokolada
chocolate bar

конфеты
konfety
hard candy

леденец на палочке
ledenets na palochke
lollipop

ириска iriska | **toffee**

нуга nuga | **nougat**

воздушный зефир
vozdushniy zefir
marshmallow

мятная конфета
myatnaya konfeta
mint

жевательная резинка
zhevatel'naya rezinka
chewing gum

желейная конфета
zheleynaya konfeta
jellybean

фруктовая жевательная конфета
fruktovaya zhevatelnaya konfeta
gumdrop

лакрица
lakritsa
licorice

другие магазины drugiye magaziny • other stores

булочная
bulochnaya
bakery

кондитерская
konditerskaya
pastry shop

мясная лавка
myasnaya lavka
butcher shop

рыбный магазин
rybniy magazin
fish counter

овощной магазин
ovoshchnoy magazin
produce stand

продуктовый магазин
produktoviy magazin
grocery store

обувной магазин
obuvnoy magazin
shoe store

хозтовары
khoztovary
hardware store

антикварный магазин
antikvarniy magazin
antique store

магазин подарков
magazin podarkov
gift shop

**туристическое
агентство**
turisticheskoye agentstvo
travel agency

ювелирный магазин
yuvelirniy magazin
jewelry store

книжный магазин
knizhniy magazin
bookstore

музыкальный магазин
muzykalny magazin
record store

винно-водочный магазин
vinno-vodochniy magazin
liquor store

зоомагазин
zoomagazin
pet store

мебельный магазин
mebel'niy magazin
furniture store

бутик
butik
boutique

словарь slovar' • vocabulary

агентство недвижимости
agentstvo nedvizhimosti
real estate office

садовый центр
sadoviy tsentr
garden center

химчистка
khimchistka
dry cleaner

прачечная
prachechnaya
laundromat

фотомагазин
fotomagazin
camera store

магазин здорового питания
magazin zdorovova pitaniya
health food store

арт-галерея
art-galereya
art supply store

комиссионный магазин
komissionny magazin
secondhand store

ателье
atel'ye
tailor shop

парикмахерская
parikmakherskaya
salon

рынок rynok | **market**

продукты питания produkti pitaniya
food

мясо myaso • meat

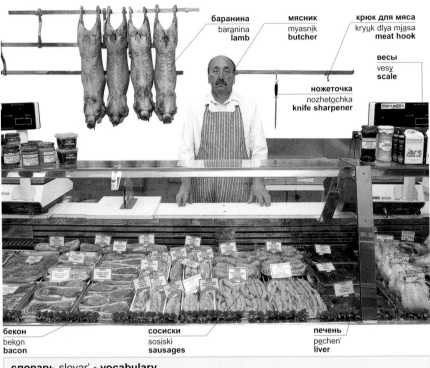

баранина
baranina
lamb

мясник
myasnik
butcher

крюк для мяса
kryuk dlya myasa
meat hook

весы
vesy
scale

ножеточка
nozhetochka
knife sharpener

бекон
bekon
bacon

сосиски
sosiski
sausages

печень
pechen'
liver

словарь slovar' • vocabulary

свинина svinina **pork**	**оленина** olenina **venison**	**требуха,** **субпродукты** trebukha, subprodukty **variety meat**	**со свободного выгула** so svobodnogo vigula **free range**	**мясо после тепловой** **обработки** myaso posle teplovoy obrabotki **cooked meat**
говядина govyadina **beef**	**крольчатина** krol'chatina **rabbit**	**солёный** solyoniy **cured**	**органическое** organicheskoye **organic**	**белое мясо** beloye myaso **white meat**
телятина telyatina **veal**	**язык** yazyk **tongue**	**копченый** kopchyoniy **smoked**	**постное мясо** postnoye myaso **lean meat**	**красное мясо** krasnoye myaso **red meat**

разделка мяса razdelka myasa • **cuts**

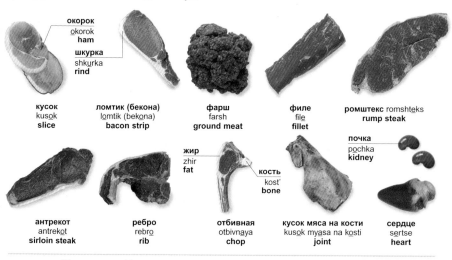

окорок
okorok
ham

шкурка
shkurka
rind

кусок
kusok
slice

ломтик (бекона)
lomtik (bekona)
bacon strip

фарш
farsh
ground meat

филе
file
fillet

ромштекс romshteks
rump steak

жир
zhir
fat

кость
kost'
bone

почка
pochka
kidney

антрекот
antrekot
sirloin steak

ребро
rebro
rib

отбивная
otbivnaya
chop

кусок мяса на кости
kusok myasa na kosti
joint

сердце
sertse
heart

птица ptitsa • **poultry**

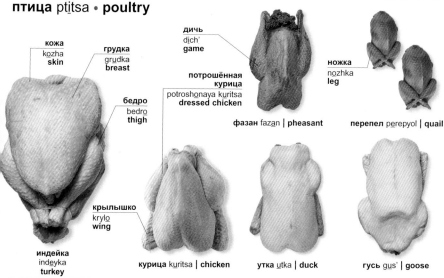

кожа
kozha
skin

грудка
grudka
breast

дичь
dich'
game

потрошённая курица
potroshonaya kuritsa
dressed chicken

ножка
nozhka
leg

бедро
bedro
thigh

фазан fazan | **pheasant**

перепел perepyol | **quail**

крылышко
krylo
wing

индейка
indeyka
turkey

курица kuritsa | **chicken**

утка utka | **duck**

гусь gus' | **goose**

рыба ryba • fish

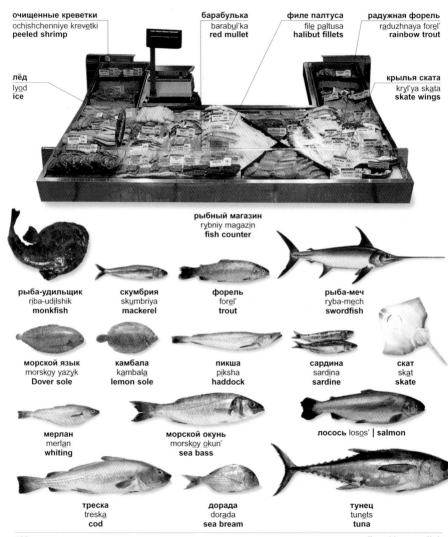

очищенные креветки
ochishchenniye krevetki
peeled shrimp

барабулька
barabul'ka
red mullet

филе палтуса
file paltusa
halibut fillets

радужная форель
raduzhnaya forel'
rainbow trout

лёд
lyod
ice

крылья ската
kryl'ya skata
skate wings

рыбный магазин
rybniy magazin
fish counter

рыба-удильщик
riba-udilshik
monkfish

скумбрия
skumbriya
mackerel

форель
forel'
trout

рыба-меч
ryba-mech
swordfish

морской язык
morskoy yazyk
Dover sole

камбала
kambala
lemon sole

пикша
piksha
haddock

сардина
sardina
sardine

скат
skat
skate

мерлан
merlan
whiting

морской окунь
morskoy okun'
sea bass

лосось losos' | **salmon**

треска
treska
cod

дорада
dorada
sea bream

тунец
tunets
tuna

морепродукты m<u>o</u>reprod<u>u</u>kty • **seafood**

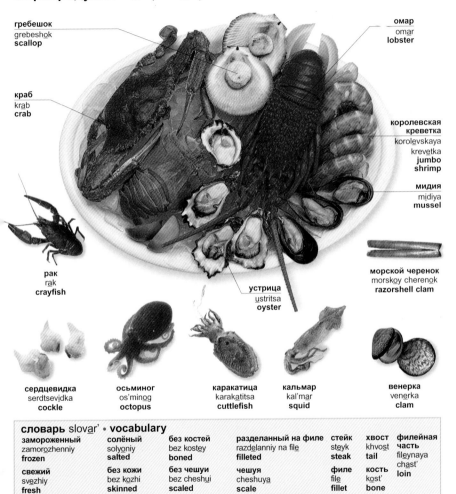

гребешок
grebesh<u>o</u>k
scallop

омар
<u>o</u>m<u>a</u>r
lobster

краб
kr<u>a</u>b
crab

**королевская
креветка**
korol<u>e</u>vskaya
kr<u>e</u>vetka
**jumbo
shrimp**

мидия
m<u>i</u>diya
mussel

рак
r<u>a</u>k
crayfish

устрица
<u>u</u>stritsa
oyster

морской черенок
morsk<u>o</u>y cher<u>e</u>nok
razorshell clam

сердцевидка
serdtsev<u>i</u>dka
cockle

осьминог
os'min<u>o</u>g
octopus

каракатица
karak<u>a</u>titsa
cuttlefish

кальмар
kal'm<u>a</u>r
squid

венерка
ven<u>e</u>rka
clam

словарь slov<u>a</u>r' • **vocabulary**

замороженный zamor<u>o</u>zhenniy **frozen**	**солёный** sol<u>yo</u>niy **salted**	**без костей** bez kost<u>e</u>y **boned**	**разделанный на филе** razd<u>e</u>lanniy na fil<u>e</u> **filleted**	**стейк** st<u>e</u>yk **steak**	**хвост** khv<u>o</u>st **tail**	**филейная часть** fil<u>e</u>ynaya ch<u>a</u>st' **loin**
свежий sv<u>e</u>zhiy **fresh**	**без кожи** bez k<u>o</u>zhi **skinned**	**без чешуи** bez cheshu<u>i</u> **scaled**	**чешуя** cheshu<u>ya</u> **scale**	**филе** fil<u>e</u> **fillet**	**кость** k<u>o</u>st' **bone**	
очищенный <u>o</u>chischenniy **cleaned**	**копчёный** kopch<u>yo</u>niy **smoked**		**Можете почистить это?** m<u>o</u>zhete poch<u>i</u>stit' <u>e</u>to? **Will you clean it for me?**			

овощи 1 ovoshchi • vegetables 1

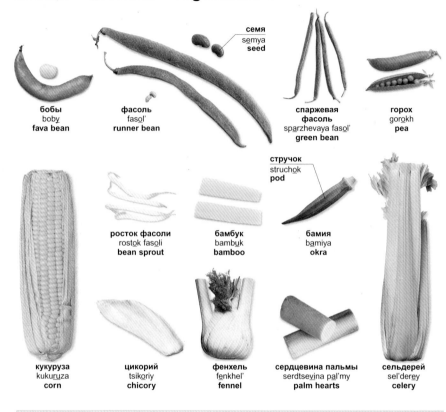

семя
semya
seed

бобы
boby
fava bean

фасоль
fasol'
runner bean

спаржевая
фасоль
sparzhevaya fasol'
green bean

горох
gorokh
pea

стручок
struchok
pod

росток фасоли
rostok fasoli
bean sprout

бамбук
bambuk
bamboo

бамия
bamiya
okra

кукуруза
kukuruza
corn

цикорий
tsikoriy
chicory

фенхель
fenkhel'
fennel

сердцевина пальмы
serdtsevina pal'my
palm hearts

сельдерей
sel'derey
celery

словарь slovar' • vocabulary

лист list **leaf**	соцветие sotsvetiye **floret**	верхушка verkhushka **tip**	органический organicheskiy **organic**	У вас есть органические овощи? u vas yest' organicheskiye ovoshchi? **Do you sell organic vegetables?**
стебель stebel' **stalk**	орешек, ядро oreshek, yadro **kernel**	сердцевина serdtsevina **heart**	пластиковый пакет plastikoviy paket **plastic bag**	Это местная продукция? eto mestnaya produktsiya? **Are these grown locally?**

рукола
rukola
arugula

водяной кресс-салат
vodyanoy kres-salat
watercress

**тревизский цикорий,
радиккио**
trevizskiy tsikoriy, radikkio
radicchio

брюссельская капуста
bryusel'skaya kapusta
Brussels sprout

листовая свёкла
listovaya svyokla
Swiss chard

листовая капуста
listovaya kapusta
kale

щавель
shchavel'
sorrel

эндивий
endiviy
endive

одуванчик
oduvanchik
dandelion

шпинат
shpinat
spinach

кольраби
kol'rabi
kohlrabi

пекинская капуста
pekinskaya kapusta
bok choy

салат-латук
salat-latuk
lettuce

брокколи
brokkoli
broccoli

капуста
kapusta
cabbage

ранняя зелень
rannyaya zelen'
spring greens

овощи 2 ovoshchi • vegetables 2

репа
repa
turnip

артишок
artishok
artichoke

цветная капуста
tsvetnaya kapusta
cauliflower

картофель
kartofel'
potato

лук
luk
onion

сладкий перец
sladkiy perets
pepper

перец чили
perets chili
chili pepper

редис
redis
radish

спаржа
sparzha
asparagus

кабачок
kabachok
squash

сахарная кукуруза
sakharnaya kukuruza
sweetcorn

словарь slovar' • vocabulary

помидор черри pomidor cherri **cherry tomato**	**сельдерей** sel'derey **celeriac**	**замороженный** zamorozhenniy **frozen**	**горький** gor'kiy **bitter**	**Один килограмм картошки, пожалуйста?** odin kilogram kartoshki, pozhalusta? **May I have one kilo of potatoes, please?**
морковь morkov' **carrot**	**корень таро** koren' taro **taro root**	**сырой** syroy **raw**	**упругий** uprugiy **firm**	
плод хлебного дерева plod khlebnogo dereva **breadfruit**	**маниок** maniok **cassava**	**пряный (острый)** pryany (ostry) **hot (spicy)**	**мякоть** myakot' **flesh**	**Сколько стоит килограмм?** skol'ko stoit kilogram? **What's the price per kilo?**
молодой картофель molodoy kartofel' **new potato**	**водяной орех** vodyanoy orekh **water chestnut**	**сладкий** sladkiy **sweet**	**корень** koren' **root**	**Как это называется?** Kak eto nazyvayetsya? **What are those called?**

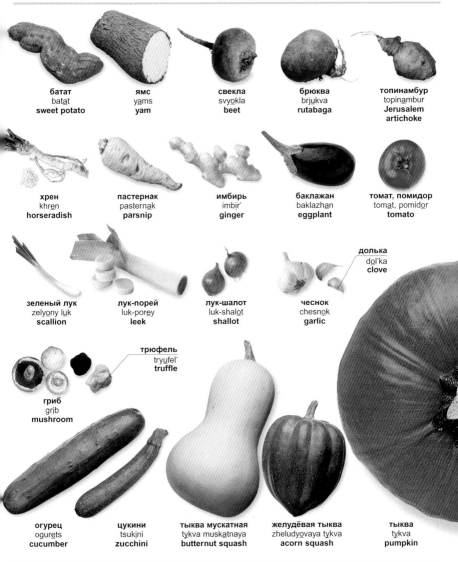

батат
batat
sweet potato

ямс
yams
yam

свекла
svyokla
beet

брюква
brjukva
rutabaga

топинамбур
topinambur
**Jerusalem
artichoke**

хрен
khren
horseradish

пастернак
pasternak
parsnip

имбирь
imbir'
ginger

баклажан
baklazhan
eggplant

томат, помидор
tomat, pomidor
tomato

зеленый лук
zelyony luk
scallion

лук-порей
luk-porey
leek

лук-шалот
luk-shalot
shallot

чеснок
chesnok
garlic

долька
dol'ka
clove

трюфель
tryufel'
truffle

гриб
grib
mushroom

огурец
ogurets
cucumber

цукини
tsukini
zucchini

тыква мускатная
tykva muskatnaya
butternut squash

желудёвая тыква
zheludyovaya tykva
acorn squash

тыква
tykva
pumpkin

фрукты 1 frukty • fruit 1

цитрусовые tsitrusoviye • citrus fruit

апельсин
apel'sin
orange

клементин
klementin
clementine

белая оболочка
belaya oblochka
pith

агли
agli
ugli fruit

грейпфрут
greypfrut
grapefruit

долька
dol'ka
segment

мандарин
mandarin
tangerine

мандарин уншиу
mandarin unshiu
satsuma

цедра
tsedra
zest

лайм
laim
lime

лимон
limon
lemon

кумкват
kumkvat
kumquat

косточковые kostochkoviye • stone fruit

персик
persik
peach

нектарин
nektarin
nectarine

абрикос
abrikos
apricot

слива
sliva
plum

вишня
vishnya
cherry

яблоко
yabloko
apple

груша
grusha
pear

корзинка с фруктами korzinka s fruktami
basket of fruit

ягоды и бахчевые yagody i bakhcheviye • berries and melons

клубника
klubnika
strawberry

малина
malina
raspberry

дыня
dynya
melon

красная смородина
krasnaya smorodina
red currant

виноград
vinograd
grapes

ежевика
yezhevika
blackberry

кожура
kozhura
rind

чёрная смородина
chyornaya smorodina
black currant

семечко
semechko
seed

клюква
klyukva
cranberry

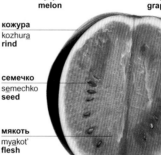

мякоть
myakot'
flesh

черника
chernika
blueberry

белая смородина
belaya smorodina
white currant

арбуз
arbuz
watermelon

ягода Логана
yagoda logana
loganberry

словарь slovar' • vocabulary

ревень reven' **rhubarb**	**кислый** kisliy **sour**	**хрустящий** khrustyashchiy **crisp**	**сок** sok **juice**		**Они спелые?** oni speliye? **Are they ripe?**
волокно volokno **fiber**	**свежий** svezhiy **fresh**	**гнилой** gniloy **rotten**	**сердцевина** serdtsevina **core**		**Можно попробовать?** mozhno poprobovat'? **Can I try one?**
сладкий sladkiy **sweet**	**сочный** sochniy **juicy**	**мякоть** myakot' **pulp**	**без косточек** bez kostochek **seedless**		**Сколько времени они хранятся?** skol'ko vremeni oni khranyatsya? **How long will they keep?**

крыжовник
kryzhovnik
gooseberry

фрукты 2 frukty • fruit 2

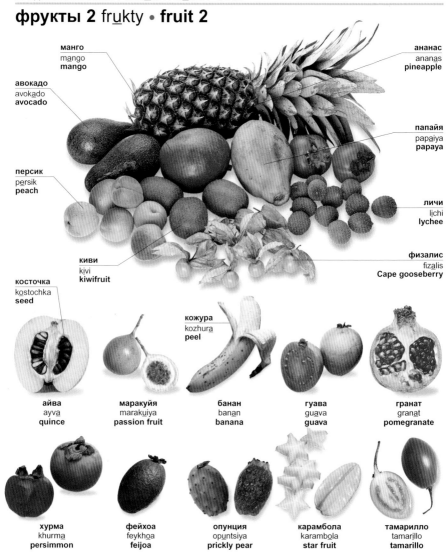

манго
mango
mango

авокадо
avokado
avocado

персик
persik
peach

косточка
kostochka
seed

киви
kivi
kiwifruit

ананас
ananas
pineapple

папайя
papaiya
papaya

личи
lichi
lychee

физалис
fizalis
Cape gooseberry

кожура
kozhura
peel

айва
ayva
quince

маракуйя
marakuiya
passion fruit

банан
banan
banana

гуава
guava
guava

гранат
granat
pomegranate

хурма
khurma
persimmon

фейхоа
feykhoa
feijoa

опунция
opuntsiya
prickly pear

карамбола
karambola
star fruit

тамарилло
tamarillo
tamarillo

Орехи и сухофрукты orekhi i sukhofrukty •
nuts and dried fruit

кедровый орех
kedroviy orekh
pine nut

фисташка
fistashka
pistachio

кешью
kesh'yu
cashew

арахис
arakhis
peanut

фундук
funduk
hazelnut

бразильский орех
brazil'skiy orekh
Brazil nut

орех-пекан
orekh-pekan
pecan

миндаль
mindal'
almond

грецкий орех
gretskiy orekh
walnut

каштан
kashtan
chestnut

макадамия
makadamiya
macadamia

инжир
inzhir
fig

финик
finik
date

чернослив
chernosliv
prune

скорлупа
skorlupa
shell

мякоть
myakot'
flesh

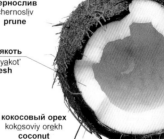

кишмиш
kishmish
sultana

изюм
izyum
raisin

коринка
korinka
currant

кокосовый орех
kokosoviy orekh
coconut

словарь slovar' • vocabulary

зеленый, незрелый zeleniy, nezreliy **green**	**твёрдый** tvyordiy **hard**	**орешек, ядро** oreshek, yadro **kernel**	**солёный** solyoniy **salted**	**жареный** zhareniy **roasted**	**очищенный** ochishchenniy **shelled**	**цукаты** tsukaty **candied fruit**
спелый speliy **ripe**	**мягкий** myahkiy **soft**	**сушёный** sushoniy **desiccated**	**сырой** syroy **raw**	**сезонный** sezonniy **seasonal**	**целый** tseliy **whole**	**тропические фрукты** tropicheskiye frukty **tropical fruit**

зерновые и бобовые культуры zernovye i bobovye kultury • grains and legumes

злаки zlaki • grains

пшеница
pshenitsa
wheat

овёс
ovyos
oats

ячмень
yachmen'
barley

просо, пшено
proso, psheno
millet

кукуруза
kukuruza
corn

киноа
kinoa
quinoa

словарь slovar' • vocabulary

зерно zerno **seed**	**душистый** dushistyy **fragranced**	**пропаренный** proparenniy **quick cooking**
шелуха shelukha **husk**	**крупа; хлопья** krupa; khlop'ya **cereal**	**длинно-зёрный** dlinnozyorniy **long-grain**
ядро yadro **kernel**	**цельнозерновой** tsel'nozernovoy **whole-grain**	**коротко-зёрный** korotkozyorniy **short-grain**
сухой sukhoy **dry**	**замачивать** zamachivat' **soak (v)**	
свежий svezhiy **fresh**		

рис ris • rice

белый рис
beliy ris
white rice

коричневый рис
korichneviy ris
brown rice

дикий рис
dikiy ris
wild rice

рис для пудинга
ris dlya pudinga
arborio rice

крупы krupy • processed grains

кускус
kuskus
couscous

крупа из плющеной пшениц
krupa iz plyushchenoy pshenitsy
cracked wheat

манная крупа
mannaya krupa
semolina

отруби
otrubi
bran

бобовые boboviye • legumes

белая фасоль лима
belaya fasol' lima
butter beans

белая фасоль неви
belaya fasol' nevi
haricot beans

красная фасоль
krasnaya fasol'
red kidney beans

адзуки
adzuki
adzuki beans

бобы
boby
fava beans

соевые бобы
soyeviye boby
soybeans

коровий горох
koroviy gorokh
black-eyed peas

фасоль пинто
fasol' pinto
pinto beans

фасоль мунг
fasol' mung
mung beans

фасоль флажолет
fasol' flazholet
flageolet beans

коричневая чечевица
korichnevaya chechevitsa
brown lentils

красная чечевица
krasnaya chechevitsa
red lentils

зелёный горошек
zelyoniy goroshek
green peas

нут; турецкий горох
nut; turetskiy gorokh
chickpeas

дроблёный горох
droblyoniy gorokh
split peas

семена semena • seeds

**тыквенные
семечки**
tykvenniye
semechki
pumpkin seed

семена горчицы
semena gorchitsy
mustard seed

тмин
tmin
caraway

семя кунжута
semya kunzhuta
sesame seed

семечки подсолнуха
semechki podsolnukha
sunflower seed

травы и пряности travy i pryanosti • herbs and spices

специи specii • spices

ваниль vanil' | **vanilla**

мускатный орех
muskatniy orekh
nutmeg

мускатный цвет
muskatniy tsvet
mace

куркума
kurkuma
turmeric

зира
zira
cumin

ароматическая
смесь
aromaticheskaya
smes'
bouquet garni

душистый перец
dushistiy perets
allspice

перец горошком
perets goroshkom
peppercorn

шамбала, пажитник
shambala, pazhitnik
fenugreek

перец чили
perets chili
chili powder

цельный
tsel'niy
whole

дроблёный
droblyoniy
crushed

шафран
shafran
saffron

кардамон
kardamon
cardamom

карри
karri
curry powder

молотый
molotiy
ground

паприка
paprika
paprika

хлопья
khlop'ya
flakes

чеснок
chesnok
garlic

пряные травы pryaniye travy • **herbs**

палочки
palochki
sticks

семена фенхеля
semena fenkhelya
fennel seeds

корица
koritsa
cinnamon

фенхель
fenkhel'
fennel

лавровый лист
lavroviy list
bay leaf

петрушка
petrushka
parsley

лимонное сорго
limonnoye sorgo
lemon grass

гвоздика
gvozdika
cloves

шнитт-лук
shnit-luk
chives

мята
myata
mint

тимьян
tim'yan
thyme

шалфей
shalfey
sage

бадьян
bad'yan
star anise

эстрагон
estragon
tarragon

майоран
mayoran
marjoram

базилик
bazilik
basil

имбирь
imbir'
ginger

душица
dushitsa
oregano

кориандр
koriandr
cilantro

укроп
ukrop
dill

розмарин
rozmarin
rosemary

бутилированные продукты
butilirovanniye produkty • **bottled foods**

масло грецкого ореха
maslo gretskava orekha
walnut oil

масло из виноградных косточек
maslo iz vinogradnykh kostochek
grapeseed oil

пробка
probka
cork

подсолнечное масло
podsolnechnoye maslo
sunflower oil

миндальное масло
mindal'noye maslo
almond oil

кунжутное масло
kunzhutnoye maslo
sesame seed oil

ореховое масло
orekhovoye maslo
hazelnut oil

оливковое масло
olivkovoye maslo
olive oil

пряные травы
pryanyye travy
herbs

ароматизированное масло
aromatizirovannoye maslo
flavored oil

масла
masla
oils

сладкие пасты sladkiye pasty •
sweet spreads

банка
banka
jar

мёд в сотах
med v sotakh
honeycomb

кристаллизованный мёд
kristalizovanniy myod
set honey

лимонный крем
limonniy krem
lemon curd

малиновое варенье
malinovoye varen'ye
raspberry jam

мармелад
marmelad
marmalade

прозрачный мёд
prozrachniy myod
clear honey

кленовый сироп
klenoviy sirop
maple syrup

соусы и заправки sousye i zapravki •
sauces and condiments

яблочный уксус
yablochniy uksus
cider vinegar

бальзамический уксус
bal'zamicheskiy uksus
balsamic vinegar

бутылка
butylka
bottle

английская горчица
angliyskaya gorchitsa
English mustard

кетчуп
ketchup
ketchup

майонез
mayonez
mayonnaise

французская горчица
frantsuskaya gorchitsa
French mustard

чатни
chatni
chutney

солодовый уксус
solodoviy uksus
malt vinegar

винный уксус
vinniy uksus
wine vinegar

соус
sous
sauce

зерновая горчица
zernovaya gorchitsa
whole-grain mustard

уксус
uksus
vinegar

банка для консервирования
banka dlya konservirovaniya
canning jar

арахисовая паста
arakhisovaya pasta
peanut butter

шоколадная паста
shokoladnaya pasta
chocolate spread

**консервированные
фрукты**
konservirovannyye frukty
preserved fruit

словарь slovar' • vocabulary

**кукурузное
масло**
kukuruznoye
maslo
corn oil

**арахисовое
масло**
arakhisovoye
maslo
peanut oil

**растительное
масло**
rastitelnoye maslo
vegetable oil

рапсовое масло
rapsovoye maslo
canola oil

**масло
холодного
отжима**
maslo kholodnava
otzhima
cold-pressed oil

молочные продукты molochniye produkty • dairy products

сыр syr • cheese

корка
korka
rind

полутвёрдый сыр
polutvyordiy syr
semi-hard cheese

тёртый сыр
tyortiy syr
grated cheese

твёрдый сыр
tvyordiy syr
hard cheese

полумягкий сыр
polumyakhkiy syr
semi-soft cheese

творог
tvorog
cottage cheese

сливочный сыр
slivochniy syr
cream cheese

голубой сыр
goluboy syr
blue cheese

мягкий сыр
myakhkiy syr
soft cheese

молодой сыр molodoy syr | **fresh cheese**

молоко moloko • milk

цельное молоко
tselnoye moloko
whole milk

полужирное молоко
poluzhirnoye moloko
reduced-fat milk

снятое (обезжиренное) молоко
snyatoye (obezzhirennoye) moloko
skim milk

пакет молока
paket moloka
milk carton

козье молоко
kozye moloko
goat's milk

сгущённое молоко
sguschyonoye moloko
condensed milk

коровье молоко korovye moloko | **cow's milk**

масло
maslo
butter

маргарин
margarin
margarine

сливки
slivki
cream

сливки к кофе
slivki k kofe
half-and-half

двойные сливки
dvoyniye slivki
heavy cream

взбитые сливки
vzbitiye slivki
whipped cream

сметана
smetana
sour cream

йогурт
yogurt
yogurt

мороженое
morozhenoye
ice cream

яйца yaytsa • eggs

желток
zheltok
yolk

белок
belok
egg white

скорлупа
skorlupa
shell

**подставка
для яиц**
podstavka
dlya yayits
eggcup

варёное яйцо varyonoye yaytso
soft-boiled egg

куриное яйцо
kurinoye yaytso
hen's egg

утиное яйцо
utinoye yaytso
duck egg

гусиное яйцо
gusinoye yaytso
goose egg

перепелиное яйцо
perepelinoye yaytso
quail egg

словарь slovar' • vocabulary

пастеризованный pasterizovanniy **pasteurized**	**овечье молоко** ovech'ye moloko **sheep's milk**	**солёный** solyoniy **salted**	**лактоза** laktoza **lactose**	**гомогенизированный** gomogenizirovanniy **homogenized**
непастеризованный nepasterizovanniy **unpasteurized**	**пахта** pakhta **buttermilk**	**несолёный** nesolyoniy **unsalted**	**обезжиренный** obezzhirenniy **fat-free**	**порошковое молоко** poroshkovoye moloko **powdered milk**
молочный коктейль molochniy kokteyl' **milk shake**	**замороженный йогурт** zamorozhenniy yogurt **frozen yogurt**			

хлеб и мука khleb i muka • breads and flours

нарезной хлеб
nareznoy khleb
sliced bread

с маком
s makom
poppy seeds

ржаной хлеб
rzhanoy khleb
rye bread

багет
baget
baguette

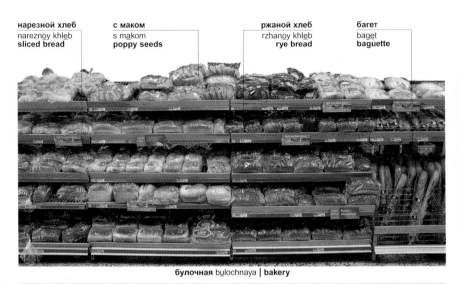

булочная bulochnaya | bakery

хлебопечение khlebopecheniye • making bread

пшеничная мука
pshenichnaya muka
white flour

ржаная мука
rzhanaya muka
brown flour

цельнозерновая мука
tselnozernovaya muka
whole-wheat flour

дрожжи
drozhzhi
yeast

просеивать proseivat'
sift (v)

смешивать smeshivat'
mix (v)

тесто
tyesto
dough

месить mesit' | knead (v)

печь pech | bake (v)

корочка
korochka
crust

буханка
bukhanka
loaf

ломтик
lomtik
slice

белый хлеб
beliy khleb
white bread

тёмный хлеб с отрубями
tyomniy khleb s otrubyami
brown bread

цельнозерновой хлеб
tsel'nozernovoy khleb
whole-wheat bread

хлеб с зёрнами
khleb s zyornami
multigrain bread

кукурузный хлеб
kukuruzniy khleb
corn bread

хлеб на соде
khleb na sode
soda bread

хлеб из дрожжевого теста
khleb iz drozzevogo testa
sourdough bread

лаваш
lavash
flat bread

бублик
bublik
bagel

мягкая булочка
myaghkaya bulochka | **bun**

булочка
bulochka | **roll**

сдоба с изюмом
sdoba s izjumom
fruit bread

зерновая булочка
zernovaya bulochka
seeded bread

наан
naan
naan bread

пита
pita
pita bread

хрустящий хлебец
khrustyashchiy khlebts
crispbread

словарь slovar' • vocabulary

обогащённая мука
obogashchennaya muka
bread flour

мука с разрыхлителем
muka s razrykhlitelem
self-rising flour

подниматься
podnimatsya
rise (v)

мука без разрыхлителя
muka bez razrykhlitelya
all-purpose flour

подходить, расстаиваться
podkhodit', rasstaivat'sya
prove (v)

глазировать
glazirovat'
glaze (v)

панировочные сухари
panirovochniye sukhari
breadcrumbs

французский багет
frantsuzskiy baget
flute

хлеборезка
khleborezka
slicer

пекарь
pekar'
baker

пирожные и десерты pirozhniye i deserty •
cakes and desserts

эклер
ekler
éclair

взбитые сливки
vzbitiye slivki
cream

начинка
nachinka
filling

заварное тесто
zavarnoye testo
choux pastry

слоёное тесто
sloyonoye testo
puff pastry

тесто фило
testo filo
phyllo dough

фруктовый пирог
fruktoviy pirog
fruitcake

**фруктовая
корзиночка**
fruktovaya
korzinochka
fruit tart

безе
beze
meringue

в шоколадной глазури
v shokoladnoy glazuri
chocolate-covered

маффин
mafin
muffin

**бисквитное
пирожное**
biskvitnoye
pirozhnoye
sponge cake

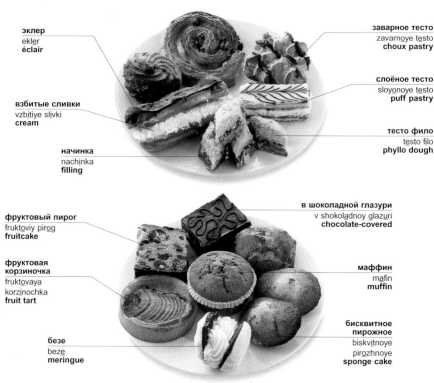

пирожные pirozhniye | cakes

словарь slovar' • vocabulary

кондитерский крем konditerskiy krem **crème pâtissière**	**сдобная булочка** sdobnaya bulochka **bun**	**выпечка** vypechka **pastry**	**рисовый пудинг** risoviy puding **rice pudding**	**Можно мне кусочек?** mozhno mne kusochek? **May I have a slice, please?**
шоколадный торт shokoladniy tort **chocolate cake**	**заварной крем** zavarnoy krem **custard**	**кусок** kusok **slice**	**праздник** praznik **celebration**	

шоколадная крошка
shokoladnaya kroshka
chocolate chip

дамские пальчики
damskiye pal'chiki
ladyfinger

флорентийское печенье
florentiyskoye pechen'ye
Florentine

трайфл
trayfl
trifle

печенье pechen'ye | cookies

мусс
mus
mousse

сорбет
sorbet
sherbet

торт с кремом
tort s kremom
cream pie

крем-карамель
krem-karamel'
crème caramel

праздничные торты prazdnichniye torty • celebration cakes

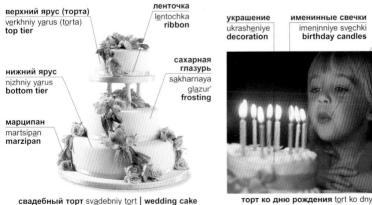

верхний ярус (торта)
verkhniy yarus (torta)
top tier

ленточка
lentochka
ribbon

нижний ярус
nizhniy yarus
bottom tier

сахарная глазурь
sakharnaya glazur'
frosting

марципан
martsipan
marzipan

свадебный торт svadebniy tort | wedding cake

украшение
ukrasheniye
decoration

именинные свечки
imeninniye svechki
birthday candles

задуть
zadut'
blow out (v)

торт ко дню рождения tort ko dnyu rozhdeniya
birthday cake

деликатесы delikatesy • delicatessen

пикантная колбаса
pikantnaya kolbasa
spicy sausage

масло
maslo
oil

флан; открытый пирог
flan; otkrytiy pirog
quiche

уксус
uksus
vinegar

сырое мясо
syroye myaso
uncooked meat

прилавок
prilavok
counter

салями
salyami
salami

пеперони; острая копчёная колбаса
peperoni; ostraya kopchonaya kolbasa
pepperoni

паштет
pashtet
pâté

моцарелла
motsarella
mozzarella

бри
bri
Brie

козий сыр
koziy syr
goat cheese

чеддер
chedder
cheddar

пармезан
parmezan
Parmesan

камамбер
kamamber
Camembert

корка
korka
rind

эдам
edam
Edam

манчего
manchego
Manchego

пироги с начинкой
pirogi s nachinkoy
potpie

черная оливка
chyornaya olivka
black olive

чили
chili
chili pepper

соус
sous
sauce

булочка
bulochka
bread roll

варёное мясо
varyonoye myaso
cooked meat

зелёная оливка
zelyonaya olivka
green olive

ветчина
vetchina
ham

витрина с бутербродами vitrina s buterbrodami
sandwich counter

копчёная рыба
kopchonaya ryba
smoked fish

каперсы
kapersy
capers

чоризо
chorizo
chorizo

прошутто
proshutto
prosciutto

фаршированная оливка
farshirovannaya olivka
stuffed olive

словарь slovar' • vocabulary

в масле v masle **in oil**	**маринованный** marinovanny **marinated**	**копчёный** kopchoniy **smoked**
в рассоле v rassole **in brine**	**солёный** solyoniy **salted**	**вяленый** vyaleniy **cured**

Возьмите номер.
vozmite nomer
Take a number, please.

Можно это попробовать?
mozhno eto poprobovat'?
Can I try some of that, please?

Можно мне шесть ломтиков этого?
mozhno mne shest' lomtikov etova?
May I have six slices of that, please?

напитки napitki • **drinks**

вода voda • **water**

вода в бутылках
voda v butylkakh
bottled water

газированная
gazirovannaya
sparkling

негазированная
negazirovannaya
still

минеральная вода
mineral'naya voda | **mineral water**

водопроводная вода
vodoprovodnaya voda
tap water

тоник
tonik
tonic water

газированная вода
gazirovannaya voda
soda water

горячие напитки goryachiye napitki • **hot drinks**

чайный пакетик
chayniy paketik
teabag

рассыпной листовой чай
rassypnoy listovoy chay
loose-leaf tea

чай
chay
tea

зёрна
zyorna
beans

молотый кофе
molotiy kofe
ground coffee

кофе
kofe
coffee

горячий шоколад
goryachiy shokolad
hot chocolate

солодовый напиток
solodoviy napitok
malted drink

безалкогольные напитки bezalkogol'nyye napitki • **soft drinks**

соломинка
solominka
straw

томатный сок
tomatny sok
tomato juice

виноградный сок
vinogradny sok
grape juice

лимонад
limonad
lemonade

апельсиновый лимонад
apelsinoviy limonad
orangeade

кола
kola
cola

алкогольные напитки alkogol'niye napitki • alcoholic drinks

джин
dzhin | **gin**

банка
banka
can

пиво
pivo
beer

сидр
sidr
hard cider

биттер
bitter
bitter

стаут; крепкий портер
staut; krepkiy porter
stout

водка
vodka | **vodka**

виски viski | **whiskey**

ром
rom
rum

бренди
brendi
brandy

портвейн
portveyn
port

сухое
sukhoe
dry

херес
kheres
sherry

кампари
kampari
Campari

розовое
rozovoye
rosé

белое
beloye
white

красное
krasnoye
red

ликёр
likyor
liqueur

текила
tekila
tequila

шампанское
shampanskoye
champagne

вино vino | **wine**

питание вне дома pitaniye vne doma
eating out

кафе kafe • café

маркиза
markiza
awning

меню
menyu
menu

зонтик
zontik
umbrella

кафе на террасе
kafe na terrase
patio café

официант
ofitsiant
server

кофемашина
kofemashina
**coffee
machine**

столик
stolik
table

уличное кафе ulichnoye kafe | **sidewalk café**

закусочная zakusochnaya | **snack bar**

кофе kofe • coffee

кофе с молоком
kofe s molokom
coffee with milk

чёрный кофе
chorniy kofe
black coffee

какао
kakao
cocoa powder

пенка
penka
froth

фильтрованный кофе
fil'trovanniy kofe
filter coffee

эспрессо
espresso
espresso

капучино
kapuchino
cappuccino

кофе-гляссе
kofe-glyasse
iced coffee

чай chay • tea

травяной чай
travyanoy chay
herbal tea

ромашковый чай
romashkoviy chay
chamomile tea

зеленый чай
zelyoniy chay
green tea

чай с молоком
chay s molokom
tea with milk

черный чай
chorniy chay
black tea

чай с лимоном
chay s limonom
tea with lemon

мятный чай
myatniy chay
mint tea

холодный чай
kholodniy chay
iced tea

соки и молочные коктейли soki i molochnyye kokteyli • juices and milkshakes

шоколадно-молочный коктейль
shokoladno-molochnyy kokteyl
chocolate milkshake

клубнично-молочный коктейль
klubnichno-molochnyy kokteyl
strawberry milkshake

кофейно-молочный коктейль
kofeyno-molochnyy kokteyl
coffee milkshake

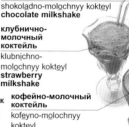

апельсиновый сок
apel'sinoviy sok
orange juice

яблочный сок
yablochniy sok
apple juice

ананасовый сок
ananasoviy sok
pineapple juice

томатный сок
tomatniy sok
tomato juice

еда yeda • food

шарик
sharik
scoop

чёрный хлеб
chorniy khleb
whole-wheat bread

тост-сэндвич
tost-sendvich
toasted sandwich

салат
salat
salad

мороженое
morozhenoye
ice cream

сладкая выпечка
sladkaya vypechka
pastry

бар bar • **bar**

стаканы;
бокалы
stakany;
bokaly
glasses

дозатор
dozator
dispenser

касса
kassa
cash register

бармен
barmen
bartender

пивной кран
pivnoy kran
beer tap

кофемашина
kofemashina
coffee machine

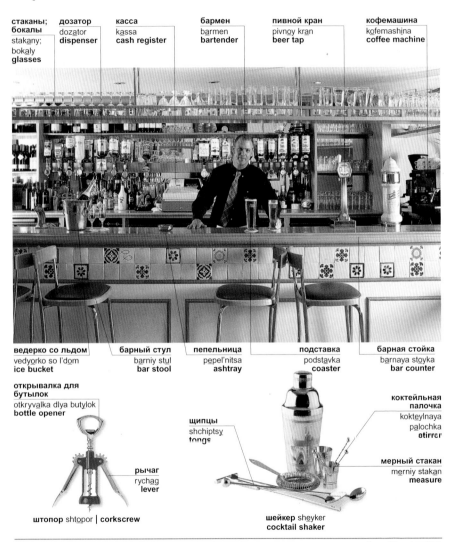

ведерко со льдом
vedyorko so l'dom
ice bucket

барный стул
barniy stul
bar stool

пепельница
pepel'nitsa
ashtray

подставка
podstavka
coaster

барная стойка
barnaya stoyka
bar counter

открывалка для
бутылок
otkryvalka dlya butylok
bottle opener

рычаг
rychag
lever

штопор shtopor | **corkscrew**

щипцы
shchiptsy
tongs

коктейльная
палочка
kokteynaya
palochka
stirrer

мерный стакан
merniy stakan
measure

шейкер sheyker
cocktail shaker

кувшин
kuvshin
pitcher

кубик льда
kubik l'da
ice cube

джин с тоником
dzhin s tonikom
gin and tonic

скотч с водой
skotch s vodoy
scotch and water

ром с колой
rom s koloy
rum and cola

водка с апельсиновым соком
vodka s apel'sinovym sokom
screwdriver

мартини
martini
martini

коктейль
kokteyl'
cocktail

вино
vino
wine

пиво pivo | beer

одинарный
odinarniy
single

двойной
dvoynoy
double

лёд и лимон
lyod i limon
ice and lemon

порция (спиртного)
portsiya (spirtnova)
shot

мерка
merka
measure

без льда
bez l'da
without ice

со льдом
so l'dom
with ice

лёгкие закуски legkiye zakuski • bar snacks

кешью
kesh'ju
cashews

арахис
arakhis
peanuts

миндаль
mindal'
almonds

чипсы chipsy | potato chips

орешки oreshki | nuts

оливки olivki | olives

ресторан restoran • restaurant

сервировка стола
servirovka stola
table setting

помощник повара
pomoshchnik povara
sous chef

шеф-повар
shef-povar
chef

бокал
bokal
glass

поднос
podnos
tray

кухня kukhnya | kitchen

официант ofitsiant | server

словарь slovar' • vocabulary

вечернее меню vecherneye menyu **dinner menu**	**фирменные блюда** firmenniye blyuda **specials**	**цена** tsena **price**	**обслуживание включено** obsluzhivaniye vklyucheno **service charge included**	**буфет** bufet **buffet**	**соль** sol' **salt**
винная карта vinnaya karta **wine list**	**а-ля карт** a-lya kart **à la carte**	**счёт** schyot **check**		**бар** bar **bar**	**перец** perets **pepper**
обеденное меню obedennoye menyu **lunch menu**	**тележка с десертами** telezhka s desertami **dessert cart**	**чек** chek **receipt** **чаевые** chayeviye **tip**	**обслуживание не включено** obsluzhivaniye ne vklyucheno **service charge not included**	**клиент** kliyent **customer**	

меню
menyu
menu

**блюдо из детского
меню**
blyudo iz detskogo menyu
child's meal

заказ zakaz | **order (v)**

(за)платить (za)platit' | **pay (v)**

блюда blyuda • courses

аперитив
aperitiv
apéritif

закуска
zakuska
appetizer

суп
sup
soup

второе блюдо
vtoroye blyudo
entrée

гарнир
garnir
side order

десерт desert | **dessert**

кофе kofe | **coffee**

Столик на двоих, пожалуйста.
stolik na dvoikh, pozhalusta
A table for two, please.

**Можно посмотреть меню/
винную карту?**
mozhno posmotret' menyu/
vinnuyu kartu?
**Can I see the menu/wine
list, please?**

**У вас есть обед по
фиксированной цене?**
u vas est' obed po fiksirovannoy tsene?
Is there a fixed-price menu?

У вас есть вегетарианские блюда?
u vas yest' vegetarianskiye blyuda?
Do you have any vegetarian dishes?

Можно счёт/чек, пожалуйста?
mozhno schyot/chek, pozhalusta?
**Could I have the check/a receipt,
please?**

Можно нам заплатить раздельно?
mozhno nam zaplatit' razdel'no?
Can we pay separately?

Простите, где здесь туалет?
prostite, gde zdes' tualet?
Where is the restroom, please?

фастфуд fastfud • **fast food**

гамбургер
gamburger
burger

соломинка
solominka
straw

безалкогольные напитки
bezalkogol'niye napitki
soft drink

картофель фри
kartofel' fri
French fries

бумажная салфетка
bumazhnaya salfetka
paper napkin

поднос
podnos
tray

бургер-комплекс burger-kompleks | **burger meal**

словарь slovar' • vocabulary

пиццерия
pitseriya
pizzeria

закусочная
zakusochnaya
burger bar

меню
menyu
menu

здесь; на месте
zdes'; na meste
eat-in

на вынос
na vynos
to go

разогреть
razogret'
reheat (v)

кетчуп
ketchup
ketchup

Можно приготовить это с собой?
mozhno prigotovit' eto s soboy?
Can I have that to go, please?

У вас есть доставка?
u vas yest' dostavka?
Do you deliver?

пицца
pitsa
pizza

прейскурант
preyskurant
price list

напиток в банке
napitok v banke
canned drink

доставка на дом dostavka na dom
home delivery

уличный киоск ulichniy kiosk
street vendor

булочка
bulochka
bun

горчица
gorchitsa
mustard

сосиска
sosiska
sausage

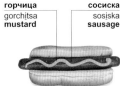

гамбургер
gamburger
hamburger

чикенбургер
chikenburger
chicken burger

вегетарианский бургер
vegetarianskiy burger
veggie burger

хот-дог khot-dog | **hot dog**

начинка
nachinka
filling

сэндвич
sendvich
sandwich

клубный сэндвич
klubniy sendvich
club sandwich

бутерброд
buterbrod
open-faced sandwich

ролл
roll
wrap

соус
sous
sauce

несладкий
nesladkiy
savory

сладкий
sladkiy
sweet

начинка
nachinka
topping

кебаб
kebab
kebab

куриные наггетсы
kuriniye nagetsy
chicken nuggets

блинчики blinchiki | **crepes**

рыба с картофелем фри
ryba s kartofelem fri
fish and chips

рёбрышки
ryobryshki
ribs

жареный цыплёнок
zharenyj tsyplenok
fried chicken

пицца
pitsa
pizza

завтрак zavtrak • breakfast

молоко
moloko
milk

хлопья; сухой завтрак
khlop'ya; sukhoy zavtrak
cereal

сухофрукты
sukhofrukty
dried fruit

ветчина
vetchina
ham

сыр
syr
cheese

хрустящий хлебец
khrustyashchij khlebets
crispbread

завтрак «шведский стол»
zavtrak shvedskij stol
breakfast buffet

мармелад
marmelad
marmalade

варенье
varen'ye
jam

паштет
pashtet
pâté

масло
maslo
butter

фруктовый сок
fruktoviy sok
fruit juice

кофе
kofe
coffee

горячий шоколад
goryachiy shokolad
hot chocolate

круассан
kruasan
croissant

чай
chay
tea

завтрак zavtrak | **breakfast table**

напитки napitki | **drinks**

помидор, томат
pomidor, tomat
tomato

кровяная колбаса
krovyanaya kolbasa
black pudding

тост
tost
toast

яичница
yaichnitsa
fried egg

сосиска
sosiska
sausage

бекон
bekon
bacon

бриошь
briosh
brioche

хлеб
khleb
bread

английский завтрак
angliyskiy zavtrak
English breakfast

копчёная рыба
kopchonaya ryba
kippers

французский тост
frantsuskiy tost
French toast

желток
zheltok
yolk

варёное яйцо
varyonoye yaytso
soft-boiled egg

яичница-болтунья
yaichnitsa-boltun'ya
scrambled eggs

взбитые
сливки
vzbutye slivki
**whipped
cream**

фруктовый йогурт
fruktoviy yogurt
fruit yogurt

блинчики
blinchiki
crepes

вафли
vafli
waffles

овсяная каша
ovsyanaya kasha
oatmeal

свежие фрукты
svezhiye frukty
fresh fruit

обед obed • dinner

суп sup | **soup**

бульон bul'yon | **broth**

рагу ragu | **stew**

карри karri | **curry**

жаркое zharkoye | **roast**

пирог с начинкой pirog s nachinkoy | **potpie**

суфле sufle | **soufflé**

кебаб kebab | **kebab**

фрикадельки frikadel'ki **meatballs**

омлет omlet | **omlet**

стир-фрай styr-frai | **stir-fry**

лапша
lapsha
noodles

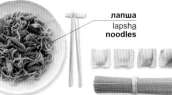

паста; макароны pasta; makarony | **pasta**

рис ris | **rice**

салат ассорти salat assorti **tossed salad**

зелёный салат zelyoniy salat | **green salad**

салатная заправка salatnaya zapravka **dressing**

способы приготовления sposoby prigotovleniya • techniques

фаршированный
farshirovanniy | **stuffed**

в соусе v souse
in sauce

жареный на гриле
zhareniy na grile | **grilled**

маринованный
marinovanniy | **marinated**

пошированный
poshirovanniy | **poached**

пюреобразный
pureobrazniy | **mashed**

запечённый
zapechyonniy | **baked**

жаренный на сковороде
zhareniy na skovorode
pan fried

жареный zhareniy | **fried**

маринованный
marinovanniy | **pickled**

копченый kopchyoniy
smoked

жаренный во фритюре
zhareniy vo frityure
deep-fried

в сиропе v sirope
in syrup

заправленный
zapravlenniy | **dressed**

на пару na paru
steamed

сушёный susheniy
cured

учёба uch<u>o</u>ba
study

школа shkola • school

доска
doska
whiteboard

учитель
uchitel'
teacher

портфель
portfel'
schoolbag

ученик
uchenik
student

парта
parta
desk

класс klas | **classroom**

школьница
shkol'nitsa
schoolgirl

школьник
shkol'nik
schoolboy

словарь slovar' • vocabulary

история istoriya **history**	**естествознание** yestestvoznaniye **science**	**физика** fizika **physics**
языки yazyki **languages**	**изобразительное** **искусство** izobrazitel'noye iskustvo **art**	**химия** khimiya **chemistry**
литература literatura **literature**	**музыка** muzyka **music**	**биология** biologiya **biology**
география geografiya **geography**	**математика** matematika **math**	**физкультура** fizkul'tura **physical** **education**

занятия zanyatiya • activities

читать chitat' | **read (v)**

писать pisat' | **write (v)**

писать по буквам pisat'
po bukvam | **spell (v)**

рисовать risovat'
draw (v)

перо
pero
nib

цветной карандаш
tsvetnoy karandash
colored pencil

точилка
tochilka
**pencil
sharpener**

цифровой проектор
tsifrovoy proyektor
digital projector

ручка
ruchka
pen

карандаш
karandash
pencil

ластик
lastik
eraser

тетрадь
tetrad'
notebook

учебник uchebnik | **textbook**

пенал penal | **pencil case**   **линейка** lineyka | **ruler**

спрашивать sprashivat'
question (v)

отвечать otvechat'
answer (v)

обсуждать obsuzhdat'
discuss (v)

учиться uchit'sya
learn (v)

словарь slovar' • **vocabulary**

директор direktor **principal**	**ответ** otvet **answer**	**отметка** otmetka **grade**
урок urok **lesson**	**домашнее задание** domashneye zadaniye **homework**	**класс** klass **year**
вопрос vopros **question**	**экзамен** ekzamen **test**	**словарь** slovar' **dictionary**
конспектировать konspektirovat' **take notes (v)**	**сочинение** sochineniye **essay**	**энциклопедия** entsiklopediya **encyclopedia**

математика matematika • math

геометрические фигуры geometricheskiye figury • shapes

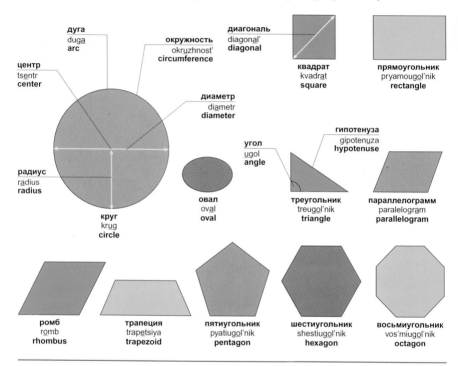

дуга
duga
arc

окружность
okruzhnost'
circumference

диагональ
diagonal'
diagonal

квадрат
kvadrat
square

прямоугольник
pryamougol'nik
rectangle

центр
tsentr
center

диаметр
diametr
diameter

гипотенуза
gipotenuza
hypotenuse

угол
ugol
angle

радиус
radius
radius

овал
oval
oval

треугольник
treugol'nik
triangle

параллелограмм
paralelogram
parallelogram

круг
krug
circle

ромб
romb
rhombus

трапеция
trapetsiya
trapezoid

пятиугольник
pyatiugol'nik
pentagon

шестиугольник
shestiugol'nik
hexagon

восьмиугольник
vos'miugol'nik
octagon

геометрические тела geometricheskiye tela • solids

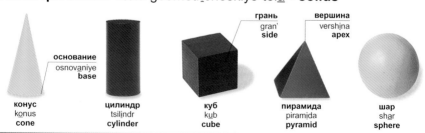

грань
gran'
side

вершина
vershina
apex

основание
osnovaniye
base

конус
konus
cone

цилиндр
tsilindr
cylinder

куб
kub
cube

пирамида
piramida
pyramid

шар
shar
sphere

линии linii • lines

прямая
pryamaya
straight

параллельная
paralel'naya
parallel

перпендикулярная
perpendikulyarnaya
perpendicular

кривая
krivaya
curved

измерения izmereniya • measurements

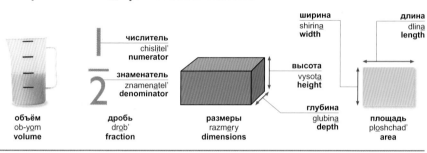

числитель
chislitel'
numerator

знаменатель
znamenatel'
denominator

ширина
shirina
width

длина
dlina
length

высота
vysota
height

глубина
glubina
depth

объём
ob-yom
volume

дробь
drob'
fraction

размеры
razmery
dimensions

площадь
ploshchad'
area

принадлежности prinadlezhnosti • equipment

угольник
ugol'nik
triangle

транспортир
transportir
protractor

линейка
lineyka
ruler

циркуль
tsirkul'
compass

калькулятор
kal'kulyator
calculator

словарь slovar' • vocabulary

геометрия geometriya **geometry**	**плюс** plyus **plus**	**умножить на** umnozhit' na **times**	**равно** ravno **equals**	**складывать** skladyvat' **add (v)**	**умножать** umnozhat' **multiply (v)**	**уравнение** uravneniye **equation**
арифметика arifmetika **arithmetic**	**минус** minus **minus**	**разделить на** razdelit' na **divided by**	**считать** schitat' **count (v)**	**вычитать** vychitat' **subtract (v)**	**делить** delit' **divide (v)**	**процент** protsent **percentage**

естественные науки yestestvenniye nauki • science

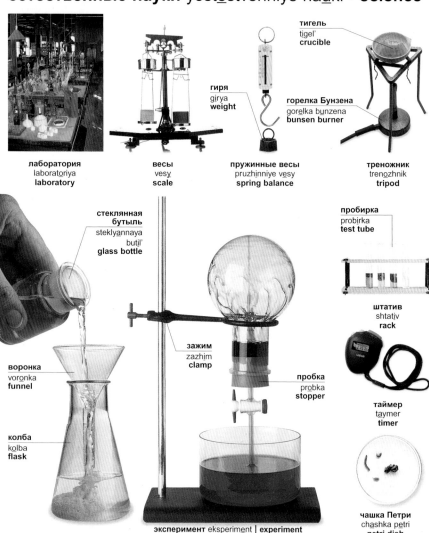

лаборатория
laboratoriya
laboratory

весы
vesy
scale

гиря
girya
weight

пружинные весы
pruzhinniye vesy
spring balance

тигель
tigel'
crucible

горелка Бунзена
gorelka bunzena
bunsen burner

треножник
trenozhnik
tripod

стеклянная бутыль
steklyannaya butil'
glass bottle

пробирка
probirka
test tube

штатив
shtativ
rack

воронка
voronka
funnel

зажим
zazhim
clamp

пробка
probka
stopper

таймер
taymer
timer

колба
kolba
flask

чашка Петри
chashka petri
petri dish

эксперимент eksperiment | **experiment**

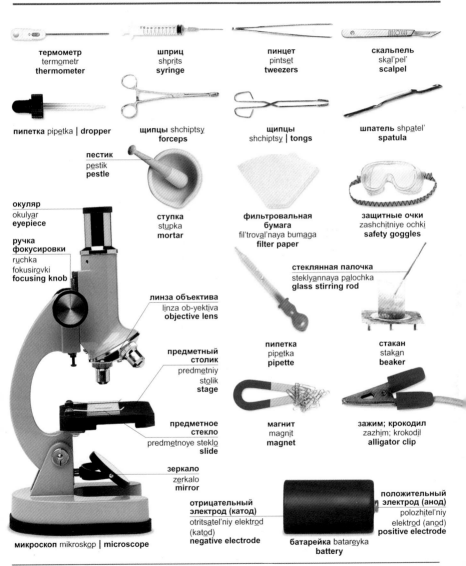

термометр
termometr
thermometer

шприц
shprits
syringe

пинцет
pintset
tweezers

скальпель
skal'pel'
scalpel

пипетка pipetka | **dropper**

щипцы shchiptsy
forceps

щипцы
shchiptsy | **tongs**

шпатель shpatel'
spatula

пестик
pestik
pestle

ступка
stupka
mortar

фильтровальная бумага
fil'troval'naya bumaga
filter paper

защитные очки
zashchitniye ochki
safety goggles

окуляр
okulyar
eyepiece

ручка фокусировки
ruchka
fokusirovki
focusing knob

линза объектива
linza ob-yektiva
objective lens

предметный столик
predmetniy
stolik
stage

предметное стекло
predmetnoye steklo
slide

зеркало
zerkalo
mirror

стеклянная палочка
steklyannaya palochka
glass stirring rod

пипетка
pipetka
pipette

стакан
stakan
beaker

магнит
magnit
magnet

зажим; крокодил
zazhim; krokodil
alligator clip

отрицательный электрод (катод)
otritsatel'niy elektrod
(katod)
negative electrode

батарейка batareyka
battery

положительный электрод (анод)
polozhitel'niy
elektrod (anod)
positive electrode

микроскоп mikroskop | **microscope**

колледж koledzh · college

приёмная комиссия
priyomnaya komisiya
admissions office

столовая
stolovaya
cafeteria

спортивно-оздоровительный комплекс
sportivno-ozdorovitel'niy kompleks
health center

спортивная площадка
sportivnaya ploshchadka
playing field

общежитие
obshchezhitiye
residence hall

библиотекарь
bibliotekar'
librarian

кампус kampus | campus

словарь slovar' · vocabulary

читательский билет chitatel'skiy bilet **library card**	**справочная** spravochnaya **help desk**	**выдача** vidacha **loan**
читальный зал chital'niy zal **reading room**	**брать в библиотеке** brat' v biblioteke **borrow (v)**	**книга** kniga **book**
список литературы spisok literaturi **reading list**	**заказывать** zakazivat' **reserve (v)**	**название** nazvaniye **title**
дата возврата data vozvrata **due date**	**продлевать** prodlevat' **renew (v)**	**проход** prokhod **aisle**

выдача книг
vidacha knig
circulation desk

книжная полка
knizhnaya polka
bookshelf

периодические издания
periodicheskiye izdaniya
periodical

журнал
zhurnal
journal

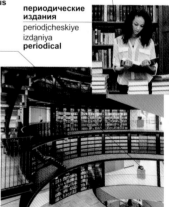

библиотека biblioteka | library

студент
student
undergraduate

лектор
lektor
professor

выпускник
vypusknik
graduate

мантия
mantiya
gown

аудитория auditoria | **lecture hall**

выпускная церемония / вручение дипломов
vypusknaya tseremoniya / vrucheniye diplomov
graduation ceremony

школы shkoly • **schools**

модель
model'
model

высшее художественное училище
vysshee khudozhestvennoe uchilishche
art school

музыкальная школа
muzykal'naya shkola
music school

танцевальная академия
tantseval'naya akademiya
dance school

словарь slovar' • **vocabulary**

стипендия stipendiya **scholarship**	**исследование** issledovaniye **research**	**диссертация** disertatsiya **dissertation**	**медицина** meditsina **medicine**	**философия** filosofiya **philosophy**
диплом diplom **diploma**	**степень магистра** stepen' magistra **master's**	**факультет** fakul'tet **department**	**зоология** zoologiya **zoology**	**литература** literatura **literature**
степень stepen' **degree**	**докторская степень** doktorskaya stepen' **doctorate**	**право** pravo **law**	**физика** fizika **physics**	**история искусств** istoriya iskustv **art history**
аспирант aspirant **postgraduate**	**диссертация** disertatsiya **thesis**	**технические науки** tekhnicheskiye nauki **engineering**	**политика** politika **political science**	**экономика** ekonomika **economics**

работа rab<u>o</u>ta
work

офис 1 <u>o</u>fis • office 1

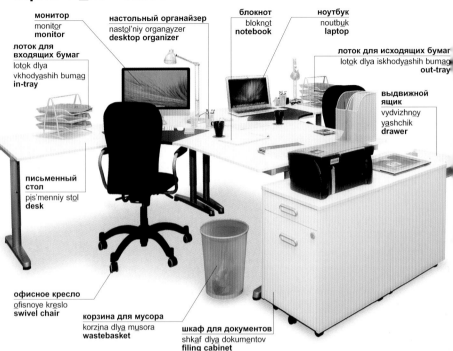

монитор
monitor
monitor

настольный органайзер
nastol'niy organ<u>a</u>yzer
desktop organizer

блокнот
blokn<u>o</u>t
notebook

ноутбук
noutb<u>u</u>k
laptop

лоток для входящих бумаг
lot<u>o</u>k dlya vkhody<u>a</u>shih bum<u>a</u>g
in-tray

лоток для исходящих бумаг
lot<u>o</u>k dlya iskhody<u>a</u>shih bum<u>a</u>g
out-tray

выдвижной ящик
vydvizhn<u>o</u>y y<u>a</u>shchik
drawer

письменный стол
pis'menniy st<u>o</u>l
desk

офисное кресло
<u>o</u>fisnoye kr<u>e</u>slo
swivel chair

корзина для мусора
korz<u>i</u>na dlya m<u>u</u>sora
wastebasket

шкаф для документов
shk<u>a</u>f dlya dokum<u>e</u>ntov
filing cabinet

офисная техника <u>o</u>fisnaya t<u>e</u>khnika • office equipment

лоток для бумаги
lot<u>o</u>k dlya bum<u>a</u>gi
paper tray

принтер pr<u>i</u>nter | **printer**

бумагорезка bum<u>a</u>gorezka
shredder

канцелярские принадлежности kantsely<u>a</u>rskie prinadl<u>e</u>zhnosti • **office supplies**

бланк
blank
letterhead

поздравительная карточка
pozdrav<u>i</u>telnaya k<u>a</u>rtochka
compliments slip

конверт
konv<u>e</u>rt
envelope

папка-регистратор
papka-registr<u>a</u>tor
box file

крепёж
krep<u>yo</u>zh
tab

разделитель
razdel<u>i</u>tel'
divider

планшетка с зажимом
plansh<u>e</u>tka s zaz<u>h</u>imom
clipboard

блокнот
blokn<u>o</u>t
notepad

подвесная папка
podvesn<u>a</u>ya p<u>a</u>pka
hanging file

папка организатор
papka-organiz<u>a</u>tor
expanding file

папка с арочным прижимом
p<u>a</u>pka s <u>a</u>rochnym priz<u>h</u>imom
binder

скобы
sk<u>o</u>by
staples

скотч
skotch
tape

чернильная подушечка
chern<u>i</u>l'naya pod<u>u</u>shechka
ink pad

личный органайзер
l<u>i</u>chniy organ<u>a</u>yzer
personal organizer

степлер
st<u>e</u>pler
stapler

держатель для скотча
derzh<u>a</u>tel' dlya sk<u>o</u>tcha
tape dispenser

дырокол
dyrok<u>o</u>l
hole punch

печать
pech<u>a</u>t'
rubber stamp

резинка
rez<u>i</u>nka
rubber band

зажим для бумаг
zaz<u>h</u>im dlya bum<u>a</u>g
bulldog clip

скрепка
skr<u>e</u>pka
paper clip

кнопка
kn<u>o</u>pka
thumbtack

доска для объявлений dosk<u>a</u> dlya ob-yavl<u>e</u>niy | **bulletin board**

офис 2 ofis · office 2

флипчарт
flipchart
flip chart

протокол
protokol
minutes

штатив
shtativ
easel

менеджер
menedzher
manager

отчёт
otchyot
report

предложение
predlozheniye
proposal

руководитель
rukovoditel'
executive

заседание, встреча zasedaniye, vstrecha | meeting

словарь slovar' · vocabulary

конференц-зал
konferents-zal
meeting room

присутствовать
prisutstvovat'
attend (v)

повестка дня
povestka dnya
agenda

председательствовать
predsedatel'stvovat'
chair (v)

Во сколько начинается встреча?
vo skol'ko nachinayetsya vstrecha?
What time is the meeting?

В какие часы работает ваш офис?
v kakie chasy rabotaet vash ofis?
What are your office hours?

докладчик
dokladchik
speaker

презентация prezentatsiya | presentation

бизнес biznes • business

бизнесмен
biznesmen
businessman

бизнесвумен
biznesvumen
businesswoman

деловой обед delovoy obed | **business lunch**

деловая поездка delovaya poyezdka | **business trip**

ежедневник ezhednevnik | **day planner**

встреча
vstrecha
appointment

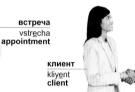

управляющий директор
upravlyayushchiy direktor
CEO

клиент
kliyent
client

сделка sdelka | **business deal**

словарь slovar' • vocabulary

компания
kompaniya
company

головной офис
golovnoy ofis
head office

филиал
filial
regional office

сотрудники
sotrudniki
staff

оклад
oklad
salary

платёжная ведомость
platyozhnaya vedomost'
payroll

бухгалтерский отдел
bukhgalterskiy otdel
accounting department

отдел маркетинга
otdel marketinga
marketing department

отдел продаж
otdel prodazh
sales department

юридический отдел
yuridicheskiy otdel
legal department

отдел по работе с клиентами
otdel po rabote s kliyentami
customer service department

отдел кадров
otdel kadrov
human resources department

компьютер komp'yuter • **computer**

принтер
printer
printer

экран
ekran
screen

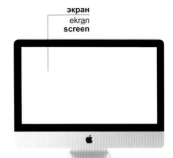

сканер
skaner
scanner

ноутбук
noutbuk | **laptop**

клавиша
klavisha
key

клавиатура
klaviatura
keyboard

мышь
mysh
mouse

динамик
dinamik
speaker

аппаратное обеспечение
aparatnoye obespecheniye
hardware

словарь slovar' • **vocabulary**

память pamyat' **memory**	**программное обеспечение** programnoye obespecheniye **software**	**сервер** server **server**
оперативная память operativnaya pamyat' **RAM**	**приложение** prilozheniye **application**	**порт** port **port**
байты bayty **bytes**	**программа** programma **program**	**процессор** protsessor **processor**
система sistema **system**	**сеть** set' **network**	**кабель питания** kabel' pitaniya **power cord**

USB-флеш-накопитель
yu-es-bi-flesh-nakopitel'
memory stick

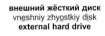

внешний жёсткий диск
vneshniy zhyostkiy disk
external hard drive

планшет
planshet
tablet

смартфон
smartfon
smartphone

рабочий стол rabochiy stol • desktop

строка меню
stroka menyu
menubar

шрифт
shrift
font

панель
инструментов
panel' instrumentov
toolbar

иконка
ikonka
icon

полоса
прокрутки
polosa
prokrutki
scrollbar

обои
oboi
wallpaper

окно
okno
window

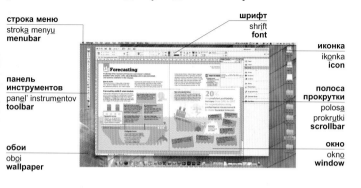

файл
fayl
file

папка
papka
folder

корзина
korzina
trash

интернет internet • internet

браузер
brauzer
browser

веб-сайт
veb-sayt
website

просматривать prosmatrivat' | **browse (v)**

электронная почта elektronnaya pochta • email

адрес электронной почты
adres elektronnoy pochty
email address

входящие
vkhodyashchiye
inbox

словарь slovar' • vocabulary

соединять soyedinyat' **connect (v)**	поставщик услуг postavshchik uslug **service provider**	входить в систему vkhodit' v sistemu **log on (v)**	загружать zagruzhat' **download (v)**	отправлять otpravlyat' **send (v)**	сохранять sokhranyat' **save (v)**
устанавливать ustanavlivat' **install (v)**	учётная запись электронной почты uchetnaya zapis' ehlektronnoj pochty **email account**	онлайн onlayn **online**	приложение prilozheniye **attachment**	получать poluchat' **receive (v)**	искать iskat' **search (v)**

средства массовой информации sr<u>e</u>dstva m<u>a</u>ssovoy inform<u>a</u>tsii • **media**

телестудия telest<u>u</u>diya • **television studio**

съёмочная площадка
s-y<u>o</u>mochnaya
ploshch<u>a</u>dka
set

ведущий
ved<u>u</u>shchiy
host

освещение
osveshch<u>e</u>nie
light

камера
k<u>a</u>mera
camera

кран-штатив
kr<u>a</u>n-shtativ
camera crane

оператор
oper<u>a</u>tor
cameraman

словарь slov<u>a</u>r' • **vocabulary**

канал kan<u>a</u>l **channel**	**новости** n<u>o</u>vosti **news**	**пресса** pr<u>e</u>ssa **press**	**мыльная опера** m<u>y</u>l'naya <u>o</u>pera **soap opera**	**мультфильм** mul'tf<u>i</u>l'm **cartoon**	**прямая трансляция** pryam<u>a</u>ya transly<u>a</u>tsiya **live**
составление программы sostavl<u>e</u>nie progr<u>a</u>mmy **programming**	**документальный фильм** dokument<u>a</u>l'niy fil'm **documentary**	**телесериал** teleseri<u>a</u>l **television series**	**игровое шоу** igrov<u>o</u>ye sh<u>o</u>u **game show**	**в записи** v z<u>a</u>pisi **prerecorded**	**транслировать** transl<u>i</u>rovat' **broadcast (v)**

интервьюер interv'yuyer
interviewer

репортёр reportyor
reporter

телесуфлёр telesuflyor
teleprompter

**ведущий/диктор
новостей** vedushchiy/
diktor novostey
anchor

актёры aktyory | **actors**

удочка для микрофона
udochka dlya mikrofona
sound boom

хлопушка khlopushka
clapper board

съёмочная площадка
s'emochnaya ploshchadka
movie set

радио radio · radio

звукооператор
zvukooperator
**sound
technician**

микшерный пульт
miksherniy pul't
mixing desk

микрофон
mikrofon
microphone

студия звукозаписи studiya zvukozapisi | **recording studio**

словарь slovar' · vocabulary

радиостанция
radiostantsiya
radio station

**трансляция;
вещание**
translyatsiya;
veshchaniye
broadcast

длина волны
dlina volny
wavelength

длинные волны
dlinniye volny
long wave

короткие волны
korotkiye volny
short wave

аналоговый
analogoviy
analog

средние волны
sredniye volny
medium wave

частота
chastota
frequency

громкость
gromkost'
volume

настраивать
nastraivat'
tune (v)

диджей
didzhey
DJ

цифровой
tsifrovoy
digital

правосудие pravosudiye • law

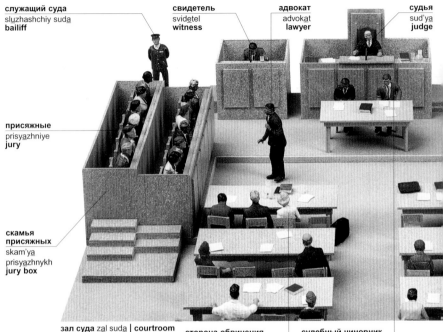

служащий суда
sluzhashchiy suda
bailiff

свидетель
svidetel
witness

адвокат
advokat
lawyer

судья
sud'ya
judge

присяжные
prisyazhniye
jury

скамья присяжных
skam'ya prisyazhnykh
jury box

зал суда zal suda | courtroom

сторона обвинения
storona obvineniya
prosecution

судебный чиновник
sudebniy chinovnik
court clerk

словарь slovar' • vocabulary

адвокатская контора advokatskaya kontora **lawyer's office**	**повестка** povestka **summons**	**судебное предписание** sudebnoye predpisaniye **writ**	**дело** delo **court case**
консультация юриста konsul'tatsiya yurista **legal advice**	**показания** pokazaniya **statement**	**дата судебного заседания** data sudebnogo zasedaniya **court date**	**обвинение** obvineniye **charge**
клиент kliyent **client**	**ордор на арост** order na arest **warrant**	**заявление ответчика** zayavleniye otvetchika **plea**	**обвиняемый** obvinyayemiy **accused**

стенографист
stenografist
stenographer

подозреваемый
podozrevayemiy
suspect

подсудимый; ответчик
podsudimiy; otvetchik
defendant

защита
zashchita
defense

преступник
prestupnik
criminal

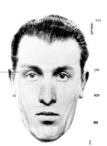

фоторобот
fotorobot | **composite sketch**

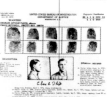

криминальное досье
kriminal'noye dos'ye
criminal record

тюремный охранник
tyuremniy okhrannik | **prison guard**

камера
kamera | **cell**

тюрьма tyur'ma | **prison**

словарь slovar' • vocabulary

улика ulika **evidence**	**виновен** vinoven **guilty**	**залог** zalog **bail**	**Я хочу встретиться с адвокатом.** ya khochu vstretit'sya s advokatom **I want to see a lawyer.**
решение суда/ приговор resheniye suda/ prigovor **verdict**	**оправдан** opravdan **acquitted**	**апелляция** apelyatsiya **appeal**	**Где находится суд?** gde nakhoditsya sud? **Where is the courthouse?**
невиновен nevinoven **innocent**	**приговор** prigovor **sentence**	**условно-досрочное освобождение** uslovno-dosrochnoye osvobozhdeniye **parole**	**Могу ли я внести залог?** mogu li ya vnesti zalog? **Can I post bail?**

ферма 1 ferma • farm 1

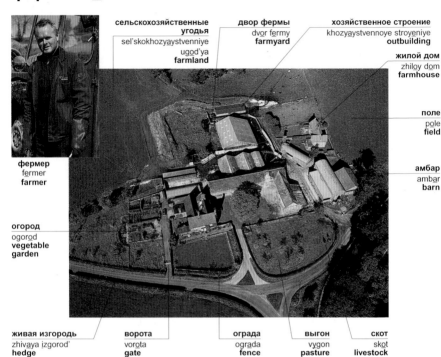

фермер
fermer
farmer

сельскохозяйственные угодья
sel'skokhozyaystvenniye ugod'ya
farmland

двор фермы
dvor fermy
farmyard

хозяйственное строение
khozyaystvennoye stroyeniye
outbuilding

жилой дом
zhiloy dom
farmhouse

поле
pole
field

амбар
ambar
barn

огород
ogorod
vegetable garden

живая изгородь
zhivaya izgorod'
hedge

ворота
vorota
gate

ограда
ograda
fence

выгон
vygon
pasture

скот
skot
livestock

культиватор
kul'tivator
cultivator

трактор traktor | tractor

зерноуборочный комбайн zernouborochnyj kombajn | combine

виды фермерских хозяйств vidy fermerskikh khozyaystv • types of farms

урожай
urozhay
crop

земледельческая ферма
zemledel'cheskaya ferma
crop farm

молочная ферма
molochnaya ferma
dairy farm

стадо
stado
flock

овцеводческая ферма
ovtsevodcheskaya ferma
sheep farm

птицеферма ptitseferma
poultry farm

свиноферма
svinoferma
pig farm

рыбоводческое хозяйство
rybovodcheskoye khozyaystvo
fish farm

плодоводческая ферма
plodovodcheskaya ferma
fruit farm

виноградная лоза
vinogradnaya loza
vine

виноградник
vinogradnik
vineyard

действия deystviya • actions

борозда
borozda
furrow

пахать
pakhat'
plow (v)

сеять
seyat'
sow (v)

доить
doit'
milk (v)

кормить
kormit'
feed (v)

поливать polivat'
water (v)

собирать урожай sobirat'
urozhay | **harvest (v)**

словарь slovar' • vocabulary

гербицид gerbitsid **herbicide**	**стадо** stado **herd**	**кормушка** kormushka **trough**
пестицид pestitsid **pesticide**	**силос** silos **silo**	**сажать** sazhat' **plant (v)**

ферма 2 ferma • farm 2

культуры kulturi • crops

пшеница
pshenitsa
wheat

кукуруза
kukuruza
corn

ячмень
yachmen'
barley

рапс
raps
rapeseed

подсолнух
podsolnukh
sunflower

тюк
tyuk
bale

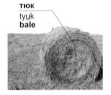

сено
seno
hay

люцерна
lyutserna
alfalfa

табак
tabak
tobacco

рис
ris
rice

чай
chay
tea

кофе
kofe
coffee

лён
lyon
flax

сахарный тростник
sakharniy trostnik
sugarcane

хлопок
khlopok
cotton

пугало
pugalo
scarecrow

скот skot • livestock

поросёнок
porosyonok
piglet

телёнок
telyonok
calf

свинья
svin'ya
pig

корова
korova
cow

бык
byk
bull

овца
ovtsa
sheep

козлёнок
kozlyonok
kid

жеребёнок
zherebyonok
foal

ягнёнок
yagnyonok
lamb

коза
koza
goat

лошадь/конь
loshad'/kon'
horse

осёл
osyol
donkey

цыплёнок
tsyplyonok
chick

утёнок
utyonok
duckling

курица
kuritsa
chicken

петух
petukh
rooster

индюк
indyuk
turkey

утка
utka
duck

стойло
stoylo
stable

загон
zagon
pen

курятник
kuryatnik
chicken coop

свинарник
svinarnik
pigsty

строительство stroitel'stvo · construction

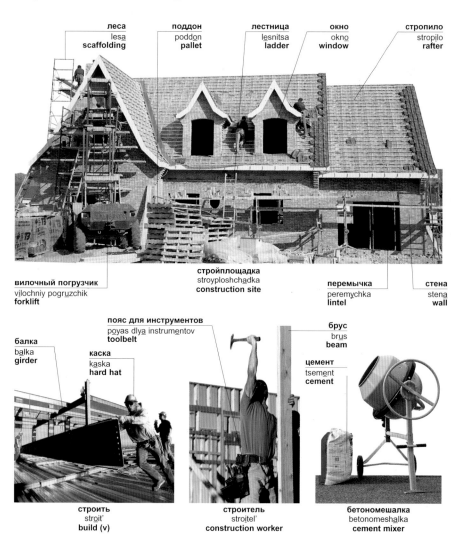

леса
lesa
scaffolding

поддон
poddon
pallet

лестница
lesnitsa
ladder

окно
okno
window

стропило
stropilo
rafter

вилочный погрузчик
vilochniy pogruzchik
forklift

стройплощадка
stroyploshchadka
construction site

перемычка
peremychka
lintel

стена
stena
wall

пояс для инструментов
poyas dlya instrumentov
toolbelt

брус
brus
beam

балка
balka
girder

каска
kaska
hard hat

цемент
tsement
cement

строить
stroit'
build (v)

строитель
stroitel'
construction worker

бетономешалка
betonomeshalka
cement mixer

материалы materi<u>a</u>ly • **materials**

кирпич
kirp<u>i</u>ch
brick

дерево
d<u>e</u>revo
lumber

черепица
cherep<u>i</u>tsa
roof tile

бетонный блок
bet<u>o</u>nniy bl<u>o</u>k
cinder block

инструменты instrum<u>e</u>nty • **tools**

строительный раствор
stro<u>i</u>tel'niy rastv<u>o</u>r
mortar

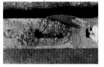 

кельма
k<u>e</u>l'ma
trowel

спиртовой уровень
spirtov<u>o</u>y <u>u</u>roven'
level

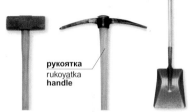

рукоятка
rukoy<u>a</u>tka
handle

кувалда
kuv<u>a</u>lda
sledgehammer

кайло
kayl<u>o</u>
pickax

лопата
lop<u>a</u>ta
shovel

техника t<u>e</u>khnika • **machinery**

каток
kat<u>o</u>k
road roller

самосвал
samosv<u>a</u>l
dump truck

выносная опора
vynosn<u>a</u>ya op<u>o</u>ra
support

крюк
kry<u>u</u>k
hook

кран kran | **crane**

дорожные работы dor<u>o</u>zhniye rab<u>o</u>ty • **roadwork**

асфальт
asf<u>a</u>l't
asphalt

конус
k<u>o</u>nus
cone

отбойный молоток
otb<u>o</u>yniy molot<u>o</u>k
jackhammer

замена дорожного покрытия
zam<u>e</u>na dor<u>o</u>zhnogo pokr<u>y</u>tiya
resurfacing

экскаватор
ekskav<u>a</u>tor
excavator

профессии 1 professiy • occupations 1

плотник
plotnik
carpenter

электрик
elektrik
electrician

сантехник
santekhnik
plumber

строитель
stroitel'
construction worker

садовник
sadovnik
gardener

пылесос
pylesos
**vacuum
cleaner**

уборщик
uborshchik
cleaner

механик
mekhanik
mechanic

мясник
myasnik
butcher

продавец рыбы
prodavets ryby
fish seller

торговец овощами
torgovets ovoshchami
produce seller

флорист
florist
florist

женский парикмахер
zhenskiy parikmakher
hairdresser

мужской парикмахер
muzhskoy parikmakher
barber

ювелир
yuvelir
jeweler

продавец-консультант
prodavets-konsul'tant
salesperson

агент по недвижимости
agent po nedvizhimosti
realtor

оптик
optik
optometrist

маска
maska
mask

зубной врач
zubnoy vrach
dentist

врач
vrach
doctor

фармацевт
farmatsevt
pharmacist

медсестра
medsestra
nurse

ветеринар
veterinar
veterinarian

фермер
fermer
farmer

рыбак
rybak
fisherman

автомат
avtomat
**machine
gun**

идентификационный
жетон
identifikatsionniy
zheton
badge

униформа
uniforma
uniform

охранник
okhrannik
security guard

моряк
moryak
sailor

солдат
soldat
soldier

полицейский
politseyskiy
police officer

пожарный
pozharniy
firefighter

профессии 2 professiy • occupations 2

модель
model'
model

юрист
yurist
lawyer

бухгалтер
bukhgalter
accountant

архитектор arkhitektor | **architect**

учёный
uchyoniy
scientist

учительница
uchitel'nitsa
teacher

библиотекарь
bibliotekar'
librarian

администратор
administrator
receptionist

**сумка
почтальона**
sumka
pochtalyona
mailbag

почтальон
pochtalyon
mail carrier

водитель автобуса
voditel' avtobusa
bus driver

водитель грузовика
voditel' gruzovika
truck driver

таксист
taksist
taxi driver

пилот
pilot
pilot

стюардесса
styuardessa
flight attendant

турагент
turagent
travel agent

**поварской
колпак**
povarskoy
kolpak
chef's hat

повар
povar
chef

пачка
pachka
tutu

музыкант
muzykant
musician

танцовщица
tantsovshchitsa
dancer

актриса
aktrisa
actress

певица
pevitsa
singer

официантка
ofitsiantka
waitress

бармен
barmen
bartender

спортсмен
sportsmen
sportsman

скульптор
skul'ptor
sculptor

заметки
zametki
notes

художник
khudozhnik
painter

фотограф
fotograf
photographer

ведущий новостей, диктор
vedushchiy novostey, diktor
anchor

журналист
zhurnalist
journalist

редактор
redaktor
editor

дизайнер
dizayner
designer

швея
shveya
seamstress

портной
portnoy
tailor

транспорт transport
transportation

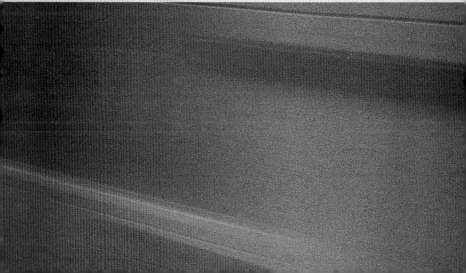

дороги dorogi • roads

шоссе
shose
freeway

пункт взимания дорожных сборов
punkt vzimaniya dorozhnykh sborov
toll booth

дорожная разметка
dorozhnaya razmetka
road markings

подъездная дорога
pod'ezdnaya doroga
on-ramp

одностороннее движение
odnostoronneye dvizheniye
one-way street

разделительная линия
razdelitel'naya liniya
divider

перекрёсток
perekrestok
interchange

светофор
svetofor
traffic light

внутренняя полоса движения
vnutrennyaya polosa dvizheniya
right lane

средняя полоса движения
srednyaya polosa dvizheniya
middle lane

внешняя полоса движения
vneshnyaya polosa dvizheniya
left lane

съезд
s'yezd
off-ramp

движение
dvizheniye
traffic

эстакада
estakada
overpass

обочина
obochina
shoulder

грузовик
gruzovik
truck

разделительная полоса
razdelitel'naya polosa
median strip

проезд под путепроводом
proyezd pod puteprovodom
underpass

аварийный телефон
avariyniy telefon
emergency phone

парковка для инвалидов
parkovka dlya invalidov
disabled parking

пробка
probka
traffic jam

пешеходный переход
peshekhodniy perekhod
crosswalk

спутниковый навигатор
sputnikoviy navigator
satnav

счётчик на стоянке
schyotchik na stoyanke
parking meter

инспектор дорожного движения
inspektor dorozhnogo dvizheniya
traffic policeman

словарь slovar' · **vocabulary**

перекресток с круговым движением
perekrestok s krugovym dvizheniem
roundabout

дорожные работы
dorozhniye raboty
roadwork

аварийное заграждение
avariynoye zagrazhdeniye
guardrail

объезд
ob-yezd
detour

автомагистраль
avtomagistral'
divided highway

парковаться
parkovatsa
park (v)

вести машину
vesti mashinu
drive (v)

давать задний ход
davat' zadniy khod
reverse (v)

обгонять
obgonyat'
pass (v)

буксировать
buksirovat'
tow away (v)

Это дорога на …?
eto doroga na …?
Is this the road to …?

Где можно припарковаться?
gde mozhno priparkovatsa?
Where can I park?

дорожные знаки dorozhniye znaki · **road signs**

въезд запрещён
v-yezd zapreshchyon
do not enter

ограничение скорости
ogranicheniye skorosti
speed limit

опасность
opasnost'
hazard

остановка запрещена
ostanovka zapreshchena
no stopping

поворот направо запрещён
povorot napravo zapreshchyon
no right turn

автобус avtobus • bus

место водителя
mesto vodjitelya
driver's seat

поручень
poruchen'
handrail

автоматическая дверь
avtomaticheskaya dver'
automatic door

переднее колесо
peredneye koleso
front wheel

багажник
bagazhnik
luggage hold

дверь dver' | **door**

междугородный автобус mezhdugorodniy avtobus | **long-distance bus**

виды автобусов vidy avtobusov • types of buses

номер маршрута
nomer marshruta
route number

водитель
voditel'
driver

двухэтажный автобус
dvukhetazhniy avtobus
double-decker bus

трамвай
tramvay
tram

троллейбус
trolleybus
streetcar

школьный автобус shkol'niy avtobus | **school bus**

кнопка остановки
knopka ostanovki
stop button

окно
okno
window

заднее колесо
zadneye koleso
rear wheel

билет
bilet
bus ticket

звонок
zvonok
bell

автовокзал
avtovokzal
bus station

**автобусная
остановка**
avtobusnaya
ostanovka
bus stop

словарь slovar' • **vocabulary**

плата за проезд
plata za proyezd
fare

расписание
raspisaniye
schedule

доступ для инвалидов-
колясочников
dostup dlya invalidov-
kolyasochnikov
wheelchair access

крытая остановка
krytaya ostanovka
bus shelter

Вы делаете
остановку на …?
vy delaete ostanovku na…?
Do you stop at …?

Какой автобус идёт на…?
kakoy avtobus idyot na…?
Which bus goes to …?

микроавтобус
mikroavtobus
minibus

туристический автобус turisticheskiy avtobus | **tour bus**

маршрутное такси
marshrutnoye taksi | **shuttle bus**

автомобиль 1 avtomobil' • car 1

вид снаружи vid snaruzhi • exterior

зеркало заднего вида
zerkalo zadneva vida
rearview mirror

лобовое стекло
lobovoye steklo
windshield

стеклоочиститель
stekloochistitel'
windshield wiper

боковое зеркало
bokovoye zerkalo
side mirror

дверь
dver'
door

багажник
bagazhnik
trunk

капот
kapot
hood

**указатель
поворота**
ukazatel'
povorota
turn signal

номерной знак
nomernoy znak
license plate

бампер
bamper
bumper

фара
fara
headlight

колесо
koleso
wheel

шина
shina
tire

багаж
bagazh
luggage

багажник на крыше
bagazhnik na kryshe
roof rack

задняя дверь
zadnyaya dver'
tailgate

ремень безопасности
remen' bezopasnosti
seat belt

детское сиденье
detskoye siden'ye
car seat

виды vidy • types

электромобиль
elektromobil'
electric car

хетчбэк
khetchbek
hatchback

седан
sedan
sedan

универсал
universal
station wagon

кабриолет
kabriolet
convertible

**спортивный
автомобиль**
sportivniy avtomobil'
sports car

**пассажирский
автомобиль**
passazhirskiy avtomobil'
minivan

полный привод
polniy privod
four-wheel drive

ретроавтомобиль,
retroavtomobil'
vintage

лимузин
limuzin
limousine

заправочная станция
zapravochnaya stantsiya •
gas station

**топливо-раздаточная
колонка**
toplivo-razdatochnaya
kolonka
gas pump

цена
tsena
price

заправочная площадка
zapravochnaya ploshchadka
forecourt

словарь slovar' • vocabulary

масло
maslo
oil

бензин
benzin
gasoline

этилированный
etilirovanniy
leaded

неэтилированный
neetilirovanniy
unleaded

гараж
garazh
garage

автомойка
avtomoyka
car wash

антифриз
antifriz
antifreeze

стеклоомыватель
stekloomyvatel'
windshield washer fluid

дизельное топливо
dizelnoye toplivo
diesel

**Пожалуйста, полный
бак.**
pozhalujsta, polnyj bak
Fill it up, please.

автомобиль 2 avtomobil' • car 2

салон salon • interior

заднее сиденье
zadneye siden'ye
backseat

подлокотник
podlokotnik
armrest

подголовник
podgolovnik
headrest

дверной замок
dvernoy zamok
door lock

ручка
ruchka
handle

словарь slovar' • vocabulary

двухдверный
dvukhdverniy
two-door

трёхдверный
tryokhdverniy
hatchback

четырёхдверный
chetyryokhdverniy
four-door

**с механической
коробкой передач**
s mekhanicheskoy
korobkoj peredach
manual

**с автоматической
коробкой передач**
s avtomaticheskoj
korobkoj peredach
automatic

зажигание
zazhiganiye
ignition

тормоз
tormoz
brake

сцепление
stsepleniye
clutch

акселератор
akselerator
accelerator

кондиционер
konditsioner
air-conditioning

Как добраться до ...?
kak dobryatsa do...?
Can you tell me the way to ...?

Где находится автостоянка?
gde nakhoditsya avtostoyanka?
Where is the parking lot?

Можно тут припарковаться?
mozhno tut priparkovat'sya?
Can I park here?

органы управления organi upravljeniya • **controls**

руль
rul'
steering wheel

звуковой сигнал
zvukovoy signal
horn

приборная панель
pribornaya panel'
dashboard

аварийная сигнализация
avariynaya signalizatsiya
hazard lights

спутниковая навигация
sputnikovaya navigatsiya
satellite navigation

леворульный автомобиль levorul'niy avtomobil' | **left-hand drive**

датчик температуры
datchik temperatury
temperature gauge

автомагнитола
avtomagnitola
car stereo

регулятор обогрева
reguljator obogreva
heater controls

ручка КПП
ruchka ka-pe-pe
gearshift

тахометр
takhometr
tachometer

спидометр
spidometr
speedometer

индикатор уровня топлива
indikator urovnya topliva
fuel gauge

переключатель освещения
pereklyuchatel' osveshcheniya
light switch

одометр
odometr
odometer

подушка безопасности
podushka bezopasnosti
air bag

праворульный автомобиль
pravorul'niy avtomobil' | **right-hand drive**

автомобиль 3 avtomobil' · car 3

механика mekhanika · mechanics

бачок омывателя
bachok omyvatelya
**washer fluid
reservoir**

щуп (масломерный)
shchup (maslomerniy)
dipstick

воздушный фильтр
vozdushniy fil'tr
air filter

бачок тормозной жидкости
bachok tormoznoy zhidkosti
brake fluid reservoir

аккумулятор
akkumulyator
battery

**кузовные
работы**
kuzovniye
raboty
bodywork

бачок охлаждающей жидкости
bachok okhlazhdayushchey zhidkosti
coolant reservoir

**головка блока
цилиндров**
golovka bloka tsilindrov
cylinder head

трубка
trubka
pipe

люк в крыше
lyuk v kryshe
sunroof

радиатор
radiator
radiator

вентилятор
ventilyator
fan

двигатель
dvigatel'
engine

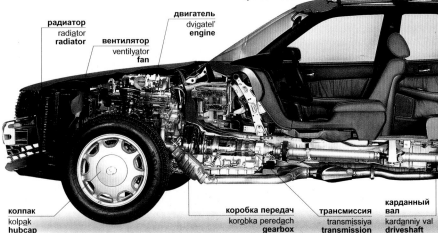

колпак
kolpak
hubcap

коробка передач
korobka peredach
gearbox

трансмиссия
transmissiya
transmission

**карданный
вал**
kardanniy val
driveshaft

прокол prok<u>o</u>l • **flat tire**

запасное колесо
zapasn<u>o</u>ye koles<u>o</u>
spare tire

гаечный ключ
gayechniy kly<u>u</u>ch
tire iron

колёсные гайки
koly<u>o</u>sniye g<u>a</u>yki
lug nuts

домкрат
domkr<u>a</u>t
jack

менять колесо
meny<u>a</u>t' koles<u>o</u>
change a tire (v)

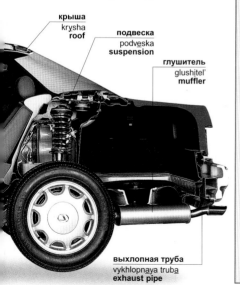

крыша
kr<u>y</u>sha
roof

подвеска
podv<u>e</u>ska
suspension

глушитель
glush<u>i</u>tel'
muffler

выхлопная труба
vykhlopn<u>a</u>ya trub<u>a</u>
exhaust pipe

словарь slov<u>a</u>r' • **vocabulary**

ДТП
de-te-p<u>e</u>
car accident

поломка
pol<u>o</u>mka
breakdown

страховка
strakh<u>o</u>vka
insurance

эвакуатор
evaku<u>a</u>tor
tow truck

механик
mekh<u>a</u>nik
mechanic

давление в шинах
davl<u>e</u>niye v sh<u>i</u>nakh
tire pressure

блок предохранителей
bl<u>o</u>k predokhran<u>i</u>teley
fuse box

свеча зажигания
svech<u>a</u> zazhig<u>a</u>niya
spark plug

ремень вентилятора
rem<u>e</u>n' ventil<u>ya</u>tora
fan belt

бензобак
benzob<u>a</u>k
gas tank

момент зажигания
mom<u>e</u>nt zazhig<u>a</u>niya
timing

турбокомпрессор
turbokompr<u>e</u>ssor
turbocharger

распределитель зажигания
raspredel<u>i</u>tel' zazhig<u>a</u>niya
distributor

шасси
shass<u>i</u>
chassis

ручной тормоз
ruchn<u>o</u>y t<u>o</u>rmoz
parking brake

генератор
gener<u>a</u>tor
alternator

ремень грм
rem<u>e</u>n' ge-er-<u>e</u>m
cam belt

Моя машина сломалась.
mo<u>ya</u> mash<u>i</u>na slomal<u>a</u>s'
My car has broken down.

Моя машина не заводится.
mo<u>ya</u> mash<u>i</u>na ne zav<u>o</u>ditsa
My car won't start.

мотоцикл mototsikl • motorcycle

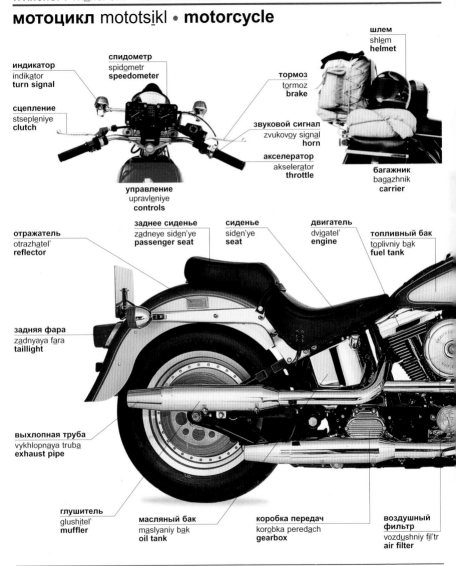

индикатор
indikator
turn signal

спидометр
spidometr
speedometer

тормоз
tormoz
brake

шлем
shlem
helmet

сцепление
stsepleniye
clutch

звуковой сигнал
zvukovoy signal
horn

акселератор
akselerator
throttle

управление
upravleniye
controls

багажник
bagazhnik
carrier

отражатель
otrazhatel'
reflector

заднее сиденье
zadneye siden'ye
passenger seat

сиденье
siden'ye
seat

двигатель
dvigatel'
engine

топливный бак
toplivniy bak
fuel tank

задняя фара
zadnyaya fara
taillight

выхлопная труба
vykhlopnaya truba
exhaust pipe

глушитель
glushitel'
muffler

масляный бак
maslyaniy bak
oil tank

коробка передач
korobka peredach
gearbox

воздушный фильтр
vozdushniy fil'tr
air filter

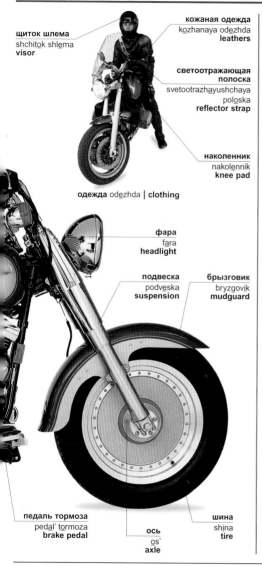

щиток шлема
shchitok shlema
visor

кожаная одежда
kozhanaya odezhda
leathers

светоотражающая полоска
svetootrazhayushchaya poloska
reflector strap

наколенник
nakolennik
knee pad

одежда odezhda | **clothing**

фара
fara
headlight

подвеска
podveska
suspension

брызговик
bryzgovik
mudguard

педаль тормоза
pedal' tormoza
brake pedal

ось
os'
axle

шина
shina
tire

типы tipy • types

гоночный мотоцикл
gonochniy mototsikl | **racing bike**

ветровое стекло
vetrovoye steklo
windshield

дорожный мотоцикл
dorozhniy mototsikl | **tourer**

кроссовый мотоцикл
krossoviy mototsikl | **dirt bike**

стойка
stoyka
stand

скутер skuter | **scooter**

велосипед velosiped · **bicycle**

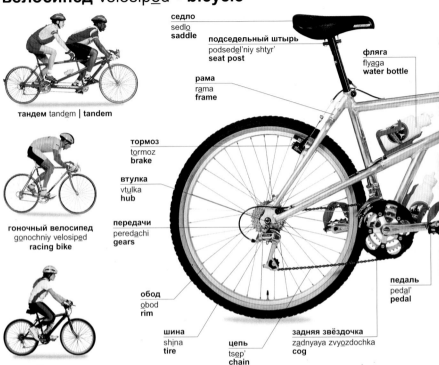

седло
sedlo
saddle

подседельный штырь
podsedel'niy shtyr'
seat post

фляга
flyaga
water bottle

рама
rama
frame

тормоз
tormoz
brake

втулка
vtulka
hub

передачи
peredachi
gears

обод
obod
rim

шина
shina
tire

цепь
tsep'
chain

задняя звёздочка
zadnyaya zvyozdochka
cog

педаль
pedal'
pedal

тандем tand**e**m | **tandem**

гоночный велосипед
gonochniy velosip**e**d
racing bike

горный велосипед
gorniy velosip**e**d
mountain bike

**туристический
велосипед**
turisticheskiy velosip**e**d
touring bike

дорожный велосипед
dorozhniy velosip**e**d
road bike

шлем
shl**e**m
helmet

велосипедная дорожка
velosipednaya dorozhka | **bike lane**

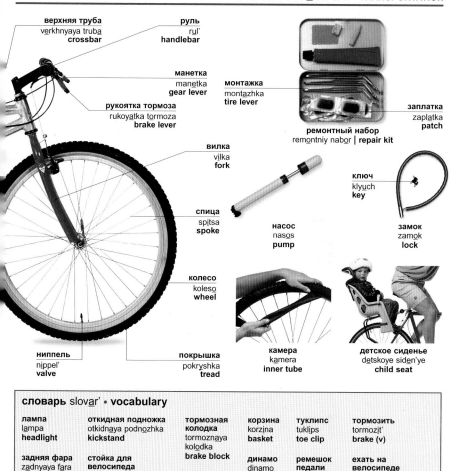

верхняя труба
verkhnyaya truba
crossbar

руль
rul'
handlebar

манетка
manetka
gear lever

монтажка
montazhka
tire lever

заплатка
zaplatka
patch

рукоятка тормоза
rukoyatka tormoza
brake lever

ремонтный набор
remontniy nabor | **repair kit**

вилка
vilka
fork

ключ
klyuch
key

спица
spitsa
spoke

насос
nasos
pump

замок
zamok
lock

колесо
koleso
wheel

ниппель
nippel'
valve

покрышка
pokryshka
tread

камера
kamera
inner tube

детское сиденье
detskoye siden'ye
child seat

словарь slovar' • vocabulary

лампа lampa **headlight**	**откидная подножка** otkidnaya podnozhka **kickstand**	**тормозная колодка** tormoznaya kolodka **brake block**	**корзина** korzina **basket**	**туклипс** tuklips **toe clip**	**тормозить** tormozit' **brake (v)**
задняя фара zadnyaya fara **rear light**	**стойка для велосипеда** stoyka dlya velosipeda **bike rack**	**тросик** trosik **cable**	**динамо** dinamo **dynamo**	**ремешок педали** remeshok pedali **toe strap**	**ехать на велосипеде** yekhat' na velosipede **cycle (v)**
отражатель otrazhatel' **reflector**	**стабилизаторы** stabilizatory **training wheels**	**звёздочка** zvyozdochka **sprocket**	**прокол** prokol **flat tire**	**крутить педали** krutit' pedali **pedal (v)**	**переключать передачу** pereklyuchat' peredachu **change gears (v)**

поезд poyezd • train

вагон
vagon
railcar

платформа
platforma
platform

тележка
telezhka
cart

**номер
платформы**
nomer platformy
platform number

пассажир
pasazhir
commuter

вокзал vokzal | train station

виды поездов vidy poyezdov • types of train

паровоз
parovoz
steam train

локомотив
lokomotiv
engine

кабина машиниста
kabina mashinista
engineer's cab

рельс
rel's
rail

дизельный поезд dizel'niy poyezd | diesel train

электро поезд
elektro poyezd
electric train

скоростной поезд
skorostnoy poyezd
high-speed train

монорельсовый поезд
monorelsoviy poyezd
monorail

поезд метро
poyezd metro
subway

трамвай
tramvay
tram

товарный поезд
tovarniy poyezd
freight train

багажная полка
bagazhnaya polka
luggage rack

окно
okno
window

путь
put'
track

дверь
dver'
door

место
mesto
seat

турникет turniket | **ticket gates**

купе
kupe | **compartment**

система оповещения пассажиров
sistema opoveshcheniya pasazhirov
public address system

расписание
raspisaniye
schedule

билет
bilet
ticket

вагон-ресторан
vagon-restoran | **dining car**

центральный зал вокзала tsentral'niy zal vokzala | **concourse**

спальное купе
spal'noye kupe
sleeping compartment

словарь slovar' • vocabulary

железнодорожная сеть
zheleznodorozhnaya set'
railroad network

скорый поезд
skoriy poezd
express train

час пик
chas pik
rush hour

карта метро
karta metro
subway map

опоздание
opozdaniye
delay

стоимость проезда
stoimost' proezda
fare

билетная касса
biletnaya kassa
ticket office

контролёр
kontrolyor
ticket inspector

делать пересадку
delat' peresadku
transfer (v)

токонесущий рельс
tokonesushchiy rels
live rail

сигнал
signal
signal

стоп-кран
stop-kran
emergency lever

воздушные суда vozdushniye suda • aircraft

авиалайнер avialayner • airliner

нос
nos
nose

кабина экипажа
kabina ekipazha
cockpit

двигатель
dvigatel'
engine

фюзеляж
fyuzelyazh
fuselage

крыло
krylo
wing

хвост
khvost
tail

руль направления
rul' napravleniya
rudder

выход
vykhod
exit

носовое колесо
nosovoye koleso
nosewheel

посадочное шасси
posadochnoye shassi
landing gear

элерон
eleron
aileron

стабилизатор
stabilizator
fin

хвостовой стабилизатор
khvostovoy stabilizator
tailplane

салон salon • cabin

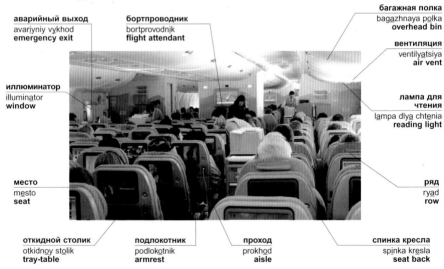

аварийный выход
avariyniy vykhod
emergency exit

бортпроводник
bortprovodnik
flight attendant

багажная полка
bagazhnaya polka
overhead bin

вентиляция
ventilyatsiya
air vent

иллюминатор
illuminator
window

лампа для чтения
lampa dlya chtenia
reading light

место
mesto
seat

ряд
ryad
row

откидной столик
otkidnoy stolik
tray-table

подлокотник
podlokotnik
armrest

проход
prokhod
aisle

спинка кресла
spinka kresla
seat back

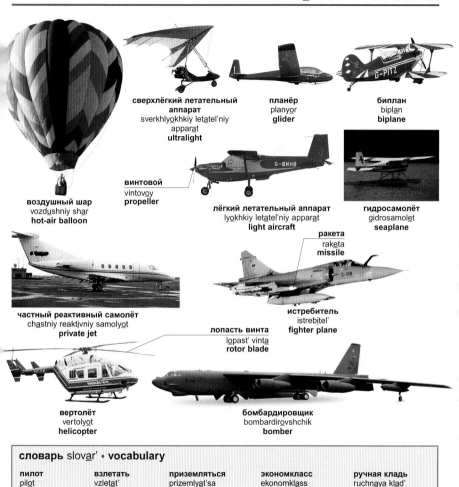

сверхлёгкий летательный аппарат
sverkhlyokhkiy letatel'niy apparat
ultralight

планёр
planyor
glider

биплан
biplan
biplane

винтовой
vintovoy
propeller

воздушный шар
vozdushniy shar
hot-air balloon

лёгкий летательный аппарат
lyokhkiy letatel'niy apparat
light aircraft

гидросамолёт
gidrosamolet
seaplane

ракета
raketa
missile

частный реактивный самолёт
chastniy reaktivniy samolyot
private jet

истребитель
istrebitel'
fighter plane

лопасть винта
lopast' vinta
rotor blade

вертолёт
vertolyot
helicopter

бомбардировщик
bombardirovshchik
bomber

словарь slovar' • vocabulary

пилот pilot **pilot**	взлетать vzletat' **take off (v)**	приземляться prizemlyat'sa **land (v)**	экономкласс ekonomklass **economy class**	ручная кладь ruchnaya klad' **carry-on luggage**
второй пилот vtoroy pilot **copilot**	лететь letet' **fly (v)**	высота vysota **altitude**	бизнес-класс biznes-klass **business class**	ремень безопасности remen' bezopasnosti **seat belt**

аэропорт aeropo<u>r</u>t · **airport**

стоянка самолётов
stoy<u>a</u>nka samoly<u>o</u>tov
apron

багажный тягач
bag<u>a</u>zhniy tyag<u>a</u>ch
baggage trailer

терминал
termin<u>a</u>l
terminal

служебный автомобиль
sluzh<u>e</u>bniy avtomobil'
service vehicle

телетрап
teletr<u>a</u>p
jetway

авиалайнер avial<u>a</u>yner | **airliner**

словарь slov<u>a</u>r' · **vocabulary**

взлётно-посадочная
полоса
vzly<u>o</u>tno-pos<u>a</u>dochnaya
pol<u>o</u>s<u>a</u>
runway

международный
рейс
mezhdunar<u>o</u>dniy reys
international flight

внутренний рейс
vn<u>u</u>trenniy reys
domestic flight

стыковка рейсов
styk<u>o</u>vka r<u>e</u>ysov
connection

номер рейса
n<u>o</u>mer r<u>e</u>ysa
flight number

иммиграционный
контроль
immigratsi<u>o</u>nniy
kontr<u>o</u>l'
immigration

таможенный
контроль
tam<u>o</u>zhenniy kontr<u>o</u>l'
customs

перевес багажа
pereves bagazh<u>a</u>
excess baggage

багажная карусель,
bag<u>a</u>zhnaya karus<u>e</u>l'
baggage carousel

охрана
okhr<u>a</u>na
security

рентгеновский аппарат
(для осмотра багажа)
rentg<u>e</u>novskiy appar<u>a</u>t (dlya
osm<u>o</u>tra bagazh<u>a</u>)
X-ray machine

туристическая брошюра
turist<u>i</u>cheskaya brosh<u>u</u>ra
travel brochure

отпуск
<u>o</u>tpusk
vacation

регистрироваться
registr<u>i</u>rovat'sya
check in (v)

диспетчерская вышка
disp<u>e</u>tcherskaya v<u>y</u>shka
control tower

бронировать рейс
bron<u>i</u>rovat' reys
book a flight (v)

ручная кладь
ruchnaya klad'
carry-on luggage

багаж
bagazh
luggage

тележка
telezhka
cart

стойка регистрации
stoyka registratsii
check-in desk

виза
viza
visa

паспорт pasport | **passport**

паспортный контроль
pasportniy kontrol'
passport control

посадочный талон
posadochniy talon
boarding pass

билет
bilet
ticket

номер выхода на посадку
nomer vykhoda na posadku
gate number

вылет
vylet
departures

зал отбытия
zal otbytia
departure lounge

пункт назначения
punkt naznacheniya
destination

прибытие
pribytie
arrivals

информационное табло
informatsionnoye tablo
information screen

магазин беспошлинной торговли
magazin besposhlinnoy torgovli
duty-free shop

выдача багажа
vydacha bagazha
baggage claim

стоянка такси
stoyanka taksi
taxi stand

прокат автомобилей
prokat avtomobiley
car rental

корабль korabl' · ship

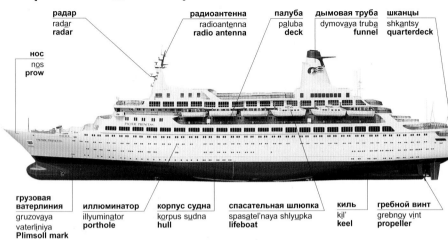

радар
radar
radar

радиоантенна
radioantenna
radio antenna

палуба
paluba
deck

дымовая труба
dymovaya truba
funnel

шканцы
shkantsy
quarterdeck

нос
nos
prow

грузовая
ватерлиния
gruzovaya
vaterliniya
Plimsoll mark

иллюминатор
illyuminator
porthole

корпус судна
korpus sudna
hull

спасательная шлюпка
spasatel'naya shlyupka
lifeboat

киль
kil'
keel

гребной винт
grebnoy vint
propeller

океанский лайнер okeanskiy layner | ocean liner

мостик
mostik
bridge

машинное отделение
mashinnoye otdeleniye
engine room

каюта
kayuta
cabin

камбуз
kambuz
galley

словарь slovar' · vocabulary

док
dok
dock

порт
port
port

сходня
skhodnya
gangway

якорь
yakor'
anchor

швартовая тумба
shvartovaya tumba
bollard

брашпиль
brashpil'
windlass

капитан
kapitan
captain

быстроходный
катер
bystrokhodniy
kater
speedboat

гребная лодка
grebnaya lodka
rowboat

каноэ
kanoe
canoe

другие суда drugiye suda • other ships

паром
parom
ferry

подвесной мотор
podvesnoy motor
outboard motor

надувная лодка
naduvnaya lodka
inflatable dinghy

судно на подводных крыльях
sudno na podvodnikh krilyakh
hydrofoil

яхта
yakhta
yacht

катамаран
katamaran
catamaran

буксирный катер
buksirniy kater
tugboat

судно на воздушной подушке
sudno na vozdushnoy podushke
hovercraft

такелаж
takelazh
rigging

трюм
tryum
hold

контейнеровоз
konteynerovoz
container ship

парусное судно
parusnoye sudno
sailboat

грузовое судно
gruzovoye sudno
freighter

нефтяной танкер
neftyanoy tanker
oil tanker

авианосец
avianosets
aircraft carrier

военный корабль
voyenniy korabl'
battleship

боевая рубка
boyevaya rubka
conning tower

подводная лодка
podvodnaya lodka
submarine

порт port • **port**

пакгауз
pakgauz
warehouse

подъёмный
кран
pod-yomniy
kran
crane

вилочный погрузчик
vilochniy pogruzchik
forklift

подъездная дорога
pod-yezdnaya doroga
access road

таможня
tamozhnya
customs house

док
dok
dock

контейнер
konteyner
container

причал
prichal
quay

груз
gruz
cargo

терминал парома
terminal paroma
ferry terminal

паром
parom
ferry

билетная касса
biletnaya kassa
ticket office

пассажир
passazhir
passenger

контейнерный порт konteynerniy port | **container port**

пассажирский порт
passazhirskiy port | **passenger port**

рыболовная сеть
rybolovnaya set'
net

рыболовное судно
rybolovnoye sudno
fishing boat

швартовка
shvartovka
mooring

яхтенный причал
yakhtenniy prichal | **marina**

рыболовный порт rybolovniy port | **fishing port**

гавань gavan' | **harbor**

пирс pirs | **pier**

мол
mol
jetty

верфь
verf'
shipyard

лампа
lampa
lamp

маяк
mayak
lighthouse

буй
buy
buoy

словарь slovar' · vocabulary

береговая охрана
beregovaya okhrana
coast guard

капитан порта
kapitan porta
harbor master

бросать якорь
brosat' yakor'
drop anchor (v)

сухой док
sukhoy dok
dry dock

пришвартовываться
prishvartovyvatsa
moor (v)

причаливать
prichalivat'
dock (v)

подниматься на борт
podnimatsya na bort
board (v)

сходить на берег
skhodit' na bereg
disembark (v)

отправляться в плавание
otpravlyatsya v plavaniye
set sail (v)

спорт sport
sports

американский футбол amerikanskiy futbol • football

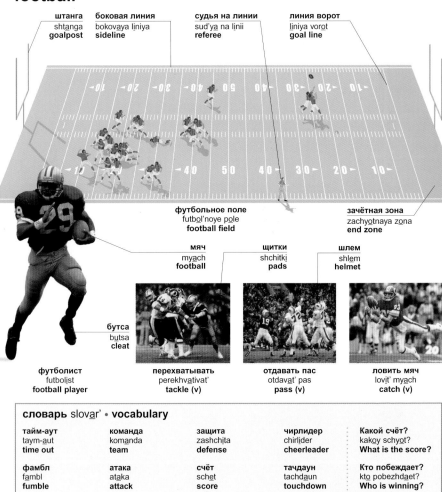

штанга
shtanga
goalpost

боковая линия
bokovaya liniya
sideline

судья на линии
sud'ya na linii
referee

линия ворот
liniya vorot
goal line

футбольное поле
futbol'noye pole
football field

зачётная зона
zachyotnaya zona
end zone

мяч
myach
football

щитки
shchitki
pads

шлем
shlem
helmet

бутса
butsa
cleat

футболист
futbolist
football player

перехватывать
perekhvativat'
tackle (v)

отдавать пас
otdavat' pas
pass (v)

ловить мяч
lovit' myach
catch (v)

словарь slovar' • vocabulary

тайм-аут taym-aut **time out**	**команда** komanda **team**	**защита** zashchita **defense**	**чирлидер** chirlider **cheerleader**	**Какой счёт?** kakoy schyot? **What is the score?**
фамбл fambl **fumble**	**атака** ataka **attack**	**счёт** schet **score**	**тачдаун** tachdaun **touchdown**	**Кто побеждает?** kto pobezhdaet? **Who is winning?**

регби regbi • rugby

площадь ворот
ploshchad' vorot
in-goal area

боковая линия
bokovaya liniya
touch line

флажок
flazhok
flag

линия мёртвого мяча
liniya myortvogo myacha
dead ball line

ворота
vorota
goal

поле для регби pole dlya regbi | **rugby field**

мяч
myach
ball

ребгийная полоска
regbiynaya poloska
rugby uniform

бросать
brosat'
throw (v)

бить по мячу
bit' po myachu
kick (v)

отдавать пас
otdavat' pas
pass (v)

производить захват
proizvodit' zakhvat
tackle (v)

попытка
popytka
try

игрок
igrok
player

рак rak | **ruck**

схватка skhvatka | **scrum**

футбол futbol • soccer

футбол
futbol
soccer ball

нападающий
napadayushchiy
forward

судья
sud'ya
referee

центральный круг
tsentral'niy krug
center circle

вратарь
vratar'
goalkeeper

футбольная полоска
futbol'naya poloska
soccer uniform

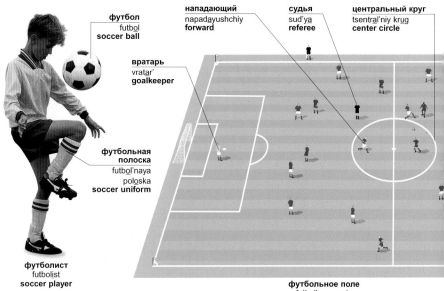

футболист
futbolist
soccer player

футбольное поле
futbol'noye pole
soccer field

штанга
shtanga
goalpost

сетка ворот
setka vorot
net

перекладина
perekladina
crossbar

гол gol | goal

вести мяч vesti myach
dribble (v)

играть головой
igrat' golovoy
head (v)

стенка
stenka
wall

штрафной удар
shtrafnoy udar | free kick

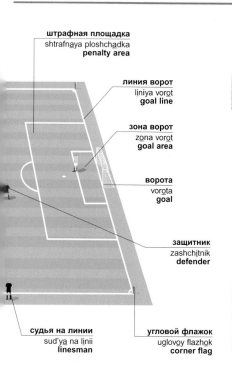

штрафная площадка
shtrafnaya ploshchadka
penalty area

линия ворот
liniya vorot
goal line

зона ворот
zona vorot
goal area

ворота
vorota
goal

защитник
zashchitnik
defender

судья на линии
sud'ya na linii
linesman

угловой флажок
uglovoy flazhok
corner flag

вбрасывание
vbrasyvaniye
throw-in

бить (по мячу) bit' (po myachu) | **kick (v)**

пасовать (мяч)
pasovat' (myach)
pass (v)

бутса
butsa
cleat

бить по воротам
bit' po vorotam
shoot (v)

брать удар
brat' udar
save (v)

отнимать мяч
otnimat' myach
tackle (v)

словарь slovar' • vocabulary

стадион stadion **stadium**	**фол** fol **foul**	**жёлтая карточка** zhyoltaya kartochka **yellow card**	**лига** liga **league**	**добавочное время** dobavochnoe vremya **extra time**
забивать гол zabivat' gol **score a goal (v)**	**угол** ugol **corner**	**офсайд,** **положение вне** **игры** ofsayd, polozheniye vne igry **offside**	**ничья** nich'ya **tie**	**запасной игрок** zapasnoy igrok **substitute**
пенальти penal'ti **penalty**	**красная карточка** krasnaya kartochka **red card**	**удаление с поля** udaleniye s polya **send off**	**тайм** tajm **halftime**	**замена** zamena **substitution**

хоккей khokey • hockey

хоккей на льду khokey na l'du • ice hockey

линия ворот
liniya vorot
goal line

зона нападения
zona napadeniya
attack zone

нейтральная зона
neytral'naya zona
neutral zone

зона защиты
zona zashchity
defending zone

вратарь
vratar'
goalkeeper

ворота
vorota
goal

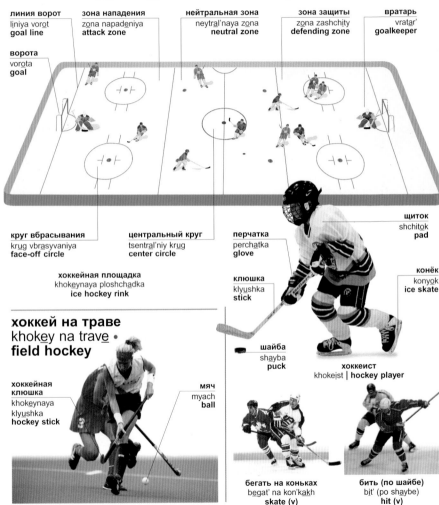

круг вбрасывания
krug vbrasyvaniya
face-off circle

центральный круг
tsentral'niy krug
center circle

перчатка
perchatka
glove

щиток
shchitok
pad

хоккейная площадка
khokeynaya ploshchadka
ice hockey rink

клюшка
klyushka
stick

конёк
konyok
ice skate

хоккей на траве
khokey na trave •
field hockey

**хоккейная
клюшка**
khokeynaya
klyushka
hockey stick

мяч
myach
ball

шайба
shayba
puck

хоккеист
khokeist | **hockey player**

бегать на коньках
begat' na kon'kakh
skate (v)

бить (по шайбе)
bit' (po shaybe)
hit (v)

крикет kriket · cricket

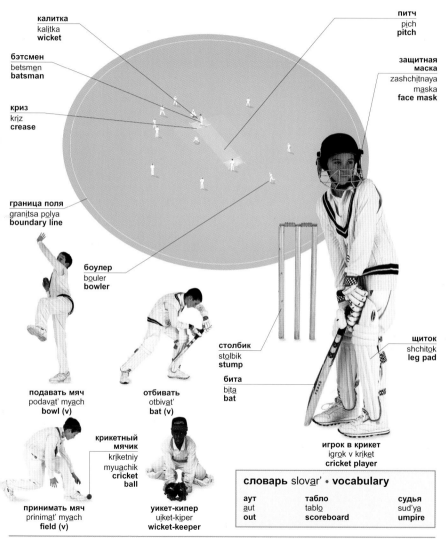

калитка
kalitka
wicket

бэтсмен
betsmen
batsman

криз
kriz
crease

граница поля
granitsa polya
boundary line

питч
pich
pitch

защитная маска
zashchitnaya maska
face mask

боулер
bouler
bowler

столбик
stolbik
stump

бита
bita
bat

щиток
shchitok
leg pad

подавать мяч
podavat' myach
bowl (v)

отбивать
otbivat'
bat (v)

крикетный мячик
kriketniy myuachik
cricket ball

принимать мяч
prinimat' myach
field (v)

уикет-кипер
uiket-kiper
wicket-keeper

игрок в крикет
igrok v kriket
cricket player

словарь slovar' · vocabulary

аут	табло	судья
aut	tablo	sud'ya
out	**scoreboard**	**umpire**

баскетбол basketbol • basketball

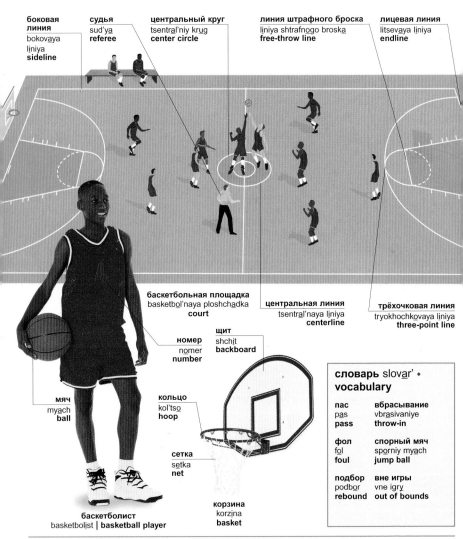

боковая линия
bokovaya liniya
sideline

судья
sud'ya
referee

центральный круг
tsentral'niy krug
center circle

линия штрафного броска
liniya shtrafnogo broska
free-throw line

лицевая линия
litsevaya liniya
endline

баскетбольная площадка
basketbol'naya ploshchadka
court

центральная линия
tsentral'naya liniya
centerline

трёхочковая линия
tryokhochkovaya liniya
three-point line

номер
nomer
number

щит
shchit
backboard

мяч
myach
ball

кольцо
kol'tso
hoop

сетка
setka
net

баскетболист
basketbolist | **basketball player**

корзина
korzina
basket

словарь slovar' • vocabulary

пас pas **pass**	**вбрасывание** vbrasivaniye **throw-in**
фол fol **foul**	**спорный мяч** sporniy myach **jump ball**
подбор podbor **rebound**	**вне игры** vne igry **out of bounds**

действия deystviya • actions

бросать
brosat'
throw (v)

ловить
lovit'
catch (v)

с силой посылать мяч
s siloy posylat' myach
shoot (v)

прыгать
prygat'
jump (v)

прикрывать
prikrivat'
mark (v)

блокировать
blokirovat'
block (v)

вести мяч
vesti myach
dribble (v)

положить сверху
polozhit' sverkhu
dunk

волейбол voleybol • volleyball

блокировать
blokirovat'
block (v)

сетка
setka
net

принимать
мяч снизу
prinimat'
myach snizu
dig (v)

судья
sud'ya
referee

наколенник
nakolennik
knee support

площадка ploshchadka | **court**

бейсбол beysbol • **baseball**

поле pole • **field**

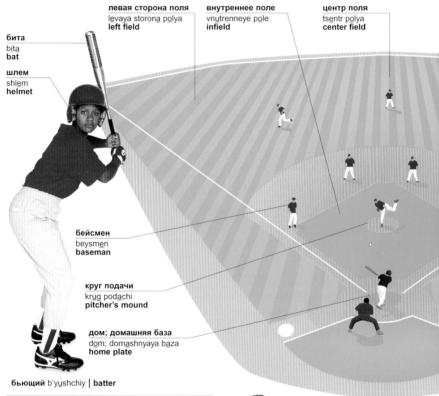

левая сторона поля
levaya storona polya
left field

внутреннее поле
vnutrenneye pole
infield

центр поля
tsentr polya
center field

бита
bita
bat

шлем
shlem
helmet

бейсмен
beysmen
baseman

круг подачи
krug podachi
pitcher's mound

дом; домашняя база
dom; domashnyaya baza
home plate

бьющий b'yushchiy | **batter**

словарь slovar' • **vocabulary**

период period **inning**	сейф seyf **safe**	фол-бол fol-bol **foul ball**
ран ran **run**	аут aut **out**	страйк strayk **strike**

мяч
myach
ball

рукавица
rukavitsa
glove

бейсбольная маска
beysbol'naya maska
mask

приёмы priyomi • **actions**

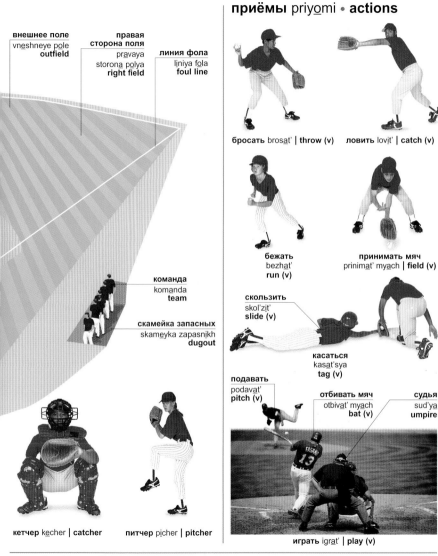

внешнее поле
vneshneye pole
outfield

правая
сторона поля
pravaya
storona polya
right field

линия фола
liniya fola
foul line

бросать brosat' | **throw (v)**

ловить lovit' | **catch (v)**

бежать
bezhat'
run (v)

принимать мяч
prinimat' myach | **field (v)**

команда
komanda
team

скамейка запасных
skameyka zapasnikh
dugout

скользить
skol'zit'
slide (v)

касаться
kasat'sya
tag (v)

подавать
podavat'
pitch (v)

отбивать мяч
otbivat' myach
bat (v)

судья
sud'ya
umpire

кетчер kecher | **catcher**

питчер picher | **pitcher**

играть igrat' | **play (v)**

теннис tenis • tennis

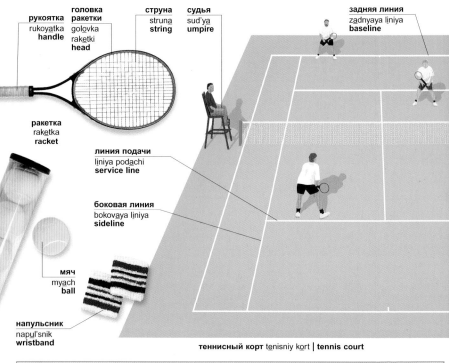

рукоятка
rukoyatka
handle

головка ракетки
golovka
raketki
head

струна
struna
string

судья
sud'ya
umpire

задняя линия
zadnyaya liniya
baseline

ракетка
raketka
racket

линия подачи
liniya podachi
service line

боковая линия
bokovaya liniya
sideline

мяч
myach
ball

напульсник
napul'snik
wristband

теннисный корт tenisniy kort | **tennis court**

словарь slovar' • vocabulary

одиночная игра odinochnaya igra **singles**	**сет** set **set**	**ноль** nol' **love**	**ошибка** oshibka **fault**	**резаный удар** rezaniy udar **slice**	**судья на линии** sud'ya na linii **linesman**
парная игра parnaya igra **doubles**	**матч** mach **match**	**ровно** rovno **deuce**	**эйс** eys **ace**	**обмен ударами** obmen udaram **rally**	**чемпионат** chempionat **championship**
гейм geym **game**	**тай-брейк** tay-breyk **tiebreaker**	**больше** bol'she **advantage**	**укороченный удар** ukorochenniy udar **dropshot**	**два мяча!** dva myacha! **let!**	**кручёный удар** kruchyoniy udar **spin**

удары udary • **strokes**

сетка
setka
net

смеш
smesh
smash

подающий мячи
podayushchiy
myachi
ball boy

подавать (мяч)
podavat' (myach)
serve (v)

**теннисные
туфли**
tenisniye tufli
tennis shoes

игрок igrok | **player**

подача
podacha
serve

удар с лёта
udar s lyota
volley

приём подачи
priyom podachi
return

свеча
svecha
lob

удар справа
udar sprava
forehand

удар слева
udar sleva
backhand

игры с ракеткой igry s raketkoy • **racket games**

волан
volan
shuttlecock

ракетка
raketka
paddle

бадминтон
badminton
badminton

настольный теннис
nastol'niy tenis
table tennis

сквош
skvosh
squash

ракетбол
raketbol
racquetball

гольф go͟l'f • golf

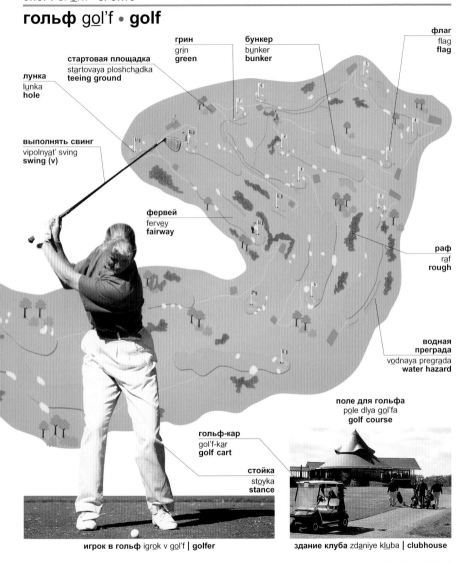

грин grin **green**

бункер bunker **bunker**

флаг flag **flag**

стартовая площадка startovaya ploshchadka **teeing ground**

лунка lu͟nka **hole**

выполнять свинг vipolnyat' sving **swing (v)**

фервей ferve͟y **fairway**

раф ra͟f **rough**

водная преграда vodnaya pregra͟da **water hazard**

поле для гольфа po͟le dlya go͟l'fa **golf course**

гольф-кар go͟l'f-ka͟r **golf cart**

стойка sto͟yka **stance**

игрок в гольф igro͟k v go͟l'f | **golfer**

здание клуба zda͟niye klu͟ba | **clubhouse**

снаряжение snaryazheniye • equipment

мячик для гольфа
myachik dlya gol'fa
golf ball

подставка
podstavka
tee

перчатка
perchatka
glove

сумка для клюшек
sumka dlya klyushek
golf bag

шипы
shipy
spikes

тележка для гольфа
telezhka dlya gol'fa
bag cart

ботинки для гольфа
botinki dlya gol'fa
golf shoe

клюшки для гольфа klyushki dlya gol'fa • golf clubs

вуд
vud
wood

паттер
patter
putter

айрон
ayron
iron

ведж
vedzh
wedge

приёмы priyomi • actions

делать первый удар
delat' perviy udar
tee-off (v)

бить драйвером
bit' drayverom
drive (v)

загонять мяч в лунку
zagonyat' myuach v lunku
putt (v)

делать короткий удар
delat' korotkiy udar
chip (v)

словарь slovar' • vocabulary

лунка за раз lunka za raz **hole in one**	**пар** par **par**	**гандикап** gandikap **handicap**	**кадди** kaddi **caddy**	**замах назад** zamakh nazad **backswing**	**удар** udar **stroke**
ниже пара nizhe para **under par**	**выше пара** vishe para **over par**	**турнир** turnir **tournament**	**зрители** zriteli **spectators**	**тренировочный замах** trenirovochniy zamakh **practice swing**	**трасса** trassa **line of play**

лёгкая атлетика lyohkaya atletika • track and field

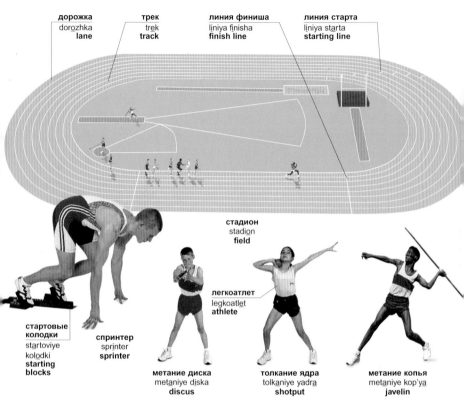

дорожка
dorozhka
lane

трек
trek
track

линия финиша
liniya finisha
finish line

линия старта
liniya starta
starting line

стадион
stadion
field

легкоатлет
legkoatlet
athlete

стартовые колодки
startoviye kolodki
starting blocks

спринтер
sprinter
sprinter

метание диска
metaniye diska
discus

толкание ядра
tolkaniye yadra
shotput

метание копья
metaniye kop'ya
javelin

словарь slovar' • vocabulary

забег zabeg **race**	**рекорд** rekord **record**	**фотофиниш** fotofinish **photo finish**	**прыжок с шестом** pryzhok s shestom **pole vault**
время vremya **time**	**бить рекорд** bit' rekord **break a record (v)**	**марафон** marafon **marathon**	**личный рекорд** lichniy rekord **personal best**

секундомер
sekundomer
stopwatch

эстафетная палочка
estafetnaya palochka
baton

планка
planka
crossbar

эстафета
estafeta
relay race

прыжок в высоту
pryzhok v vysotu
high jump

прыжок в длину
pryzhok v dlinu
long jump

бег с препятствиями
beg s prepyatstviyami
hurdles

гимнастика gimnastika • **gymnastics**

гимнастический мостик
gimnasticheskiy mostik
springboard

гимнастка
gimnastka
gymnast

гимнастический конь
gimnasticheskiy kon'
horse

сальто
sal'to
somersault

бревно brevno | **beam**

лента
lenta
ribbon

мат
mat
mat

опорный прыжок
oporniy pryzhok
vault

упражнения на ковре
uprazhneniya na kovrye
floor exercises

колесо
koleso
cartwheel

ритмическая гимнастика
ritmicheskaya gimnastika
rhythmic gymnastics

словарь slovar' • **vocabulary**

перекладина perekladina **horizontal bar**	**гимнастический конь** gimnasticheskiy kon' **pommel horse**	**кольца** kol'tsa **rings**	**медали** medali **medals**	**серебро** serebro **silver**
параллельные брусья paralel'niye brus'ya **parallel bars**	**разновысокие брусья** raznovysokiye brus'ya **asymmetric bars**	**пьедестал почёта** pyedestal pocheta **podium**	**золото** zoloto **gold**	**бронза** bronza **bronze**

спортивные единоборства sportivniye yedinoborstva • **combat sports**

противник
protivnik
opponent

защитный шлем
zashchitniy shlem
guard

перчатка
perchatka
glove

пояс
poyas
belt

тхэквондо tkhekvondo | **tae kwon do**

маска
maska
mask

меч
mech
sword

карате karate | **karate**

дзюдо dzyudo | **judo**

кунг-фу kun-fu | **kung fu**

айкидо aykido | **aikido**

кендо kendo | **kendo**

кикбоксинг
kikboksing | **kickboxing**

борьба bor'ba | **wrestling**

бокс boks | **boxing**

приёмы priyomi • actions

падение padeniye | **fall**

захват zakhvat | **hold**

бросок brosok | **throw**

удержание
uderzhaniye | **pin**

удар ногой
udar nogoy | **kick**

удар кулаком
udar kulakom | **punch**

удар udar | **strike**

прыжок pryzhok | **jump**

блок blok | **block**

рубящий удар
rubyashchiy udar | **chop**

словарь slovar' • vocabulary

боксёрский ринг boksyorskiy ring **boxing ring**	**раунд** raund **round**	**кулак** kulak **fist**	**чёрный пояс** chyorniy poyas **black belt**	**капоэйра** kapoeyra **capoeira**
боксёрские перчатки boksyorskiye perchatki **boxing gloves**	**поединок** poyedinok **bout**	**нокаут** nokaut **knockout**	**самозащита** samozashchita **self-defense**	**борьба сумо** bor'ba sumo **sumo wrestling**
капа kapa **mouth guard**	**спарринг** sparring **sparring**	**боксёрская груша** boksyorskaya grusha **punching bag**	**боевые искусства** boyeviye iskustva **martial arts**	**тай-чи** tai-chi **tai chi**

плавание plavaniye • swimming

спортивный инвентарь sportivniy inventar' • equipment

нарукавник для плавания
narukavnik dlya plavaniya
water wings

очки для плавания
ochki dlya plavaniya | **goggles**

носовой зажим
nosovoy zazhim
nose clip

плавательная доска
plavatel'naya doska
kickboard

купальник
kupal'nik
swimsuit

дорожка
dorozhka
lane

вода
voda
water

стартовая тумба
startovaya tumba
starting block

шапочка
shapochka
swimming cap

плавки
plavki
trunks

плавательный бассейн plavatel'niy baseyn | **swimming pool**

трамплин
tramplin
diving board

ныряльщик
nyryal'shchik
diver

пловец plovets | **swimmer**

нырять nyryat' | **dive (v)**

плавать plavat' | **swim (v)**

поворот povorot | **turn**

стили плавания stili plavaniya • **styles**

кроль krol' | **front crawl**

брасс bras | **breaststroke**

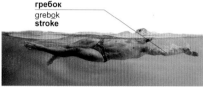

гребок
grebok
stroke

плавание на спине plavaniye na spine | **backstroke**

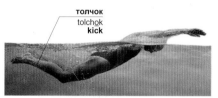

толчок
tolchok
kick

баттерфляй baterflyay | **butterfly**

дайвинг с аквалангом dayving s akvalangom • **scuba diving**

гидрокостюм
gidrokostyum
wetsuit

ласт
last
fin

грузовой пояс
gruzovoy poyas
weight belt

баллон акваланга
balon akvalanga
air cylinder

маска
maska
mask

регулятор
regulyator
regulator

**дыхательная
трубка**
dykhatel'naya trubka
snorkel

словарь slovar' • **vocabulary**

прыжок в воду pryzhok v vodu **dive**	**плыть стоя** plyt' stoya **tread water (v)**	**шкафчики для одежды** shkafchiki dlya odezhdy **lockers**	**водное поло** vodnoye polo **water polo**	**мелкая сторона бассейна** melkaya storona basseyna **shallow end**	**судорога** sudoroga **cramp**
прыжок с трамплина pryzhok s vishki **high dive**	**стартовый прыжок** startoviy pryzhok **racing dive**	**спасатель** spasatel' **lifeguard**	**глубокая сторона бассейна** glubokaya storona basseyna **deep end**	**синхронное плавание** sinkhronnoye plavaniye **synchronized swimming**	**тонуть** tonut' **drown (v)**

парусный спорт parusniy sport • sailing

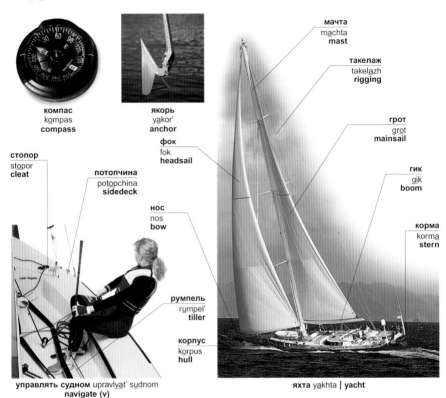

компас
kompas
compass

якорь
yakor'
anchor

мачта
machta
mast

такелаж
takelazh
rigging

грот
grot
mainsail

фок
fok
headsail

гик
gik
boom

стопор
stopor
cleat

потопчина
potopchina
sidedeck

нос
nos
bow

корма
korma
stern

румпель
rumpel'
tiller

корпус
korpus
hull

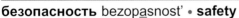

управлять судном upravlyat' sudnom
navigate (v)

яхта yakhta | **yacht**

безопасность bezopasnost' • safety

фальшфейер
fal'shfeiyer
flare

спасательный круг
spasatel'niy krug
life buoy

спасательный жилет
spasatel'niy zhilet
life jacket

спасательная лодка
spasatelnaya lodka
life raft

водные виды спорта vodniye vidy sporta • **watersports**

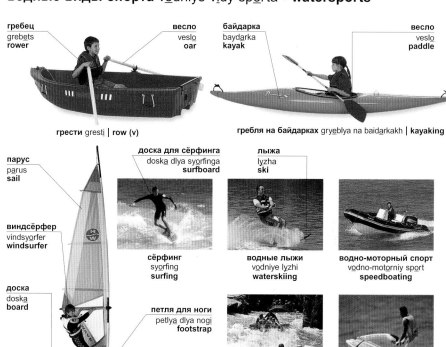

гребец grebets **rower** — **весло** veslo **oar**

байдарка baydarka **kayak** — **весло** veslo **paddle**

грести gresti | **row (v)**

гребля на байдарках gryeblya na baidarkakh | **kayaking**

парус parus **sail**

виндсёрфер vindsyorfer **windsurfer**

доска doska **board**

доска для сёрфинга doska dlya syorfinga **surfboard**

сёрфинг syorfing **surfing**

лыжа lyzha **ski**

водные лыжи vodniye lyzhi **waterskiing**

водно-моторный спорт vodno-motorniy sport **speedboating**

петля для ноги petlya dlya nogi **footstrap**

виндсёрфинг vindsyorfing | **windsurfing**

рафтинг rafting **rafting**

катание на гидроцикле kataniye na gidrotsikle **jet skiing**

словарь slovar' • **vocabulary**

воднолыжник vodnolyzhnik **waterskier**	**команда, экипаж** komanda, ekipazh **crew**	**ветер** veter **wind**	**прибой** priboy **surf**	**шкот** shkot **sheet**	**шверт** shvert **centerboard**
сёрфер syorfer **surfer**	**менять курс** menyat' kurs **tack (v)**	**волна** volna **wave**	**пороги реки** porogi reki **rapids**	**руль** rul' **rudder**	**опрокидываться** oprokidyvat'sya **capsize (v)**

конный спорт konniy sport • **horseback riding**

жокейская шапочка
zhokeyskaya shapochka
riding hat

грива
griva
mane

наездник
nayeznik
rider

поводья
povod'ya
reins

седло
sedlo
saddle

конь
kon'
horse

джодпуры
dzhodpury
jodhpurs

хвост
khvost
tail

подпруга
podpruga
girth

**сапог для
верховой езды**
sapog dlya
verkhovoy yezdy
riding boot

стремя
stremya
stirrup

копыто
kopyto
hoof

лука
luka
pommel

налобник
nalobnik
browband

нахрапник
nakhrapnik
noseband

удила
udila
bit

**седельная
подушка**
sedelnaya
podushka
seat

подкова
podkova
horseshoe

дамское седло
damskoye sedlo
sidesaddle

уздечка uzdechka | **bridle**

хлыст khlust | **riding crop**

соревнования sorevnovaniya • events

скаковая лошадь
skakovaya loshad'
racehorse

скачки
skachki
horse race

родео
rodeo
rodeo

конный туризм
konniy turizm | **trail riding**

препятствие
prepyuatstviye
fence

скачки с препятствиями
skachki s prepyatstviyami
steeplechase

конкур
konkur
showjumping

выездка viyezdka | **dressage**

рысистые бега
rysistiye bega
harness race

соревнования конных упряжек
sorevnovaniya konnykh upryazhek
carriage race

поло polo | **polo**

словарь slovar' • vocabulary

шаг shag **walk**	кентер kenter **canter**	прыжок pryzhok **jump**	недоуздок nedouzdok **halter**	выгул vygul **paddock**	скачки без препятствий skachki bez prepyatstviy **flat race**
рысь rys' **trot**	галоп galop **gallop**	конюх konyukh **groom**	конюшня konyushnya **stable**	арена arena **arena**	ипподром ipodrom **racecourse**

рыбная ловля rybnaya lovlya • **fishing**

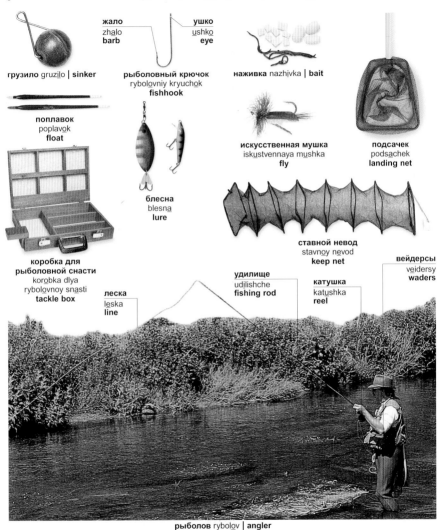

грузило gruzilo | **sinker**

жало
zhalo
barb

ушко
ushko
eye

рыболовный крючок
rybolovniy kryuchok
fishhook

наживка nazhivka | **bait**

поплавок
poplavok
float

искусственная мушка
iskustvennaya mushka
fly

подсачек
podsachek
landing net

блесна
blesna
lure

**коробка для
рыболовной снасти**
korobka dlya
rybolovnoy snasti
tackle box

ставной невод
stavnoy nevod
keep net

вейдерсы
veidersy
waders

удилище
udilishche
fishing rod

катушка
katushka
reel

леска
leska
line

рыболов rybolov | **angler**

СПОРТ SPORT • SPORTS

виды рыбной ловли vidy rybnoy lovli • types of fishing

пресноводная рыбалка
presnovodnaya ribalka
freshwater fishing

ловля рыбы нахлыстом
lovlya ryby nakhlystom
fly fishing

спортивное рыболовство
sportivnoye rybolovstvo
sport fishing

морское рыболовство
morskoye ribolovstvo
deep sea fishing

морская береговая рыбалка
morskaya beregovaya
rybalka | **surfcasting**

действия deystviya • activities

забрасывать
zabrasivat'
cast (v)

ловить
lovit'
catch (v)

наматывать
namatyvat'
reel in (v)

ловить сетью
lovit' set'yu
net (v)

отпускать
otpuskat'
release (v)

словарь slovar' • vocabulary

приманивать primanivat' **bait (v)**	**рыболовные снасти** rybolovniye snasti **tackle**	**непромокаемая одежда** nepromokayemaya odezhda **rain gear**	**лицензия на рыбную ловлю** licenziya na rybnuyu lovlyu **fishing license**	**верша** versha **creel**
клевать klevat' **bite (v)**	**катушка** katushka **spool**	**багор** bagor **pole**	**морская рыбалка** morskaya ribalka **marine fishing**	**подводная охота** podvodnaya okhota **spearfishing**

русский ruskiy • english   245

лыжный спорт lyzhniy sport • skiing

горнолыжный склон
gornolyzhniy sklon
ski slope

кресельный
подъёмник
kresel'niy
pod-yomnik
chairlift

вагон
фуникулёра
vagon
funikulyora
cable car

лыжня
lyzhnya
ski run

защитное
ограждение
zashchitnoye
ograzhdeniye
safety barrier

лыжная палка
lyzhnaya palka
ski pole

перчатка
perchatka
glove

ребро лыжи
rebro lyzhi
edge

лыжа
lyzha
ski

лыжная куртка
lyzhnaya kurtka
ski jacket

носок лыжи
nosok lyzhi
tip

лыжный ботинок
lyzhniy botinok
ski boot

лыжник
lyzhnik
skier

дисциплины distsiplini • events

скоростной спуск
skorostnoy spusk
downhill skiing

ворота
vorota
gate

слалом
slalom
slalom

прыжки на лыжах
prizhki na lizhakh
ski jump

лыжные гонки
lyzhniye gonki
cross-country skiing

зимние виды спорта zimniye vidy sporta • winter sports

ледолазание
ledolazaniye
ice climbing

конькобежный спорт
kon'kobezhniy sport
ice-skating

защитные лыжные очки
zashchitniye lyzhniye ochki
goggles

конёк
konyok
skate

фигурное катание
figurnoye kataniye
figure skating

сноубординг
snoubording
snowboarding

бобслей
bobsley
bobsled

санный спорт
sanniy sport
luge

мотосани
motosani
snowmobile

катание на санях
kataniye na sanykh
sledding

словарь slovar' • vocabulary

горнолыжный спорт
gornolyzhniy sport
alpine skiing

гигантский слалом
gigantskiy slalom
giant slalom

вне трасс
vne tras
off-piste

кёрлинг
kyorling
curling

езда на собачьих упряжках
ezda na sobach'ikh upryazhkakh
dogsledding

скоростной бег на коньках
skorostnoy beg na kon'kakh
speed skating

биатлон
biatlon
biathlon

лавина
lavina
avalanche

другие виды спорта drugiye vidy sporta • other sports

планёр
planyor
glider

дельтаплан
del'taplan
hang-glider

планеризм
planerizm
gliding

парашют
parashyut
parachute

дельтапланеризм
del'taplanerizm
hang-gliding

альпинистская верёвка
alpinistskaya
verevka
rope

альпинизм
al'pinizm
rock climbing

прыжки с парашютом
prizhki s parashutom
parachuting

параглайдинг
paraglayding
paragliding

затяжные прыжки с парашютом
zatyazhniye pryzhki s parashyutom
skydiving

спуск по верёвке
spusk po verevke
rappelling

банджи-джампинг
bandzhi-dzhamping
bungee jumping

ралли
ralli
rally driving

гонщик
gonshchik
race-car driver

автомобильные гонки
avtomobil'niye gonki
auto racing

мотокросс
motokros
motocross

мотогонки
motogonki
motorcycle racing

скейтборд
skeytbord
skateboard

скейтбординг
skeytbording
skateboarding

катание на роликовых коньках
kataniye na rolikovykh kon'kakh
inline skating

стик
stik
stick

лакросс
lakros
lacrosse

маска
maska
mask

рапира
rapira
foil

фехтование
fekhtovaniye
fencing

кегля
keglya
pin

боулинг
bouling
bowling

шар для боулинга
shar dlya boulinga
bowling ball

лук
luk
bow

стрела
strela
arrow

колчан
kolchan
quiver

стрельба из лука
strel'ba iz luka
archery

мишень
mishen'
target

спортивная стрельба
sportivnaya strel'ba
target shooting

пул
pul
pool

снукер
snuker
snooker

фитнес fitnes • fitness

велотренажёр
velotrenazhyor
exercise bike

тренажёр
trenazher
gym machine

скамья
skamya
bench

свободные веса
svobodniye vesa
free weights

гриф
grif
bar

тренажёрный зал
trenazhyorniy zal
gym

гребной тренажёр
grebnoy trenazhyor
rowing machine

беговая дорожка
begovaya dorozhka
treadmill

кросстренажёр
krosstrenazher
elliptical trainer

персональный тренер
personal'niy trener
personal trainer

степ-тренажёр
step-trenazhyor
stair machine

плавательный бассейн
plavatel'niy baseyn
swimming pool

сауна
sauna
sauna

упражнения uprazhn<u>e</u>niya • exercises

растяжка
rast<u>ya</u>zhka
stretch

выпад
v<u>y</u>pad
lunge

трико
trik<u>o</u>
tights

отжимание
otzhim<u>a</u>niye
push-up

гантель
gant<u>e</u>l'
dumbbell

приседание
prised<u>a</u>niye
squat

подъём туловища
pod-y<u>o</u>m t<u>u</u>lovishcha
sit-up

подъём на бицепс
pod-y<u>o</u>m na b<u>i</u>tseps
bicep curl

жим ногами
zhim nog<u>a</u>mi
leg press

жим лёжа
zhim l<u>yo</u>zha
chest press

гриф штанги
grif sht<u>a</u>ngi
weight bar

силовые тренировки
silov<u>i</u>ye treni<u>ro</u>vki
weight training

тренировочная обувь
treni<u>ro</u>vochnaya <u>o</u>buv'
sneakers

бег трусцой
beg trusts<u>o</u>y
jogging

пилатес
pil<u>a</u>tes
Pilates

словарь slov<u>a</u>r' • vocabulary

тренироваться
treni<u>ro</u>vat'sya
train (v)

разогреваться
razogrev<u>a</u>t'sya
warm up (v)

бежать на месте
bezh<u>a</u>t' na m<u>e</u>ste
jog in place (v)

сгибать
sgib<u>a</u>t'
flex (v)

растягивать
rast<u>ya</u>givat'
extend (v)

подтягиваться
podt<u>ya</u>givat'sya
pull up (v)

прыжки со скакалкой
pryzhk<u>i</u> so skak<u>a</u>lkoj
jumping rope

боксерсайз
bokser<u>sa</u>yz
boxercise

круговая тренировка
krugov<u>a</u>ya treni<u>ro</u>vka
circuit training

досуг dos<u>ug</u>
leisure

театр te<u>a</u>tr · **theater**

занавес
z<u>a</u>naves
curtain

кулисы
kul<u>i</u>sy
wings

декорации
dekor<u>a</u>tsii
set

зрители
zr<u>i</u>teli
audience

оркестр
ork<u>e</u>str
orchestra

сцена sts<u>e</u>na | **stage**

место
m<u>e</u>sto
seat

верхний ярус
v<u>e</u>rkhniy y<u>a</u>rus
balcony seats

ряд
ry<u>a</u>d
row

ложа
l<u>o</u>zha
box

бельэтаж
bel'et<u>a</u>zh
mezzanine

балкон
balk<u>o</u>n
balcony

проход
prokh<u>o</u>d
aisle

партер
part<u>e</u>r
**orchestra
seats**

схема зала
skh<u>e</u>ma z<u>a</u>la | **seating**

словарь slov<u>a</u>r' · **vocabulary**

актёрский состав akt<u>e</u>rskiy sost<u>a</u>v **cast**	сценарий stsen<u>a</u>riy **script**	премьера prem'y<u>e</u>ra **opening night**
актёр akty<u>o</u>r **actor**	задник z<u>a</u>dnik **backdrop**	антракт antr<u>a</u>kt **intermission**
актриса aktr<u>i</u>sa **actress**	режиссёр rezhisy<u>o</u>r **director**	программа progr<u>a</u>mma **program**
пьеса p'y<u>e</u>sa **play**	продюсер prody<u>u</u>ser **producer**	оркестровая яма orkestr<u>o</u>vaya y<u>a</u>ma **orchestra pit**

концерт kontsert | **concert**

мюзикл myuzikl | **musical**

костюм
kostyum
costume

балет balet | **ballet**

словарь slovar' • vocabulary

капельдинер kapel'diner **usher**	фонограмма fonogramma **soundtrack**	Когда он начинается? kogda on nachinayetsya? **What time does it start?**
классическая музыка klasicheskaya muzyka **classical music**	аплодировать aplodirovat' **applaud (v)**	Мне два билета на сегодняшний спектакль. mne dva bileta na segodnyashniy spektakl' **I'd like two tickets for tonight's performance.**
музыка к спектаклю; партитура muzyka k spektaklyu; partitura **musical score**	(на) бис (na) bis **encore**	

опера
opera | **opera**

кино kino • movies

попкорн
popkorn
popcorn

вестибюль
vestibyul'
lobby

касса
kassa
box office

афиша
afisha
poster

кинозал
kinozal
movie theater

экран
ekran
screen

словарь slovar' • vocabulary

комедия komediya **comedy**	мелодрама melodrama **romance**
триллер triller **thriller**	научно-фантастический фильм nauchno-fantasticheskiy fil'm **science fiction movie**
фильм ужасов fil'm uzhasov **horror movie**	приключенческий фильм priklyuchencheskiy fil'm **adventure movie**
вестерн vestern **Western**	мультфильм mul'tfil'm **animated movie**

оркестр orkestr • orchestra

струнные инструменты strunniye instrumenty • strings

арфа
arfa
harp

дирижёр
dirizhor
conductor

контрабас
kontrabas
double bass

скрипка
skripka
violin

подиум
podium
podium

альт
al't
viola

виолончель
violonchel'
cello

партитура
partitura
score

скрипичный ключ
skripichniy klyuch
treble clef

нота
nota
note

нотный стан
notniy stan
staff

басовый ключ
basoviy klyuch
bass clef

Andante

rit.

нотное письмо notnoye pis'mo | **notation**

пианино pianino | **piano**

словарь slovar' • vocabulary

увертюра uvertyura **overture**	соната sonata **sonata**	знак паузы znak pauzi **rest**	диез diez **sharp**	бекар bekar **natural**	гамма gamma **scale**
симфония simfoniya **symphony**	музыкальные инструменты muzikalnie instrumenti **instruments**	высота звука vysota zvuka **pitch**	бемоль bemol' **flat**	тактовая черта wtaktovaya cherta **bar**	дирижёрская палочка dirizhorskaya palochka **baton**

деревянные духовые инструменты derevyanniye dukhoviye instrumenty • **woodwind**

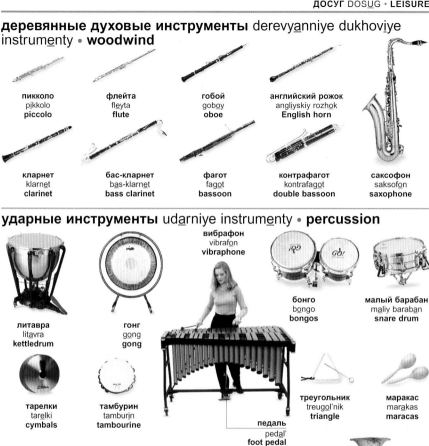

пикколо
pikkolo
piccolo

флейта
fleyta
flute

гобой
goboy
oboe

английский рожок
angliyskiy rozhok
English horn

кларнет
klarnet
clarinet

бас-кларнет
bas-klarnet
bass clarinet

фагот
fagot
bassoon

контрафагот
kontrafagot
double bassoon

саксофон
saksofon
saxophone

ударные инструменты udarniye instrumenty • **percussion**

вибрафон
vibrafon
vibraphone

бонго
bongo
bongos

малый барабан
maliy baraban
snare drum

литавра
litavra
kettledrum

гонг
gong
gong

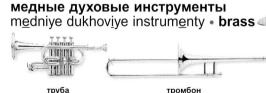

тарелки
tarelki
cymbals

тамбурин
tamburin
tambourine

треугольник
treugol'nik
triangle

маракас
marakas
maracas

педаль
pedal'
foot pedal

медные духовые инструменты medniye dukhoviye instrumenty • **brass**

труба
truba
trumpet

тромбон
trombon
trombone

валторна
valtorna
French horn

туба
tuba
tuba

концерт kontsert • concert

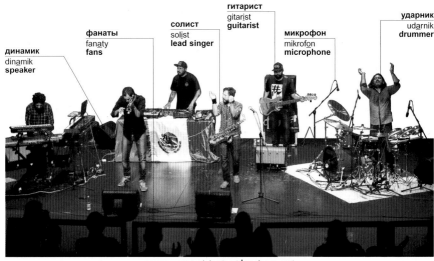

динамик
dinamik
speaker

фанаты
fanaty
fans

солист
solist
lead singer

гитарист
gitarist
guitarist

микрофон
mikrofon
microphone

ударник
udarnik
drummer

рок-концерт rok-kontsert | **rock concert**

инструменты yuèqì • instruments

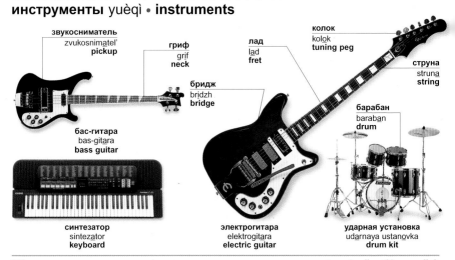

звукосниматель
zvukosnimatel'
pickup

гриф
grif
neck

лад
lad
fret

колок
kolok
tuning peg

струна
struna
string

бридж
bridzh
bridge

барабан
baraban
drum

бас-гитара
bas-gitara
bass guitar

синтезатор
sintezator
keyboard

электрогитара
elektrogitara
electric guitar

ударная установка
udarnaya ustanovka
drum kit

музыкальные стили muzykal'niye stili • musical styles

джаз dzhaz | jazz

блюз blyuz | blues

панк-рок pank-rok | punk

фолк folk | folk music

поп pop | pop

танцевальная музыка
tantseval'naya muzyka | dance

рэп rep | rap

хеви-метал
khevi-metal | heavy metal

классическая музыка
klasicheskaya muzyka
classical music

словарь slovar' • vocabulary

песня	текст песни	мелодия	ритм; темп	регги	кантри	прожектор
pesnya	tekst pesni	melodiya	ritm; temp	reggi	kantri	prozhektor
song	**lyrics**	**melody**	**beat**	**reggae**	**country**	**spotlight**

осмотр достопримечательностей osmotr
dostoprimechatelnostey • **sightseeing**

турист
turist
tourist

маршрут
marshrut
itinerary

с открытым верхом
s otkrytym verkhom
open-top

туристический автобус
turisticheskiy avtobus | **tour bus**

гид
gid
tour guide

статуэтка
statuetka
figurine

достопримечательность
dostoprimechatel'nost' | **tourist attraction**

**организованная
экскурсия**
organizovannaya ekskursiya
guided tour

сувениры
suveniry
souvenirs

словарь slovar' • **vocabulary**

открыто otkryto **open**	путеводитель putevoditel' **guidebook**	видеокамера videokamera **camcorder**	слева; налево; левый sleva; nalevo; leviy **left**	**Где находится…?** gde nakhoditsya…? **Where is …?**
закрыто zakryto **closed**	фотоплёнка fotoplyonka **film**	фотоаппарат fotoaparat **camera**	справа; направо; правый sprava; napravo; praviy **right**	**Я заблудился/ заблудилась.** ya zabludilsya/zabludilas' **I'm lost.**
входная плата vkhodnaya plata **entrance fee**	батарейки batareyki **batteries**	указатели направления ukazateli napravlenia **directions**	прямо pryamo **straight ahead**	**Как пройти/проехать к …?** kak proyti/proyekhat' k…? **Can you tell me the way to …?**

достопримечательности dostoprimechatel'nosti • **attractions**

картина
kartina
painting

экспонат
eksponat
exhibit

выставка
vystavka
exhibition

исторические развалины
istoricheskiye razvaliny
famous ruin

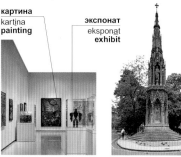

художественная галерея
khudozhestvennaya galereya
art gallery

памятник
pamyatnik
monument

музей
muzey
museum

историческое здание
istoricheskoye zdaniye
historic building

казино
kazino
casino

парк
park
gardens

национальный парк
natsional'niy park
national park

информация informatsiya • **information**

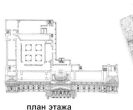

время
vremya
times

план этажа
plan etazha
floor plan

карта
karta
map

расписание
raspisaniye
schedule

туристский информационный центр
turistskiy informatsionniy tsentr
tourist information

отдых на открытом воздухе otdykh na otkrytom vozdukhe • outdoor activities

тропинка
tropinka
footpath

солнечные часы
solnechnyye chasy
sundial

кафе
kafe
café

парк park | **park**

трава
trava
grass

скамейка
skameyka
bench

сад в классическом стиле
sad v klasicheskom stile
formal gardens

американские горки
amerikanskiye gorki
roller coaster

территория ярмарки
teritoriya yarmarki
fairground

ярмарочная площадь
yarmarochnaya ploshchad'
theme park

сафари-парк
safari-park
safari park

зоопарк
zoopark
zoo

занятия zanyatiya • **activities**

катание на велосипеде
kataniye na velosipede
cycling

бег трусцой
beg trustsoy
jogging

катание на скейтборде
kataniye na skeytborde
skateboarding

катание на роликах
kataniye na rolikakh
rollerblading

верховая тропа
verkhovaya tropa
bridle path

наблюдение за птицами
nablyudeniye za ptitsami
bird-watching

верховая езда
verkhovaya yezda
horseback riding

пешеходный туризм
peshekhodniy turizm
hiking

корзинка для пикника
korzinka dlya piknika
hamper

пикник
piknik
picnic

детская площадка detskaya ploshchadka • **playground**

песочница
pesochnitsa
sandbox

детский бассейн
detskiy baseyn
wading pool

качели
kacheli
swing

доска-качели
doska-kacheli | **seesaw**

детская горка detskaya gorka | **slide**

лесенка lesenka | **climbing frame**

пляж plyazh • beach

гостиница	пляжный зонт	пляжный домик	песок	волна	море
gostinitsa	plyazhniy zont	plyazhniy domik	pesok	volna	more
hotel	**beach umbrella**	**beach hut**	**sand**	**wave**	**sea**

пляжная сумка
plyazhnaya sumka
beach bag

бикини
bikini
bikini

загорать zagorat' | sunbathe (v)

спасательная вышка
spasatel'naya vyshka
lifeguard tower

спасатель
spasatel'
lifeguard

ветролом
vetrolom
windbreak

набережная
naberezhnaya
boardwalk

шезлонг
shezlong
deck chair

солнцезащитные очки
solntsezashchitnyie ochki
sunglasses

шляпа от солнца
shlyapa ot sontsa
sun hat

крем для загара
krem dlya zagara
suntan lotion

солнцезащитный крем
solntsezashchitniy krem
sunblock

пляжный мяч
plyazhniy myach
beach ball

плавательный круг
plavatel'niy krug
inflatable ring

купальник
kupal'nik
swimsuit

лопатка
lopatka
shovel

ведёрко
vedyorko
pail

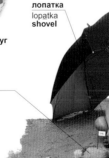

песочный замок
pesochniy zamok
sandcastle

пляжное полотенце
plyazhnoye polotentse
beach towel

ракушка
rakushka
shell

кемпинг kemping • camping

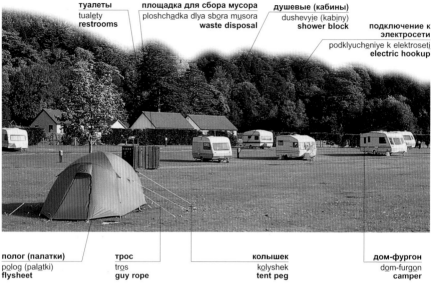

туалеты
tualety
restrooms

площадка для сбора мусора
ploshchadka dlya sbora musora
waste disposal

душевые (кабины)
dushevyie (kabiny)
shower block

подключение к электросети
podklyucheniye k elektroseti
electric hookup

полог (палатки)
polog (palatki)
flysheet

трос
tros
guy rope

колышек
kolyshek
tent peg

дом-фургон
dom-furgon
camper

площадка для кемпинга ploshchadka dlya kempinga | campground

словарь slovar' • vocabulary

разбивать лагерь
razbivat' lager'
camp (v)

администрация кемпинга
administratsia kempinga
site manager's office

Есть свободные места
yest' svobodniye mesta
sites available

мест нет
mest net
full

место для палатки
mesto dlya palatki
site

ставить палатку
stavit' palatku
pitch a tent (v)

палаточная стойка
palatochnaya stoika
tent pole

походная кровать
pokhodnaya krovat'
camp bed

скамейка для пикника
skameika dlya piknika
picnic bench

гамак
gamak
hammock

автодом
avtodom
camper van

прицеп
pritsep
trailer

уголь
ugol'
charcoal

растопка
rastopka
firelighter

разводить костёр
razvodit' kostyor
light a fire (v)

костёр
kostyor
campfire

каркас
karkas
frame

подстилка
podstilka
ground sheet

рюкзак
ryukzak
backpack

термос
termos
vacuum flask

фляжка
flyazhka
water bottle

палатка
palatka
tent

репеллент
repelent
insect repellent

фонарик
fonarik
flashlight

москитная сетка
moskitnaya setka
mosquito net

термобельё
termobel'yo
thermal underwear

туристические ботинки
turisticheskiye botinki
hiking boots

непромокаемая одежда
nepromokayemaya odezhda
rain gear

спальный мешок
spal'niy meshok
sleeping bag

туристический коврик
turisticheskiy kovrik
sleeping mat

походная плита
pokhodnaya plita
camping stove

барбекю
barbekyu
barbecue grill

надувной матрац naduvnoy matrats | **air mattress**

домашняя аудио- и видеоаппаратура domashnyaya audio- i videoapparatura • home entertainment

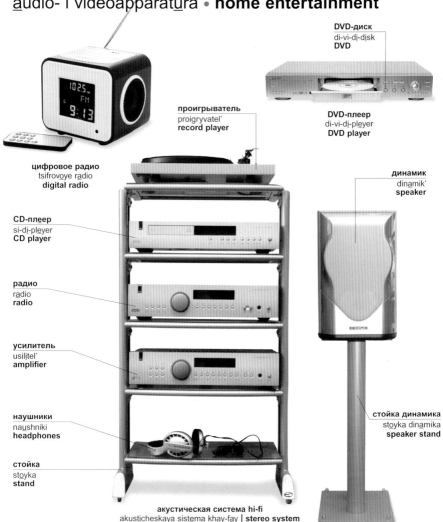

DVD-диск
di-vi-di-disk
DVD

проигрыватель
proigryvatel'
record player

DVD-плеер
di-vi-di-pleyer
DVD player

цифровое радио
tsifrovoye radio
digital radio

динамик
dinamik'
speaker

CD-плеер
si-di-pleyer
CD player

радио
radio
radio

усилитель
usilitel'
amplifier

наушники
naushniki
headphones

стойка динамика
stoyka dinamika
speaker stand

стойка
stoyka
stand

акустическая система hi-fi
akusticheskaya sistema khay-fay | **stereo system**

экран
ekran
screen

наглазник
naglaznik
eyecup

цифровая приставка
tzifrovaya pristavka
DTV converter box

видеокамера
videokamera
camcorder

спутниковая тарелка
sputnikovaya tarelka
satellite dish

телевизор с плоским экраном
televizor s ploskim ekranom
flatscreen TV

игровая приставка
igrovaya pristavka
console

быстрая перемотка вперёд
bystraya peremotka vperyod
fast-forward

запись
zapis'
record

громкость
gromkost'
volume

перемотка назад
peremotka nazad
rewind

стоп
stop
stop

контроллер
kontroller
controller

воспроизведение
vosproizvedeniye
play

пауза
pauza
pause

видеоигра videoigra | **video game**

пульт дистанционного управления
pul't distantsionnogo upravleniya | **remote control**

словарь slovar' • vocabulary

компакт-диск
kompakt-disk
CD

потоковый
potokoviy
streaming

высокое разрешение
viysokoye razresheniye
high-definition

кассетный плеер
kassetniy pleyer
cassette player

платный канал
platniy kanal
pay-per-view channel

реклама
reklama
advertisement

цифровой
tsifrovoy
digital

кассета
kasseta
cassette tape

программа
programma
program

стерео
stereo
stereo

кабельное телевидение
kabelnoye televideniye
cable television

вай-фай
vay-fay
Wi-Fi

художественный фильм
khudozhestvenniy fil'm
feature film

переключать канал
pereklyuchat' kanal
change channel (v)

настраивать радио (на канал/волну)
nastraivat' radio (na kanal/volnu)
tune the radio (v)

смотреть телевизор
smotret' televizor
watch television (v)

выключать телевизор
vyklyuchat' televizor
turn off the television (v)

включать телевизор
vklyuchat' televizor
turn on the television (v)

фотография fotografiya • photography

спуск затвора
spusk zatvora
shutter release

регулятор диафрагмы
regulator diafragmi
aperture dial

объектив
ob-yektiv
lens

фильтр
fil'tr
filter

крышка объектива
kryshka ob-yektiva
lens cap

зеркальный фотоаппарат
zerkalniy fotoapparat | **SLR camera**

лампа-вспышка
lampa-vspyshka
flash gun

экспонометр
eksponometr
light meter

зум-объектив
zum-ob-yektiv
zoom lens

штатив
shtativ
tripod

типы фотоаппаратов tipy fotoaparatov • types of camera

вспышка
vspyshka
flash

поляроид
polyaroid
Polaroid camera

цифровой фотоаппарат
tsifrovoy fotoaparat
digital camera

телефон с камерой
telefon s kameroj
camera phone

одноразовый фотоаппарат
odnorazoviy fotoaparat
disposable camera

фотографировать fotografirovat' • photograph (v)

катушка плёнки
katushka plyonki
film roll

плёнка
plyonka
film

фокусировать
fokusirovat'
focus (v)

проявлять
proyavlyat'
develop (v)

негатив
negativ
negative

пейзаж
peyzazh
landscape

портрет
portret
portrait

фотография fotografiya | **photograph**

фотоальбом
fotoal'bom
photo album

фоторамка
fotoramka
picture frame

проблемы problemy • problems

недоэкспонированный
nedoeksponirovanniy
underexposed

переэкспонированный
pereeksponirovanniy
overexposed

нерезкий
nerezkiy
out of focus

красные глаза
krasniye glaza
red eye

словарь slovar' • vocabulary

видоискатель
vidoiskatel'
viewfinder

чехол камеры
chekhol kamery
camera case

экспозиция
ekspozitsiya
exposure

проявочная; тёмная комната
proyavochnaya; tyomnaya komnata
darkroom

печать; отпечаток
pechat'; otpechatok
print

матовый
matoviy
matte

глянцевый
glyantseviy
gloss

увеличение
uvelicheniye
enlargement

Мне нужно проявить эту плёнку.
mne nuzhno proyavit' etu plyonku
I'd like this film processed.

игры igry • games

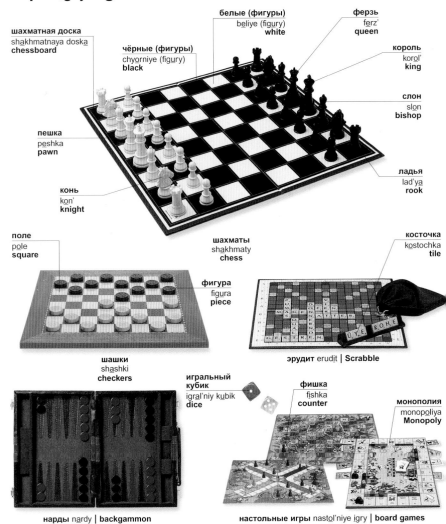

шахматная доска
shakhmatnaya doska
chessboard

чёрные (фигуры)
chyorniye (figury)
black

белые (фигуры)
beliye (figury)
white

ферзь
ferz'
queen

король
korol'
king

слон
slon
bishop

пешка
peshka
pawn

конь
kon'
knight

ладья
lad'ya
rook

поле
pole
square

шахматы
shakhmaty
chess

косточка
kostochka
tile

фигура
figura
piece

шашки
shashki
checkers

эрудит erudit | **Scrabble**

игральный кубик
igral'niy kubik
dice

фишка
fishka
counter

монополия
monopoliya
Monopoly

нарды nardy | **backgammon**

настольные игры nastol'niye igry | **board games**

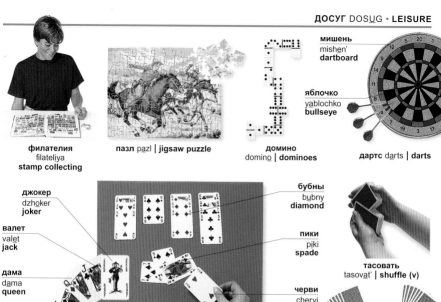

мишень
mishen'
dartboard

яблочко
yablochko
bullseye

филателия
filateliya
stamp collecting

пазл pazl | **jigsaw puzzle**

домино
domino | **dominoes**

дартс darts | **darts**

джокер
dzhoker
joker

валет
valet
jack

дама
dama
queen

король
korol'
king

туз
tuz
ace

карты karty | **cards**

бубны
bubny
diamond

пики
piki
spade

черви
chervi
heart

трефы
trefy
club

тасовать
tasovat' | **shuffle (v)**

сдавать sdavat' | **deal (v)**

словарь slovar' · vocabulary

ход khod **move**	**выигрывать** vyigryvat' **win (v)**	**проигравший** proigravshiy **loser**	**очко** ochko **point**	**бридж** bridzh **bridge**	**Бросай кубик.** brosay kubik **Roll the dice.**
играть igrat' **play (v)**	**победитель** pobeditel' **winner**	**игра** igra **game**	**счёт** schyot **score**	**колода карт** koloda kart **deck of cards**	**Чья очередь?** ch'ya ochered'? **Whose turn is it?**
игрок igrok **player**	**проигрывать** proigryvat' **lose (v)**	**пари** pari **bet**	**покер** poker **poker**	**масть** mast' **suit**	**Твой ход.** tvoy khod **It's your move.**

искусства и ремёсла 1 iskustva i remyosla • arts and crafts 1

художница
khudozhnitsa
artist

картина
kartina
painting

мольберт
mol'bert
easel

холст
kholst
canvas

кисть
kist'
brush

палитра
palitra
palette

живопись zhivopis' | painting

краски kraski • paints

масляные краски
maslyaniye kraski
oil paint

акварель
akvarel'
watercolor paint

пастель
pastel'
pastels

акриловая краска
akrilovaya kraska
acrylic paint

гуашь
guash' | poster paint

цвета tsveta • colors

красный
krasniy | red

синий siniy | blue

жёлтый
zhyoltiy | yellow

зелёный
zelyoniy | green

оранжевый
oranzheviy | orange

фиолетовый
fioletoviy | purple

белый
beliy | white

чёрный
chyorniy | black

серый seriy | gray

розовый
rozoviy | pink

коричневый
korichneviy
brown

индиго
indigo | indigo

другие умения drugiye umenia • other crafts

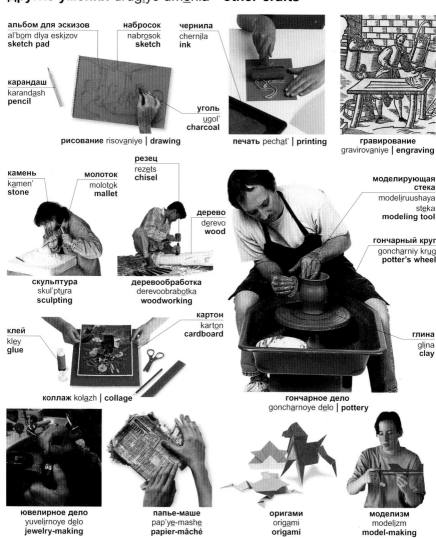

альбом для эскизов
al'bom dlya eskizov
sketch pad

набросок
nabrosok
sketch

чернила
chernila
ink

карандаш
karandash
pencil

уголь
ugol'
charcoal

рисование risovaniye | **drawing**

печать pechat' | **printing**

гравирование
gravirovaniye | **engraving**

камень
kamen'
stone

молоток
molotok
mallet

резец
rezets
chisel

дерево
derevo
wood

скульптура
skul'ptura
sculpting

деревообработка
derevoobrabotka
woodworking

моделирующая стека
modeliruushaya steka
modeling tool

гончарный круг
goncharniy krug
potter's wheel

клей
kley
glue

картон
karton
cardboard

глина
glina
clay

коллаж kolazh | **collage**

гончарное дело
goncharnoye delo | **pottery**

ювелирное дело
yuvelirnoye delo
jewelry-making

папье-маше
pap'ye-mashe
papier-mâché

оригами
origami
origami

моделизм
modelizm
model-making

искусство и ремёсла 2 iskustvo i remyosla 2 · arts and crafts 2

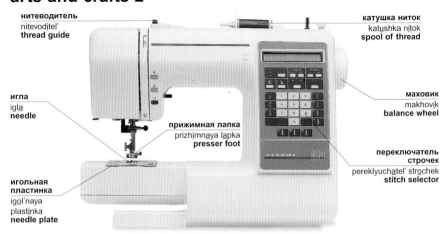

нитеводитель
nitevoditel'
thread guide

катушка ниток
katushka nitok
spool of thread

игла
igla
needle

маховик
makhovik
balance wheel

прижимная лапка
prizhimnaya lapka
presser foot

игольная пластинка
igol'naya plastinka
needle plate

переключатель строчек
pereklyuchatel' strochek
stitch selector

швейная машина shveynaya mashina | **sewing machine**

ножницы
nozhnitsy
scissors

выкройка
vykroyka
pattern

булавка
bulavka
pin

сантиметр
santimetr
tape measure

ткань
tkan'
material

игольница
igol'nitsa
pincushion

корзинка для шитья
korzinka dlya shit'ya | **sewing basket**

нитки
nitki
thread

петля
petlya
eye

шпулька
shpul'ka
bobbin

крючок
kryuchok
hook

напёрсток
napyorstok
thimble

портновский мелок
portnovskiy melok
tailor's chalk

манекен
maneken
tailor's dummy

вдевать
vdevat'
thread (v)

стежок
stezhok
stitch

шить
shit'
sew (v)

штопать
shtopat'
darn (v)

примётывать
primyotyvat'
tack (v)

резать
rezat'
cut (v)

гобелен
gobelen
needlepoint

вышивка
vyshivka
embroidery

крючок
kryuchok
**crochet
hook**

вязание крючком
vyazaniye
kryuchkom
crochet

макраме
makrame
macramé

лоскутное шитьё
loskutnoye shit'e
patchwork

подбивка ватой
podbivka vatoy
quilting

коклюшка
koklyushka
lace bobbin

плетение кружев
pleteniye kruzhev
lace-making

ткацкий станок
tkatskiy stanok
loom

ткачество
tkachestvo
weaving

вязальная спица
vyazal'naya spitsa
knitting needle

вязание спицами
vyazaniye spitsami | **knitting**

шерсть
sherst'
yarn

моток пряжи
motok pryazhi | **skein**

словарь slovar' • vocabulary

распарывать	нейлон
rasparyvat'	neylon
unpick (v)	**nylon**
ткань	шёлк
tkan'	shyolk
fabric	**silk**
хлопок	дизайнер
khlopok	dizayner
cotton	**designer**
лён	мода
lyon	moda
linen	**fashion**
полиэстер	застёжка-молния
poliester	zastyozhka-molniya
polyester	**zipper**

окружающая среда okruzhayushchaya sreda
environment

космос kosmos • **space**

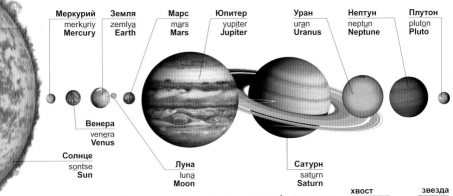

Меркурий
merkuriy
Mercury

Земля
zemlya
Earth

Марс
mars
Mars

Юпитер
yupiter
Jupiter

Уран
uran
Uranus

Нептун
neptun
Neptune

Плутон
pluton
Pluto

Венера
venera
Venus

Солнце
sontse
Sun

Луна
luna
Moon

Сатурн
saturn
Saturn

Солнечная система solnechnaya sistema | **solar system**

хвост
khvost
tail

звезда
zvezda
star

галактика
galaktika
galaxy

туманность
tumannost'
nebula

астероид
asteroid
asteroid

комета
kometa
comet

словарь slovar' • **vocabulary**

вселенная vselennaya **universe**	**чёрная дыра** chyornaya dyra **black hole**	**полнолуние** polnoluniye **full moon**
орбита orbita **orbit**	**планета** planeta **planet**	**новолуние** novoluniye **new moon**
гравитация gravitatsiya **gravity**	**метеор** meteor **meteor**	**лунный серп** lunniy serp **crescent moon**

затмение zatmeniye | **eclipse**

исследование космоса issl**e**dovaniye k**o**smosa • **space exploration**

шаттл
sh**a**tl
space shuttle

ускоритель
uskoritel'
booster

манёвровый двигатель
manevr**o**viy dvigatel'
thruster

скафандр
skaf**a**ndr
space suit

радар
radar
radar

люк для экипажа
lyuk dlya
ekip**a**zha
crew hatch

астронавт
astron**a**vt | **astronaut**

лунный модуль lunniy m**o**dul' | **lunar module**

стартовый комплекс
st**a**rtoviy
k**o**mpleks
launch pad

запуск
z**a**pusk
launch

спутник
sp**u**tnik
satellite

космическая станция
kosm**i**cheskaya st**a**ntsiya
space station

астрономия astron**o**miya • **astronomy**

созвездие
sozv**e**zdiye
constellation

бинокль
bin**o**kl'
binoculars

телескоп
telesk**o**p
telescope

штатив
shtat**i**v
tripod

Земля zemlya • Earth

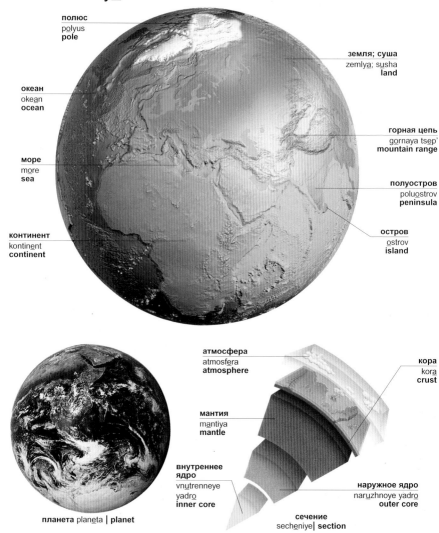

полюс
polyus
pole

земля; суша
zemlya; susha
land

океан
okean
ocean

горная цепь
gornaya tsep'
mountain range

море
more
sea

полуостров
poluostrov
peninsula

континент
kontinent
continent

остров
ostrov
island

атмосфера
atmosfera
atmosphere

кора
kora
crust

мантия
mantiya
mantle

внутреннее
ядро
vnutrenneye
yadro
inner core

наружное ядро
naruzhnoye yadro
outer core

планета planeta | **planet**

сечение
secheniye| **section**

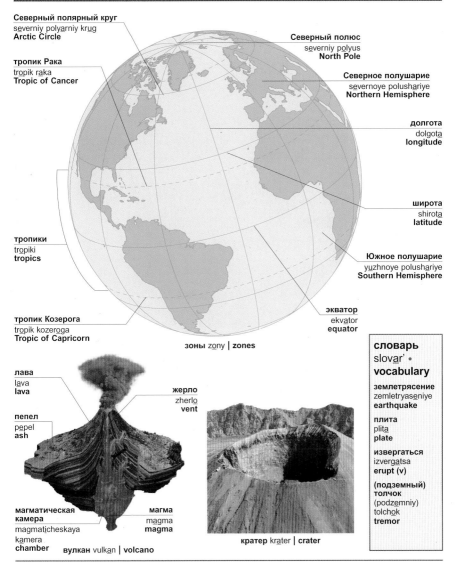

Северный полярный круг
severniy polyarniy krug
Arctic Circle

тропик Рака
tropik raka
Tropic of Cancer

тропики
tropiki
tropics

тропик Козерога
tropik kozeroga
Tropic of Capricorn

Северный полюс
severniy polyus
North Pole

Северное полушарие
severnoye polushariye
Northern Hemisphere

долгота
dolgota
longitude

широта
shirota
latitude

Южное полушарие
yuzhnoye polushariye
Southern Hemisphere

экватор
ekvator
equator

зоны zony | zones

лава
lava
lava

пепел
pepel
ash

жерло
zherlo
vent

магматическая камера
magmaticheskaya kamera
chamber

магма
magma
magma

вулкан vulkan | volcano

кратер krater | crater

словарь
slovar' •
vocabulary

землетрясение
zemletryaseniye
earthquake

плита
plita
plate

извергаться
izvergatsa
erupt (v)

(подземный) толчок
(podzemniy) tolchok
tremor

русский ruskiy • **english**

283

ландшафт landsh<u>a</u>ft • **landscape**

гора
gor<u>a</u>
mountain

склон
sklon
slope

берег
bereg
bank

река
rek<u>a</u>
river

пороги
por<u>o</u>gi
rapids

скалы
sk<u>a</u>ly
rocks

ледник ledn<u>i</u>k | **glacier**

долина dol<u>i</u>na | **valley**

холм
kh<u>o</u>lm
hill

плато
plat<u>o</u>
plateau

ущелье
ushch<u>e</u>l'ye
gorge

пещера
peshch<u>e</u>ra
cave

равнина
ravnina | **plain**

пустыня
pustynya | **desert**

(густой) лес
(gustoy) les | **forest**

лес les | **woods**

тропический лес
tropicheskiy les
rain forest

болото
boloto
swamp

луг
lug
meadow

травянистая местность
travyanistaya mesnost'
grassland

водопад
vodopad
waterfall

ручей
ruchey
stream

озеро
ozero
lake

гейзер
geyzer
geyser

побережье
poberezh'ye
coast

утёс
utyos
cliff

коралловый риф
koraloviy rif
coral reef

устье
ust'ye
estuary

погода pog̲oda • **weather**

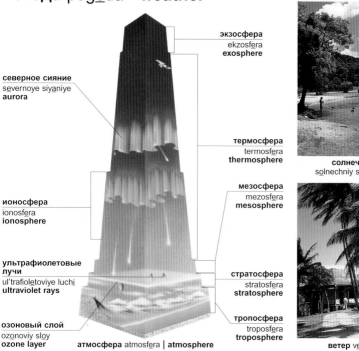

экзосфера
ekzosf̲era
exosphere

северное сияние
severnoye siy̲aniye
aurora

термосфера
termosf̲era
thermosphere

мезосфера
mezosf̲era
mesosphere

ионосфера
ionosf̲era
ionosphere

ультрафиолетовые лучи
ul'trafiol̲etoviye luch̲i
ultraviolet rays

стратосфера
stratosf̲era
stratosphere

озоновый слой
oz̲onoviy sl̲oy
ozone layer

тропосфера
troposf̲era
troposphere

атмосфера atmosf̲era | **atmosphere**

солнечный свет
s̲olnechniy sv̲et | **sunshine**

ветер v̲eter | **wind**

словарь slov̲ar' • **vocabulary**

дождь со снегом dozhd' so sn̲egom **sleet**	**ливень** liven' **shower**	**жарко** zh̲arko **hot**	**сухо** s̲ukho **dry**	**ветрено** v̲etreno **windy**	**Мне жарко/холодно.** mne zh̲arko/kh̲olodno **I'm hot/cold.**
град gr̲ad **hail**	**солнечно** s̲olnechno **sunny**	**холодно** kh̲olodno **cold**	**дождливо** dozhdl̲ivo **wet**	**буря** b̲urya **gale**	**Идёт дождь.** idy̲ot dozhd' **It's raining.**
гром gr̲om **thunder**	**облачно** obl̲achno **cloudy**	**тепло** tepl̲o **warm**	**влажно** vl̲azhno **humid**	**температура** temperat̲ura **temperature**	**Сейчас… градусов.** seych̲as… gr̲adusov **It's … degrees.**

облако oblako | **cloud**

дождь dozhd' | **rain**

молния
molniya
lightning

гроза groza | **storm**

лёгкий туман
lekhkiy tuman | **mist**

густой туман
gustoy tuman | **fog**

радуга raduga | **rainbow**

снег sneg | **snow**

иней iney | **frost**

лёд lyod | **ice**

сосулька
sosul'ka
icicle

холод kholod | **freeze**

ураган
uragan | **hurricane**

торнадо
tornado | **tornado**

муссон
muson | **monsoon**

наводнение
navodneniye | **flood**

горные породы gorniye porody • rocks

магматическая
magmaticheskaya • **igneous**

гранит
granit
granite

обсидиан
obsidian
obsidian

базальт
bazal't
basalt

пемза
pemza
pumice

осадочная osadochnaya • **sedimentary**

песчаник
peschanik
sandstone

известняк
izvesnyak
limestone

мел
mel
chalk

кремень
kremen'
flint

конгломерат
konglomerat
conglomerate

уголь
ugol'
coal

метаморфическая
metamorficheskaya • **metamorphic**

аспидный сланец
aspidniy slanets
slate

слюдяной сланец
sljudanoy slanets
schist

гнейс
gneys
gneiss

мрамор
mramor
marble

драгоценные камни dragotsenniye kamni • **gems**

рубин rubin **ruby**

аквамарин akvamarin **aquamarine**

аметист ametist **amethyst**

алмаз almaz **diamond**

нефрит nefrit **jade**

гагат gagat **jet**

изумруд izumrud **emerald**

опал opal **opal**

сапфир sapfir **sapphire**

лунный камень lunniy kamen' **moonstone**

гранат granat **garnet**

топаз topaz **topaz**

турмалин turmalin **tourmaline**

минералы miner**a**ly • **minerals**

кварц	слюда	сера	гематит	кальцит
kv**a**rts	slyud**a**	s**e**ra	gematit	kal'ts**i**t
quartz	**mica**	**sulfur**	**hematite**	**calcite**

малахит	бирюза	оникс	агат	графит
malakh**i**t	biryuz**a**	**o**niks	ag**a**t	graf**i**t
malachite	**turquoise**	**onyx**	**agate**	**graphite**

металлы met**a**lly • **metals**

золото	серебро	платина	никель	железо
z**o**loto	serebr**o**	pl**a**tina	n**i**kel'	zhel**e**zo
gold	**silver**	**platinum**	**nickel**	**iron**

медь	олово	алюминий	ртуть	цинк
m**e**d'	**o**lovo	alyum**i**niy	rt**u**t'	ts**i**nk
copper	**tin**	**aluminum**	**mercury**	**zinc**

ЖИВОТНЫЕ 1 zhivotniye • animals 1
млекопитающие mlekopitayushchiye • mammals

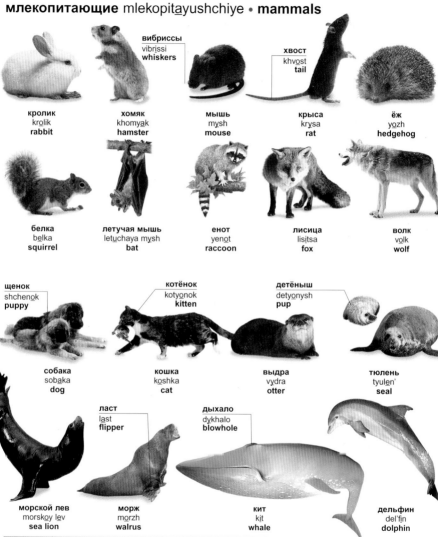

вибриссы
vibrissi
whiskers

хвост
khvost
tail

кролик
krolik
rabbit

хомяк
khomyak
hamster

мышь
mysh
mouse

крыса
krysa
rat

ёж
yozh
hedgehog

белка
belka
squirrel

летучая мышь
letuchaya mysh
bat

енот
yenot
raccoon

лисица
lisitsa
fox

волк
volk
wolf

щенок
shchenok
puppy

котёнок
kotyonok
kitten

детёныш
detyonysh
pup

собака
sobaka
dog

кошка
koshka
cat

выдра
vydra
otter

тюлень
tyulen'
seal

ласт
last
flipper

дыхало
dykhalo
blowhole

морской лев
morskoy lev
sea lion

морж
morzh
walrus

кит
kit
whale

дельфин
del'fin
dolphin

олений рог
oleniy r<u>og</u>
antler

грива
griva
mane

копыто
kop<u>y</u>to
hoof

горб
gorb
hump

олень
ol<u>e</u>n'
deer

зебра
zebra
zebra

жираф
zhir<u>a</u>f
giraffe

верблюд
verbl<u>yu</u>d
camel

хобот
kh<u>o</u>bot
trunk

бивень
biv<u>e</u>n'
tusk

рог
r<u>og</u>
horn

бегемот
begem<u>o</u>t
hippopotamus

слон
sl<u>o</u>n
elephant

носорог
nosor<u>og</u>
rhinoceros

тигр
tigr
tiger

грива
griva
mane

лев
l<u>e</u>v
lion

обезьяна
obez'<u>ya</u>na
monkey

горилла
gor<u>i</u>la
gorilla

коала
ko<u>a</u>la
koala

сумка
s<u>u</u>mka
pouch

панда
p<u>a</u>nda
panda

коготь
k<u>og</u>ot'
claw

кенгуру
kengur<u>u</u>
kangaroo

медведь
medv<u>e</u>d'
bear

белый медведь
beliy medv<u>e</u>d'
polar bear

животные 2 zhivotniye • animals 2
птицы ptitsy • birds

хвост
khvost
tail

канарейка; кенар
kanareyka; kenar
canary

воробей
vorobey
sparrow

колибри
kolibri
hummingbird

ласточка
lastochka
swallow

ворона
vorona
crow

голубь
golub'
pigeon

дятел
dyatel
woodpecker

сокол
sokol
falcon

сова
sova
owl

чайка
chayka
gull

орёл
oryol
eagle

пеликан
pelikan
pelican

фламинго
flamingo
flamingo

аист
aist
stork

журавль
zhuravl'
crane

пингвин
pingvin
penguin

страус
straus
ostrich

русский ruskiy • english

гусь g<u>us</u>' | **goose**

лебедь
l<u>e</u>bed'
swan

павлин
pavl<u>i</u>n
peacock

фазан
faz<u>a</u>n
pheasant

индюк
indy<u>u</u>k
turkey

клюв
kly<u>u</u>v
beak

перо
per<u>o</u>
feather

крыло
kryl<u>o</u>
wing

какаду
kakad<u>u</u>
cockatoo

коготь
k<u>o</u>got'
claw

попугай
popug<u>a</u>y
parrot

пресмыкающиеся
presmyk<u>a</u>yushchiesya • **reptiles**

чешуя
cheshuy<u>a</u>
scales

аллигатор
alig<u>a</u>tor
alligator

ящерица
y<u>a</u>shcheritsa
lizard

игуана
igu<u>a</u>na
iguana

панцирь
p<u>a</u>ntsir'
shell

морская черепаха
morsk<u>a</u>ya cherep<u>a</u>kha
turtle

сухопутная черепаха
sukhop<u>u</u>tnaya cherep<u>a</u>kha
tortoise

змея
zmey<u>a</u>
snake

морда
m<u>o</u>rda
snout

крокодил
krokod<u>i</u>l
crocodile

животные 3 zhivotniye • animals 3

земноводные zemnovodniye • amphibians

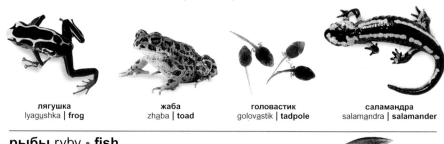

лягушка
lyagushka | **frog**

жаба
zhaba | **toad**

головастик
golovastik | **tadpole**

саламандра
salamandra | **salamander**

рыбы ryby • fish

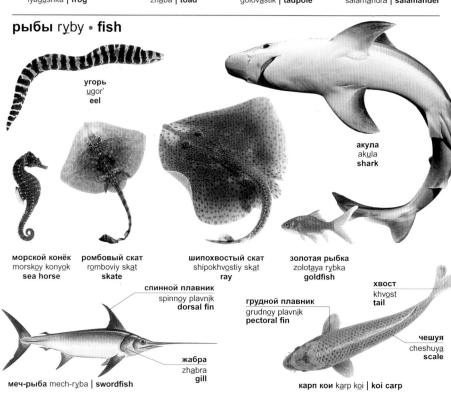

угорь
ugor'
eel

акула
akula
shark

морской конёк
morskoy konyok
sea horse

ромбовый скат
romboviy skat
skate

шипохвостый скат
shipokhvostiy skat
ray

золотая рыбка
zolotaya rybka
goldfish

спинной плавник
spinnoy plavnik
dorsal fin

грудной плавник
grudnoy plavnik
pectoral fin

хвост
khvost
tail

чешуя
cheshuya
scale

жабра
zhabra
gill

меч-рыба mech-ryba | **swordfish**

карп кои karp koi | **koi carp**

беспозвоночные bespozvon<u>o</u>chniye • *invertebrates*

муравей
mura<u>vey</u>
ant

термит
ter<u>mit</u>
termite

пчела
pchel<u>a</u>
bee

оса
os<u>a</u>
wasp

жук
zh<u>u</u>k
beetle

таракан
tara<u>kan</u>
cockroach

мотылёк
moty<u>lyok</u>
moth

усик
<u>u</u>sik
antenna

бабочка
b<u>a</u>bochka
butterfly

кокон
k<u>o</u>kon
cocoon

гусеница
gus<u>e</u>nitsa
caterpillar

сверчок
sverch<u>o</u>k | **cricket**

кузнечик
kuzn<u>e</u>chik
grasshopper

богомол
bogom<u>o</u>l
praying mantis

жало
zh<u>a</u>lo
sting

скорпион
skorpi<u>o</u>n
scorpion

сороконожка
sorokon<u>o</u>zhka
centipede

стрекоза
strekoz<u>a</u>
dragonfly

муха
m<u>u</u>kha
fly

комар
kom<u>a</u>r
mosquito

божья коровка
b<u>o</u>zh'ya kor<u>o</u>vka
ladybug

паук
pa<u>u</u>k
spider

слизень
sl<u>i</u>zen'
slug

улитка
ul<u>i</u>tka
snail

червяк cherv<u>ya</u>k | **worm**

морская звезда
morsk<u>a</u>ya zvezd<u>a</u>
starfish

мидия
m<u>i</u>diya
mussel

краб
kr<u>a</u>b | **crab**

лобстер
l<u>o</u>bster | **lobster**

осьминог
os'min<u>o</u>g | **octopus**

кальмар
kal'm<u>a</u>r | **squid**

медуза
med<u>u</u>za | **jellyfish**

растения rasteniya • **plants**

дерево derevo • **tree**

лист
list
leaf

ветка
vetka
branch

кора
kora
bark

веточка
vetochka
twig

ива
iva
willow

корень
koren'
root

ствол
stvol
trunk

дуб dub | **oak**

тополь
topol'
poplar

эвкалипт
evkalipt
eucalyptus

лиственница
listvennitsa
larch

бук
buk
beech

берёза
beryoza
birch

сосна
sosna
pine

кедр
kedr
cedar

ягода
yagoda
berry

клён
klyon
maple

вяз
vyaz
elm

липа
lipa
lime

остролист
ostrolist
holly

пальма
pal'ma
palm

цветущее растение tsvetushchee rasteniye • flowering plant

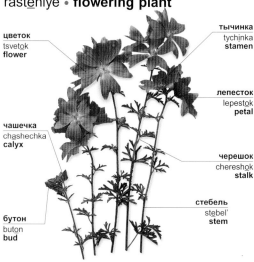

цветок
tsvetok
flower

чашечка
chashechka
calyx

бутон
buton
bud

тычинка
tychinka
stamen

лепесток
lepestok
petal

черешок
chereshok
stalk

стебель
stebel'
stem

лютик
lyutik
buttercup

ромашка
romashka
daisy

чертополох
chertopolokh
thistle

одуванчик
oduvanchik
dandelion

вереск
veresk
heather

мак
mak
poppy

наперстянка
naperstyanka
foxglove

жимолость
zhimolost'
honeysuckle

подсолнух
podsolnukh
sunflower

клевер
klever
clover

колокольчики
kolokol'chiki
bluebells

примула
primula
primrose

люпин
lyupin
lupines

крапива
krapiva
nettle

город gorod • city

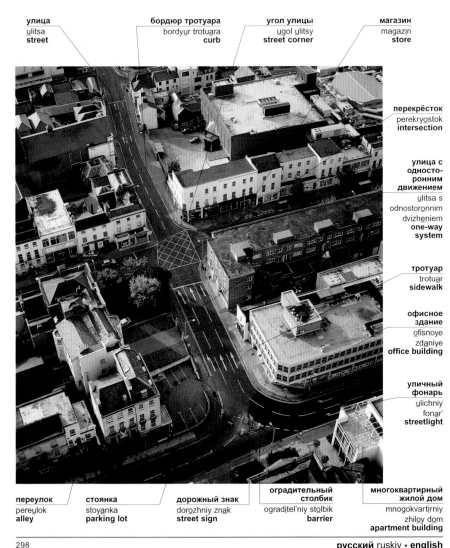

улица
ulitsa
street

бордюр тротуара
bordyur trotuara
curb

угол улицы
ugol ulitsy
street corner

магазин
magazin
store

перекрёсток
perekryostok
intersection

улица с
односто-
ронним
движением
ulitsa s
odnostoronnim
dvizheniem
**one-way
system**

тротуар
trotuar
sidewalk

офисное
здание
ofisnoye
zdaniye
office building

уличный
фонарь
ulichniy
fonar'
streetlight

переулок
pereulok
alley

стоянка
stoyanka
parking lot

дорожный знак
dorozhniy znak
street sign

оградительный
столбик
ograditel'niy stolbik
barrier

многоквартирный
жилой дом
mnogokvartirniy
zhiloy dom
apartment building

здания zd<u>a</u>niya • **buildings**

ратуша
r<u>a</u>tusha
town hall

библиотека
biblio<u>te</u>ka
library

кинотеатр
kinoте<u>a</u>tr
movie theater

театр
те<u>a</u>tr
theater

университет
universi<u>te</u>t
university

небоскрёб
neboskry<u>ob</u>
skyscraper

школа
shk<u>o</u>la
school

районы ray<u>o</u>ny • **areas**

промышленная зона
prom<u>y</u>shlennaya z<u>o</u>na
industrial park

город
g<u>o</u>rod
city

пригород
pr<u>i</u>gorod
suburb

деревня
der<u>e</u>vnya
village

словарь slov<u>a</u>r' • **vocabulary**

пешеходная зона peshekh<u>o</u>dnaya z<u>o</u>na **pedestrian zone**	боковая улица bok<u>o</u>vaya <u>u</u>litsa **side street**	канализационный колодец kanalizats<u>io</u>nniy kol<u>o</u>dets **manhole**	водосточный жёлоб vodost<u>o</u>chniy zh<u>o</u>lob **gutter**	церковь ts<u>e</u>rkov' **church**
проспект prosp<u>e</u>kt **avenue**	площадь pl<u>o</u>shchad' **square**	автобусная остановка avt<u>o</u>busnaya ostan<u>o</u>vka **bus stop**	фабрика f<u>a</u>brika **factory**	водосток vodost<u>o</u>k **drain**

архитектура arkhitektura • architecture

здания и сооружения zdaniya i sooruzheniya • buildings and structures

башенка
bashenka
turret

шпиль
shpil'
spire

фиал
fial
finial

крепостной ров
krepostnoy rov
moat

небоскрёб
neboskryob
skyscraper

замок
zamok
castle

купол
kupol
dome

фронтон
fronton
gable

церковь
tserkov'
church

мечеть
mechet' | **mosque**

башня
bashnya
tower

свод
svod
vault

храм
khram
temple

синагога
sinagoga
synagogue

карниз
karniz
cornice

колонна
kolonna
pillar

плотина
plotina
dam

мост
most
bridge

собор sobor | **cathedral**

стили stili • styles

архитрав
arkhitrav
architrave

барокко
barokko
Baroque

готический
goticheskiy | **Gothic**

Возрождение
vozrozhdeniye
Renaissance

арка
arka
arch

фриз
friz
frieze

хор
khor
choir

рококо
rokoko
Rococo

фронтон
fronton
pediment

контрфорс
kontrfors
buttress

неоклассический стиль
neoklasicheskiy stil'
Neoclassical

ар-нуво
ar-nuvo
Art Nouveau

ар-деко
ar-deko
Art Deco

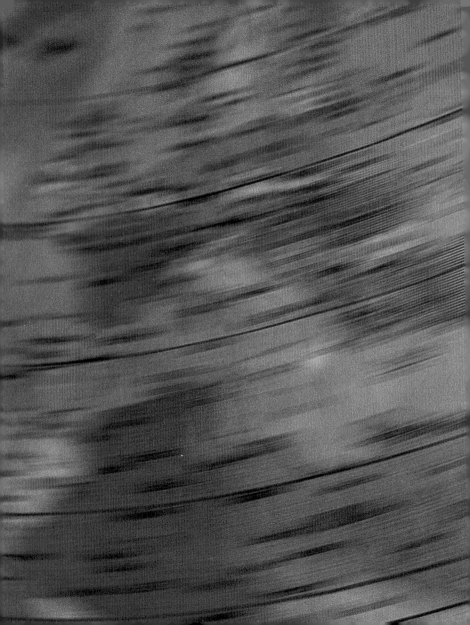

справка spr<u>a</u>vka
reference

время vremya • time

минутная стрелка
minutnaya strelka
minute hand

часовая стрелка
chasovaya strelka
hour hand

часы
chasy
clock

словарь slovar' • vocabulary

секунда sekunda **second**	сейчас seychas **now**	четверть часа chetvert' chasa **a quarter of an hour**
минута minuta **minute**	позже pozhe **later**	двадцать минут dvatsat' minut **twenty minutes**
час chas **hour**	полчаса polchasa **half an hour**	сорок минут sorok minut **forty minutes**

Который час?
kotoriy chas?
What time is it?

Три часа.
Tri chasa
It's three o'clock.

пять минут второго
pyat' minut vtorogo
five past one

десять минут второго
desyat' minut vtorogo
ten past one

четверть второго
chetvert' vtorogo
quarter past one

двадцать минут второго
dvatsat' minut vtorogo
twenty past one

секундная
стрелка
sekundnaya
strelka
second hand

двадцать пять минут
второго
dvatsat' pyat' minut vtorogo
twenty-five past one

половина второго
polovina vtorogo
one thirty

без двадцати пяти два
bez dvatsati pyati dva
twenty-five to two

без двадцати два
bez dvatsati dva
twenty to two

без четверти два
bez chetverti dva
quarter to two

без десяти два
bez desyati dva
ten to two

без пяти два
bez pyati dva
five to two

два часа
dva chasa
two o'clock

день и ночь den' i noch' • night and day

полночь
polnoch' | **midnight**

восход voskhod | **sunrise**

рассвет rassvet | **dawn**

утро utro | **morning**

закат
zakat
sunset

полдень
polden'
noon

сумерки sumerki | **dusk**

вечер vecher | **evening**

день den' | **afternoon**

словарь slovar' • vocabulary

рано
rano
early

вовремя
vovremya
on time

поздно
pozno
late

Вы пришли рано.
vy prishli rano
You're early.

Вы опоздали.
vy opozdali
You're late.

Я скоро буду там.
ya skoro budu tam
I'll be there soon.

Пожалуйста, приходите вовремя.
pozhaluysta, prikhodite vovremya
Please be on time.

Увидимся позже.
uvidimsya pozzhe
I'll see you later.

Во сколько начало?
vo skolko nachalo?
What time does it start?

Когда это заканчивается?
kogda eto zakanchivayetsya?
What time does it end?

Уже поздно.
uzhe pozno
It's getting late.

Сколько это продлится?
skol'ko eto prodlitsya?
How long will it last?

календарь kalend<u>a</u>r' • calendar

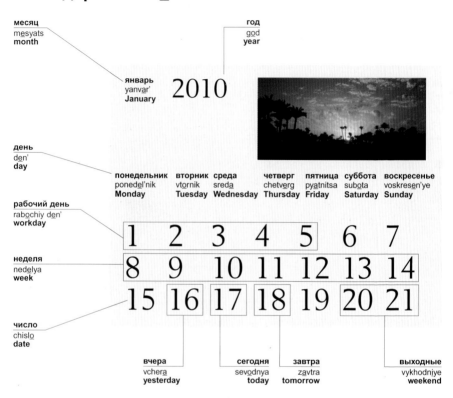

месяц
m<u>e</u>syats
month

год
g<u>o</u>d
year

январь
yanv<u>a</u>r'
January

2010

день
d<u>e</u>n'
day

понедельник	вторник	среда	четверг	пятница	суббота	воскресенье
ponedel'nik	vt<u>o</u>rnik	sr<u>e</u>da	chetv<u>e</u>rg	p<u>ya</u>tnitsa	sub<u>o</u>ta	voskres<u>e</u>n'ye
Monday	**Tuesday**	**Wednesday**	**Thursday**	**Friday**	**Saturday**	**Sunday**

рабочий день
rab<u>o</u>chiy d<u>e</u>n'
workday

| 1 | 2 | 3 | 4 | 5 | 6 | 7 |

неделя
ned<u>e</u>lya
week

| 8 | 9 | 10 | 11 | 12 | 13 | 14 |

| 15 | 16 | 17 | 18 | 19 | 20 | 21 |

число
chisl<u>o</u>
date

вчера
vcher<u>a</u>
yesterday

сегодня
sev<u>o</u>dnya
today

завтра
z<u>a</u>vtra
tomorrow

выходные
vykhodn<u>i</u>ye
weekend

словарь slov<u>a</u>r' • vocabulary

январь	март	май	июль	сентябрь	ноябрь
yanv<u>a</u>r'	m<u>a</u>rt	m<u>a</u>y	iy<u>u</u>l'	sent<u>ya</u>br'	no<u>ya</u>br'
January	**March**	**May**	**July**	**September**	**November**
февраль	апрель	июнь	август	октябрь	декабрь
fevr<u>a</u>l'	apr<u>e</u>l'	iy<u>u</u>n'	<u>a</u>vgust	okt<u>ya</u>br'	dek<u>a</u>br'
February	**April**	**June**	**August**	**October**	**December**

годы go_dy • years

1900 — **тысяча девятисотый год** tysyacha devyatiso_tiy god • **nineteen hundred**

1901 — **тысяча девятьсот первый год** tysyacha devyat'so_t pe_rviy god • **nineteen hundred and one**

1910 — **тысяча девятьсот десятый год** tysyacha devyat'so_t desya_tiy god • **nineteen ten**

2000 — **двухтысячный год** dvukhty_syachniy god • **two thousand**

2001 — **две тысячи первый год** dve_tysya_chi pe_rviy god • **two thousand and one**

времена года vremen_a go_da • seasons

весна
vesn_a
spring

лето
le_to
summer

осень
o_sen'
fall

зима
zim_a
winter

словарь slovar' • vocabulary

век; столетие
ve_k; stole_tiye
century

десятилетие
desyatile_tiye
decade

тысячелетие
tysyachele_tiye
millennium

две недели
dve_ nede_li
two weeks

на этой неделе
na e_toy nede_le
this week

на прошлой неделе
na pro_shloy nede_le
last week

на следующей неделе
na sle_duyushchey nede_le
next week

позавчера
pozavchera_
the day before yesterday

послезавтра
poslezavtra
the day after tomorrow

еженедельно
yezhenede_l'no
weekly

ежемесячно
yezheme_syachno
monthly

ежегодно
yezhego_dno
annual

Какое сегодня число?
kako_ye sevo_dnya chislo_?
What's the date today?

сегодня седьмое февраля, две тысячи семнадцатого года.
segodnya sed'mo_ye fevralya_, dve_ tysyachi semn_atsatogo go_da
It's February seventh, two thousand and seventeen.

числа chisla • **numbers**

0	ноль nol' • **zero**	20	двадцать dvatsat' • **twenty**
1	один odin • **one**	21	двадцать один dvatsat' odin • **twenty-one**
2	два dva • **two**	22	двадцать два dvatsat' dva • **twenty-two**
3	три tri • **three**	30	тридцать tritsat' • **thirty**
4	четыре chetyre • **four**	40	сорок sorok • **forty**
5	пять pyat' • **five**	50	пятьдесят pyat'desyat • **fifty**
6	шесть shest' • **six**	60	шестьдесят shest'desyat • **sixty**
7	семь sem' • **seven**	70	семьдесят sem'desyat • **seventy**
8	восемь vosem' • **eight**	80	восемьдесят vosem'desyat • **eighty**
9	девять devyat' • **nine**	90	девяносто devyanosto • **ninety**
10	десять desyat' • **ten**	100	сто sto • **one hundred**
11	одиннадцать odinatsat' • **eleven**	110	сто десять sto desyat' • **one hundred and ten**
12	двенадцать dvenatsat' • **twelve**	200	двести dvesti • **two hundred**
13	тринадцать trinatsat' • **thirteen**	300	триста trista • **three hundred**
14	четырнадцать chetyrnatsat' • **fourteen**	400	четыреста chetyresta • **four hundred**
15	пятнадцать pyatnatsat' • **fifteen**	500	пятьсот pyat'sot • **five hundred**
16	шестнадцать shesnatsat' • **sixteen**	600	шестьсот shest'sot • **six hundred**
17	семнадцать semnatsat' • **seventeen**	700	семьсот sem'sot • **seven hundred**
18	восемнадцать vosemnatsat' • **eighteen**	800	восемьсот vosem'sot • **eight hundred**
19	девятнадцать devyatnatsat' • **nineteen**	900	девятьсот devyat'sot • **nine hundred**

русский ruskiy • **english**

1,000	(одна) тысяча (odna) tysyacha • **one thousand**
10,000	десять тысяч desyat' tysyach • **ten thousand**
20,000	двадцать тысяч dvatsat' tysyach • **twenty thousand**
50,000	пятьдесят тысяч pyat'desyat tysyach • **fifty thousand**
55,500	пятьдесят пять тысяч пятьсот pyat'desyat pyat' tysyach pyat'sot • **fifty-five thousand five hundred**
100,000	сто тысяч sto tysyach • **one hundred thousand**
1,000,000	(один) миллион (odin) milion • **one million**
1,000,000,000	(один) миллиард (odin) miliard • **one billion**

первый perviy • **first**

второй vtoroy • **second**

третий tretiy • **third**

четвёртый chetvyortiy • **fourth**

пятый pyatiy • **fifth**

шестой shestoy • **sixth**

седьмой sed'moy • **seventh**

восьмой vos'moy • **eighth**

девятый devyatiy • **ninth**

десятый desyatiy • **tenth**

одиннадцатый odinatsatiy • **eleventh**

двенадцатый dvenatsatiy • **twelfth**

тринадцатый trinatsatiy • **thirteenth**

четырнадцатый chetyrnatsatiy • **fourteenth**

пятнадцатый pyatnatsatiy • **fifteenth**

шестнадцатый shestnatsatiy • **sixteenth**

семнадцатый semnatsatiy • **seventeenth**

восемнадцатый vosemnatsatiy • **eighteenth**

девятнадцатый devyatnatsatiy • **nineteenth**

двадцатый dvatsatiy • **twentieth**

двадцать первый dvatsat' perviy • **twenty-first**

двадцать второй dvatsat' vtoroy • **twenty-second**

двадцать третий dvatsat' tretiy • **twenty-third**

тридцатый tritsatiy • **thirtieth**

сороковой sorokovoy • **fortieth**

пятидесятый pyatidesyatiy • **fiftieth**

шестидесятый shestidesyatiy • **sixtieth**

семидесятый semidesyatiy • **seventieth**

восьмидесятый vos'midesyatiy • **eightieth**

девяностый devyanostiy • **ninetieth**

сотый sotiy • **(one) hundredth**

меры и веса m<u>e</u>ry i ves<u>a</u> • **weights and measures**

площадь
pl<u>o</u>shchad' • **area**

квадратный фут	**квадратный метр**
kvadr<u>a</u>tniy fut	kvadr<u>a</u>tniy m<u>e</u>tr
square foot	**square meter**

расстояние
rasstoy<u>a</u>niye • **distance**

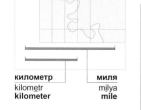

километр	**миля**
kil<u>o</u>metr	m<u>i</u>lya
kilometer	**mile**

чаша весов
ch<u>a</u>sha ves<u>o</u>v
pan

фунт
f<u>u</u>nt
pound

унция
<u>u</u>ntsiya
ounce

килограмм
kil<u>o</u>gr<u>a</u>m
kilogram

грамм
gr<u>a</u>m
gram

весы vesy | **scale**

словарь slov<u>a</u>r' • **vocabulary**

ярд	тонна	измерять
yard	t<u>o</u>nna	izmery<u>a</u>t'
yard	**ton**	**measure (v)**
метр	миллиграмм	взвешивать
m<u>e</u>tr	millig<u>a</u>m	vzv<u>e</u>shivat'
meter	**milligram**	**weigh (v)**

длина dlin<u>a</u> • **length**

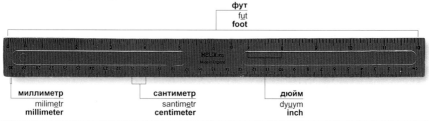

фут
f<u>u</u>t
foot

миллиметр
milim<u>e</u>tr
millimeter

сантиметр
santim<u>e</u>tr
centimeter

дюйм
dy<u>uy</u>m
inch

ёмкость yomkost' • capacity

пол-литра
pol-litra
half-liter

пинта
pinta
pint

объём
ob-yom
volume

миллилитр
mililitr
milliliter

мерная кружка mernaya kruzhka
measuring cup

мера жидкостей mera zhidkostey
liquid measure

контейнер konteyner • container

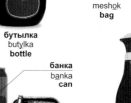

мешок
meshok
bag

картонная упаковка
kartonnaya upakovka
carton

пакет
paket
packet

бутылка
butylka
bottle

банка
banka
can

пластиковая коробка
plastikovaya korobka
tub

банка banka | **jar**

банка banka | **tin**

распылитель
raspylitel' | **spray bottle**

кусок
kusok
bar

тюбик
tyubik
tube

рулон
rulon
roll

пачка
pachka
pack

аэрозольный баллончик
aerozol'niy balonchik
spray can

карта мира karta mira · **world map**

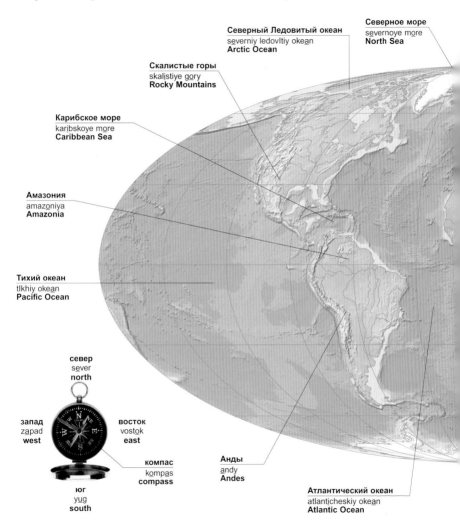

Северный Ледовитый океан
severniy ledovltiy okean
Arctic Ocean

Северное море
severnoye more
North Sea

Скалистые горы
skalistiye gory
Rocky Mountains

Карибское море
karibskoye more
Caribbean Sea

Амазония
amazoniya
Amazonia

Тихий океан
tlkhiy okean
Pacific Ocean

север
sever
north

запад
zapad
west

восток
vostok
east

компас
kompas
compass

Анды
andy
Andes

юг
yug
south

Атлантический океан
atlanticheskiy okean
Atlantic Ocean

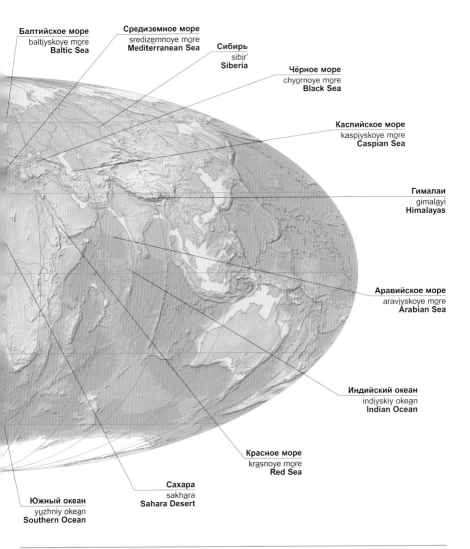

Балтийское море
baltiyskoye more
Baltic Sea

Средиземное море
sredizemnoye more
Mediterranean Sea

Сибирь
sibir'
Siberia

Чёрное море
chyornoye more
Black Sea

Каспийское море
kaspiyskoye more
Caspian Sea

Гималаи
gimalayi
Himalayas

Аравийское море
araviyskoye more
Arabian Sea

Индийский океан
indiyskiy okean
Indian Ocean

Красное море
krasnoye more
Red Sea

Сахара
sakhara
Sahara Desert

Южный океан
yuzhniy okean
Southern Ocean

Северная и Центральная Америка severnaya i tsentral'naya amerika • North and Central America

Барбадос barbados • **Barbados**

Канада kanada • **Canada**

Коста-Рика kosta-rika • **Costa Rica**

Куба kuba • **Cuba**

Ямайка yamayka • **Jamaica**

Мексика meksika • **Mexico**

Панама panama • **Panama**

Тринидад и Тобаго trinidad i tobago • **Trinidad and Tobago**

Соединённые Штаты Америки soyedinyonniye shtaty ameriki • **United States of America**

Аляска alyaska • **Alaska**

Антигуа и Барбуда antigua i barbuda • **Antigua and Barbuda**

Багамы bagamy • **Bahamas**

Барбадос barbados • **Barbados**

Белиз beliz • **Belize**

Канада kanada • **Canada**

Коста-Рика kosta-rika • **Costa Rica**

Куба kuba • **Cuba**

Доминика dominika • **Dominica**

Доминиканская Республика dominikanskaya respublika • **Dominican Republic**

Эль-Сальвадор el'-sal'vador • **El Salvador**

Гренландия grenlandiya • **Greenland**

Гренада grenada • **Grenada**

Гватемала gvatemala • **Guatemala**

Гаити gaiti • **Haiti**

Гавайи gavayi • **Hawaii**

Гондурас gonduras • **Honduras**

Ямайка yamayka • **Jamaica**

Мексика meksika • **Mexico**

Никарагуа nikaragua • **Nicaragua**

Панама panama • **Panama**

Пуэрто-Рико puerto-riko • **Puerto Rico**

Сент-Китс и Невис sent-kits i nevis • **St. Kitts and Nevis**

Сент-Люсия sent-lyusiya • **St. Lucia**

Сент-Винсент и Гренадины sent-vinsent i grenadiny • **St. Vincent and The Grenadines**

Тринидад и Тобаго trinidad i tobago • **Trinidad and Tobago**

Соединённые Штаты Америки soyedinyonniye shtaty ameriki • **United States of America**

Южная Америка yuzhnaya amerika • **South America**

Аргентина argentina •
Argentina

Боливия boliviya • **Bolivia**

Бразилия braziliya •
Brazil

Чили chili • **Chile**

Колумбия kolumbiya •
Colombia

Эквадор ekvador •
Ecuador

Перу peru • **Peru**

Уругвай urugvay •
Uruguay

Венесуэла venesuela •
Venezuela

Аргентина argentina •
Argentina

Боливия boliviya • **Bolivia**

Бразилия braziliya • **Brazil**

Чили chili • **Chile**

Колумбия kolumbiya •
Colombia

Эквадор ekvador • **Ecuador**

Фолклендские острова
folklendskiye ostrova •
Falkland Islands

Французская Гвиана
frantsuzskaya gviana •
French Guiana

Галапагосские острова
galapagosskiye ostrova •
Galápagos Islands

Гайана gayana • **Guyana**

Парагвай paragvay • **Paraguay**

Перу peru • **Peru**

Суринам surinam • **Suriname**

Уругвай urugvay • **Uruguay**

Венесуэла venesuela •
Venezuela

словарь slovar' • vocabulary		
страна strana **country**	**территория** teritoriya **territory**	**регион** region **region**
нация natsiya **nation**	**колония** koloniya **colony**	**столица** stolitsa **capital**
континент continent **continent**	**княжество** knyazhestvo **principality**	
государство gosudarstvo **state**	**зона** zona **zone**	
провинция provintsiya **province**	**район** rayon **district**	

Европа yevropa · Europe

Франция frantsiya · **France**

Германия germaniya · **Germany**

Италия italiya · **Italy**

Польша pol'sha · **Poland**

Португалия portugaliya · **Portugal**

Испания ispaniya · **Spain**

Албания albaniya · **Albania**

Андорра andorra · **Andorra**

Австрия avstriya · **Austria**

Балеарские острова balearskiye ostrova · **Balearic Islands**

Беларусь belarus' · **Belarus**

Бельгия bel'giya · **Belgium**

Босния и Герцеговина bosniya i gertsegovina · **Bosnia and Herzegovina**

Болгария bolgariya · **Bulgaria**

Корсика korsika · **Corsica**

Хорватия khorvatiya · **Croatia**

Чехия chekhiya · **Czech Republic**

Дания daniya · **Denmark**

Эстония estoniya · **Estonia**

Финляндия finlyandiya · **Finland**

Франция frantsiya · **France**

Германия germaniya · **Germany**

Греция gretsiya · **Greece**

Венгрия vengriya · **Hungary**

Исландия islandiya · **Iceland**

Ирландия irlandiya · **Ireland**

Италия italiya · **Italy**

Калининград kaliningrad · **Kaliningrad**

Косово kosovo · **Kosovo**

Латвия latviya · **Latvia**

Лихтенштейн likhtenshteyn · **Liechtenstein**

Литва litva · **Lithuania**

Люксембург lyuksemburg · **Luxembourg**

Македония makedoniya · **Macedonia**

Мальта mal'ta · **Malta**

Молдова moldova · **Moldova**

Монако monako · **Monaco**

Черногория chernogoriya · **Montenegro**

Нидерланды niderlandy · **Netherlands**

Норвегия norvegiya · **Norway**

Польша pol'sha · **Poland**

Португалия portugaliya · **Portugal**

Румыния rumyniya · **Romania**

Российская Федерация rosiyskaya federatsiya · **Russian Federation**

Сан-Марино san-marino · **San Marino**

Сардиния sardiniya · **Sardinia**

Сербия serbiya · **Serbia**

Сицилия sitsiliya · **Sicily**

Словакия slovakiya · **Slovakia**

Словения sloveniya · **Slovenia**

Испания ispaniya · **Spain**

Швеция shvetsiya · **Sweden**

Швейцария shveytsariya · **Switzerland**

Украина ukraina · **Ukraine**

Великобритания velikobritaniya · **United Kingdom**

Ватикан vatikan · **Vatican City**

Африка afrika · **Africa**

Египет yegipet · **Egypt**

Эфиопия efiopiya · **Ethiopia**

Кения keniya · **Kenya**

Нигерия nigeriya · **Nigeria**

Южно-Африканская Республика yuzhno-afrikanskaya respublika · **South Africa**

Уганда uganda · **Uganda**

Алжир alzhir · **Algeria**

Ангола angola · **Angola**

Бенин benin · **Benin**

Ботсвана botsvana · **Botswana**

Буркина-Фасо burkina faso · **Burkina Faso**

Бурунди burundi · **Burundi**

Кабинда kabinda · **Cabinda**

Камерун kamerun · **Cameroon**

Центральноафриканская Республика tsentral'noafrikanskaya respublika · **Central African Republic**

Чад chad · **Chad**

Коморы komory · **Comoros**

Конго kongo · **Congo**

Демократическая Республика Конго demokraticheskaya respublika kongo · **Democratic Republic of the Congo**

Джибути dzhibuti · **Djibouti**

Египет yegipet · **Egypt**

Экваториальная Гвинея ekvatorial'naya gvineya · **Equatorial Guinea**

Эритрея eritreya · **Eritrea**

Эфиопия efiopiya · **Ethiopia**

Габон gabon · **Gabon**

Гамбия gambiya · **Gambia**

Гана gana · **Ghana**

Гвинея gvineya · **Guinea**

Гвинея-Бисау gvineya-bisau · **Guinea-Bissau**

Кот-д'Ивуар kot-d-ivuar · **Ivory Coast**

Кения keniya · **Kenya**

Лесото lesoto · **Lesotho**

Либерия liberiya · **Liberia**

Ливия liviya · **Libya**

Мадагаскар madagaskar · **Madagascar**

Малави malavi · **Malawi**

Мали mali · **Mali**

Мавритания mavritaniya · **Mauritania**

Маврикий mavrikiy · **Mauritius**

Марокко marokko · **Morocco**

Мозамбик mozambik · **Mozambique**

Намибия namibiya · **Namibia**

Нигер niger · **Niger**

Нигерия nigeriya · **Nigeria**

Руанда ruanda · **Rwanda**

Сан-Томе и Принсипи san-tome i prinsipi · **São Tomé and Principe**

Сенегал senegal · **Senegal**

Сьерра-Леоне s'yerra-leone · **Sierra Leone**

Сомали somali · **Somalia**

Южно-Африканская Республика yuzhno-afrikanskaya respublika · **South Africa**

Южный Судан yuzhniy sudan · **South Sudan**

Судан sudan · **Sudan**

Свазиленд svazilend · **Swaziland**

Танзания tanzaniya · **Tanzania**

Того togo · **Togo**

Тунис tunis · **Tunisia**

Уганда uganda · **Uganda**

Западная Сахара zapadnaya sakhara · **Western Sahara**

Замбия zambiya · **Zambia**

Зимбабве zimbabve · **Zimbabwe**

Азия aziya · Asia

Бангладеш bangladesh · **Bangladesh**

Китай kitay · **China**

Индия indiya · **India**

Япония yaponiya · **Japan**

Иордания iordaniya · **Jordan**

Филиппины filipiny · **Philippines**

Южная Корея yuzhnaya koreya · **South Korea**

Таиланд tailand · **Thailand**

Турция turtsiya · **Turkey**

Афганистан afganistan · **Afghanistan**

Армения armeniya · **Armenia**

Азербайджан azerbaydzhan · **Azerbaijan**

Бахрейн bakhreyn · **Bahrain**

Бангладеш bangladesh · **Bangladesh**

Бутан butan · **Bhutan**

Бруней bruney · **Brunei**

Камбоджа kambodzha · **Cambodia**

Китай kitay · **China**

Кипр kipr · **Cyprus**

Восточный Тимор vostochniy timor · **East Timor**

Фиджи fidzhi · **Fiji**

Грузия gruziya · **Georgia**

Индия indiya · **India**

Индонезия indoneziya · **Indonesia**

Иран iran · **Iran**

Ирак irak · **Iraq**

Израиль izrail' · **Israel**

Япония yaponiya · **Japan**

Иордания iordaniya · **Jordan**

Казахстан kazakhstan · **Kazakhstan**

Кувейт kuveyt · **Kuwait**

Киргизия kirgizia · **Kyrgyzstan**

Лаос laos · **Laos**

Ливан livan · **Lebanon**

Малайзия malayziya · **Malaysia**

Мальдивы mal'divy · **Maldives**

Монголия mongoliya · **Mongolia**

Мьянма (Бирма) m'yanma (birma) · **Myanmar (Burma)**

Непал nepal · **Nepal**

Северная Корея severnaya koreya · **North Korea**

Оман oman · **Oman**

Пакистан pakistan · **Pakistan**

Папуа - Новая Гвинея papua novaya gvineya · **Papua New Guinea**

Филиппины filipiny · **Philippines**

Катар katar · **Qatar**

Саудовская Аравия saudovskaya araviya · **Saudi Arabia**

Сингапур singapur · **Singapore**

Соломоновы Острова solomonovy ostrova · **Solomon Islands**

Южная Корея yuzhnaya koreya · **South Korea**

Шри-Ланка shri-lanka · **Sri Lanka**

Индонезия indon<u>e</u>ziya ·
Indonesia

Саудовская Аравия s<u>au</u>dovskaya ar<u>a</u>viya · **Saudi Arabia**

Вьетнам v'yetn<u>a</u>m · **Vietnam**

Сирия s<u>i</u>riya · **Syria**

Таджикистан tadzhikist<u>a</u>n · **Tajikistan**

Таиланд tail<u>a</u>nd · **Thailand**

Турция t<u>u</u>rtsiya · **Turkey**

Туркменистан turkmenist<u>a</u>n · **Turkmenistan**

Объединённые Арабские Эмираты ob-yedin<u>yo</u>nniye ar<u>a</u>bskiye emir<u>a</u>ty · **United Arab Emirates**

Узбекистан uzbekist<u>a</u>n · **Uzbekistan**

Вануату vanu<u>a</u>tu · **Vanuatu**

Вьетнам v'yetn<u>a</u>m · **Vietnam**

Йемен y<u>e</u>men · **Yemen**

Австралазия avstral<u>a</u>ziya · Australasia

Австралия avstr<u>a</u>liya · **Australia**

Новая Зеландия n<u>o</u>vaya zel<u>a</u>ndiya · **New Zealand**

Австралия avstr<u>a</u>liya · **Australia**

Новая Зеландия n<u>o</u>vaya zel<u>a</u>ndiya · **New Zealand**

Тасмания tasm<u>a</u>niya · **Tasmania**

частицы и антонимы chastitsy i antonimi •
particles and antonyms

к k **to**	**от** ot **from**	**для** dlya **for**	**на** na **toward**
над nad **over**	**под** pod **under**	**вдоль** vdol' **along**	**поперёк, через** poperyok, cherez **across**
впереди, перед vperedi, pered **in front of**	**позади, сзади** pozadi, zzadi **behind**	**с** s **with**	**без** bez **without**
на (поверхность) na (poverkhnost') **onto**	**в** v; vnutr' **into**	**перед** pered **before**	**после** posle **after**
в v **in**	**из** iz **out**	**к** k **by**	**до** do **until**
над, (с)выше nad, (s)vyshe **above**	**под** pod **below**	**рано** rano **early**	**поздно** pozdno **late**
внутри vnutri **inside**	**снаружи** snaruzhi **outside**	**сейчас** seychas **now**	**позже** pozhe **later**
вверх vverkh **up**	**вниз** vniz **down**	**всегда** vsegda **always**	**никогда** nikogda **never**
у, около u, okolo **at**	**за** za **beyond**	**часто** chasto **often**	**редко** redko **rarely**
сквозь, через skvoz', cherez **through**	**вокруг** vokrug **around**	**вчера** vchera **yesterday**	**завтра** zavtra **tomorrow**
наверху naverkhu **on top of**	**рядом с** ryadom s **beside**	**сначала** snachala **first**	**в последнюю очередь** v poslednyuyu ochered' **last**
между mezhdu **between**	**напротив** naprotiv **opposite**	**каждый** kazhdiy **every**	**некоторый, несколько** nekotoriy, neskolki **some**
близко blizko **near**	**далеко** daleko **far**	**около** okolo **about**	**точно** tochno **exactly**
здесь zdes' **here**	**там** tam **there**	**немного** nemnogo **a little**	**много** mnogo **a lot**

большой
bol'shoy
large

маленький
malen'kiy
small

горячий
goryachiy
hot

холодный
kholodniy
cold

широкий
shirokiy
wide

узкий
uzkiy
narrow

открытый
otkrytiy
open

закрытый
zakrytiy
closed

высокийа
vysokiy
tall

короткий
korotkiy
short

полный
polniy
full

пустой
pustoy
empty

высокий
vysokiy
high

низкий
nizkiy
low

новый
noviy
new

старый
stariy
old

густой
gustoy
thick

тонкий
tonkiy
thin

светлый
svetliy
light

тёмный
tyomniy
dark

лёгкий
lyohkiy
light

тяжёлый
tyazholiy
heavy

простой
prostoy
easy

сложный
slozhniy
difficult

твёрдый
tvyordiy
hard

мягкий
myahkiy
soft

свободный
svobodniy
free

занятый
zanyatiy
occupied

мокрый
mokriy
wet

сухой
sukhoy
dry

сильный
sil'niy
strong

слабый
slabiy
weak

хороший
khoroshiy
good

плохой
plokhoy
bad

толстый
tolstiy
fat

худой
khudoy
thin

быстрый
bystriy
fast

медленный
medlenniy
slow

молодой
molodoy
young

старый
stariy
old

правильный
pravil'niy
correct

неправильный
nepravil'niy
wrong

лучше
luchshe
better

хуже
khuzhe
worse

чистый
chistiy
clean

грязный
gryazniy
dirty

чёрный
chyorniy
black

белый
beliy
white

красивый
krasiviy
beautiful

уродливый
urodliviy
ugly

интересный
interesniy
interesting

скучный
skuchniy
boring

дорогой
dorogoy
expensive

дешёвый
deshyoviy
cheap

больной
bol'noy
sick

здоровый
zdoroviy
well

тихий
tikhiy
quiet

шумный
shumniy
noisy

начало
nachalo
beginning

конец
konets
end

полезные фразы polezniye frazy · useful phrases

**необходимые
фразы**
neobkhodimiye frazy ·
essential phrases

Да
da
Yes

Нет
net
No

Возможно
vozmozhno
Maybe

Пожалуйста
pozhaluysta
Please

Спасибо
spasibo
Thank you

Пожалуйста
pozhaluysta
You're welcome

Простите
prostite
Excuse me

Мне очень жаль!
mnye ochen' zhal
I'm sorry

Не надо
ne nado
Don't

OK, хорошо
okey, khorosho
OK

Хорошо
khorosho
That's fine

**(Это) верно/
правильно**
(eto) verno/ pravil'no
That's correct

**Вы ошибаетесь/
Это не так**
vy oshibayetes'/ eto
ne tak
That's wrong

приветствия
privetstviya · **greetings**

Здравствуйте
zdrastvuyte
Hello

До свидания
do svidaniya
Goodbye

Доброе утро
dobroye utro
Good morning

Добрый день
dobriy den'
Good afternoon

Добрый вечер
dobriy vecher
Good evening

Спокойной ночи
spokoynoy nochi
Good night

Как дела?
kak dela?
How are you?

Меня зовут…
menya zovut…
My name is …

Как Вас/тебя зовут?
kak vas/tebya zovut?
**What is your
name?**

Как его/её зовут?
kak yego/yeyo zovut?
**What is his/her
name?**

**Разрешите
представить …?**
razhreshite predstavit'
May I introduce …

Это…
eto…
This is …

**Приятно
познакомиться**
priyatno poznakomit'sya
Pleased to meet you

увидимся
uvidimsya
See you later

объявления
ob-yavleniya ·
signs

Туристическое бюро
turisticheskoye byuro
Tourist information

Вход
vkhod
Entrance

Выход
vykhod
Exit

**Запасной/ аварийный
выход**
zapasnoy/ avariyniy
vykhod
Emergency exit

От себя
ot sebya
Push

Опасность
opasnost'
Danger

Не курить!
ne kurit'
No smoking

Не работает
ne rabotayet
Out of order

Часы работы
chasy raboty
Opening times

Вход бесплатный
vkhod besplatniy
Free dmission

Сниженная цена
snizhennaya tsena
Reduced

Распродажа
rasprodazha
Sale

Без стука не входить
bez stuka ne vkhodit'
Knock before entering

По газонам не ходить
po gazonam ne khodit'
Keep off the grass

помощь
pomoshch' · **help**

**Не могли бы
Вы мне помочь?**
ne mogli by
vy mne pomoch'?
Can you help me?

(Я) не понимаю
(ya) ne ponimayu
I don't understand

(Я) не знаю
(ya) ne znayu
I don't know

по-английски
ya govoryu po-angliyski
I speak English

**Вы говорите
по-английски**
vy govorite po-angliyski?
Do you speak English?

**Пожалуйста, говорите
помедленней**
pozhaluysta, govorite
pomedlenney
Please speak more slowly

**Пожалуйста, запишите
мне это**
pozhaluysta, zapishite mne eto
**Please write it down
for me**

Я потерял...
ya poteryal...
I have lost ...

направление
napravleniya ·
directions

Я заблудился
ya zabludilsya
I am lost

Где (находится)...?
gde (nakhoditsya)...?
Where is the ...?

Где ближайший/
ближайшее/
ближайшая ...?
gde blizhayshiy/
blizhayshee/
blizhayshaya ...?
**Where is the
nearest ...?**

Где (находятся)
туалеты?
gde (nakhodyatsya)
tualety?
**Where is the
restroom?**

Как добраться до...?
kak dobrat'sya do...?
How do I get to ...?

Направо
napravo
To the right

Налево
nalevo
To the left

Прямо
pryamo
Straight ahead

Далеко ли до ...?
daleko li do ...?
How far is ...?

**дорожные знаки
и указатели**
dorozhniye znaki i
ukazateli · **road signs**

Внимание
vnimaniye
Caution

Въезд запрещён
v-yezd zapreshchyon
Do not enter

Снизь(те) скорость
sniz'(te) skorost'
Slow down

Объезд
ob-yezd
Detour

Держитесь правой
стороны
derzhites' pravoy storony
Keep right

автострада
avtostrada
Freeway

Парковка запрещена
parkovka zapreshchena
No parking

Тупик
tupik
Dead end

Дорога с
односторонним
движением
doroga s odnostoronnim
dvizheniyem
One-way street

Уступи дорогу
ustupi dorogu
Yield

Только для жителей
tol'ko dlya zhiteley
Residents only

Дорожные работы
dorozhniye raboty
Roadwork

Опасный поворот
opasniy povorot
Dangerous curve

Ночлег
nochleg ·
accommodation

У меня заказан номер
u menya zakazan nomer
I have a reservation
Где находится
столовая?
gde nakhoditsya stolovaya?
**Where is the dining
room?**

В какое время/когда
завтрак?
v kakoye vremya/kogda
zavtrak?
What time is breakfast?

Я вернусь в ... часов
ya vernus' v ... chasov
I'll be back at ... o'clock

Я уезжаю завтра
ya uyezhayu zavtra
I'm leaving tomorrow

приём пищи priyom
pishchi · **eating
and drinking**

Твоё здоровье!
tvoyo zdorov'ye!
Cheers!

Это очень вкусно/не
очень вкусно
eto ochen vkusno/ne
ochen vkusno
It's delicious/awful

Я не курю/пью
ya ne kuryu/p'yu
I don't drink/smoke

Я не ем мясо
ya ne yem myaso
I don't eat meat

Спасибо, для меня
достаточно
spasibo, dlya menya
dostatochno
**No more for me,
thank you**

Можно мне ещё
немного?
mozhno mne yeshchyo
nemnogo?
May I have some more?
Можно счёт?

mozhno schyot?
**May we have
the check?**
Можно чек?
mozhno chek?
Can I have a receipt?

Место для курения
mesto dlya kureniya
Smoking area

здоровье
zdorov'ye · **health**

Мне нехорошо
mne nekhorosho
I don't feel well

Меня тошнит
menya toshnit
I feel sick

Здесь больно/болит
zdes' bol'no/bolit
It hurts here

У меня температура
u menya temperatura
I have a fever

Я на ... месяце
беременности
ya na ... mesyatse
beremennosti
I'm ... months pregnant

Мне нужен рецепт
на...
mne nuzhen retsept na...
**I need a prescription
for ...**

Обычно я
принимаю...
obychno ya prinimayu...
I normally take ...

У меня аллергия
на...
u menya alergiya na...
I'm allergic to ...

Он/она будет в
порядке?
on/ona budet v
poryadke?
**Will he/she be
all right?**

русский указатель ruskiy ukazatel' • **Russian index**

ruskiy

РУССКИЙ УКАЗАТЕЛЬ RUSKIY UKAZATEL' • RUSSIAN INDEX

ruskiy

ruskiy

ruskiy

ruskiy

английский указатель angliyskiy ukazatel' • English index

english

english

english

english

english

english

groom 243
ground 60, 132
ground coffee 144
ground meat 119
ground cover 87
ground floor 104
ground sheet 267
group therapy 55
grout 83
guard 236
guardrail 195
Guatemala 314
guava 128
guest 64, 100
guidebook 260
guided tour 260
guilty 181
Guinea 317
Guinea-Bissau 317
guitarist 258
gull 292
gum 50
gumdrop 113
gun 94
gurney 48
gutter 58, 299
guy rope 266
Guyana 315
gym 101, 250
gym machine 250
gymnast 235
gymnastics 235
gynecologist 52
gynecology 49
gypsophila 110

H

hacksaw 81
haddock 120
hemorrhage 46
hail 286
hair 14, 38
hair dye 40
hair straightener 38
hairdresser 38, 188
hairspray 38
Haiti 314
half an hour 304
half-and-half 137
half-liter 311
halftime 223
halibut fillets 120
Halloween 27
halter 243
halter neck 35
ham 119, 143, 156
hammer 80
hammer v 79
hammock 266
hamper 263
hamster 290
hamstring 16
hand 13, 15
hand drill 81

hand fork 89
hand rail 59, 196
hand towel 73
handbag 37
handcuffs 94
handicap 233
handkerchief 36
handle 36, 88, 106, 187, 200, 230
handlebar 207
handles 37
handsaw 81, 89
handset 99
hang v 82
hang-glider 248
hang-gliding 248
hanging basket 84
hanging file 173
happy 25
harbor 217
harbor master 217
hard 129, 321
hard candy 113
hard cheese 136
hard cider 145
hard hat 186
hardboard 79
hardware 176
hardware store 114
hardwood 79
haricot beans 131
harness race 243
harp 256
harvest v 91, 183
hat 36
hatchback 199, 200
have a baby v 26
Hawaii 314
hay 184
hay fever 44
hazard 195
hazard lights 201
hazelnut 129
hazelnut oil 134
head 12, 19, 81, 230
head v 222
head injury 46
head office 175
headache 44
headband 39
headboard 70
headlight 198, 205, 207
headphones 268
headrest 200
headsail 240
health 44
health center 168
health food store 115
heart 18, 119, 122, 273
heart attack 44
heater controls 201
heather 297
heating element 61

heavy 321
heavy cream 137
heavy metal 259
hedge 85, 90, 182
hedgehog 290
heel 13, 15, 37
height 165
helicopter 211
hello 322
helmet 95, 204, 206, 220, 224, 228
help desk 168
hem 34
hematite 289
hen's egg 137
herb 55, 86
herb garden 84
herbaceous border 85
herbal remedies 108
herbal tea 149
herbalism 55
herbicide 183
herbs 133, 134
herbs and spices 132
herd 183
hexagon 164
high 321
high chair 75
high-definition 269
high dive 239
high-heeled shoe 37
high jump 235
high speed train 208
highlights 39
hiking 263
hiking boot 37, 267
hill 284
Himalayas 313
hip 12
hippopotamus 291
historic building 261
history 162
hit v 224
hob 67
hockey 224
hockey stick 224
hoe 88
hold 215, 237
hole 232
hole in one 233
hole punch 173
holly 296
home 58
home delivery 154
home entertainment 268
home furnishings 105
home plate 228
homeopathy 55
homework 163
homogenized 137
Honduras 314
honeycomb 135
honeymoon 26

honeysuckle 297
hood 31, 75, 198
hoof 242, 291
hook 187, 276
hoop 226, 277
horizontal bar 235
hormone 20
horn 201, 204, 291
horror movie 255
horse 185, 235, 242
horse race 243
horseback riding 242, 263
horseradish 125
horseshoe 242
hose 89, 95
hose reel 89
hosepipe 89
hospital 48
host 64, 178
hostess 64
hot 124, 286, 321
hot-air balloon 211
hot chocolate 144, 156
hot dog 155
hot drinks 144
hot faucet 72
hot-water bottle 70
hotel 100, 264
hour 304
hour hand 304
house 58
household current 60
household products 107
hovercraft 215
hub 206
hubcap 202
hull 214, 240
human resources department 175
humerus 17
humid 286
hummingbird 292
hump 291
hundred 308
hundred and ten 308
hundred thousand 308
hundredth 309
Hungary 316
hungry 64
hurdles 235
hurricane 287
husband 22
husk 130
hydrant 95
hydrofoil 215
hydrotherapy 55
hypnotherapy 55
hypoallergenic 41
hypotenuse 164

I

ice 120, 287
ice and lemon 151
ice bucket 150
ice climbing 247
ice cream 137, 149
ice-cream scoop 68
ice cube 151
ice hockey 224
ice hockey player 224
ice hockey rink 224
ice maker 67
ice skate 224
ice-skating 247
iced coffee 148
iced tea 149
Iceland 316
icicle 287
icon 177
identity tag 53
igneous 288
ignition 200
iguana 293
illness 44
immigration 212
impotent 20
in 320
in brine 143
in front of 320
in oil 143
in sauce 159
in syrup 159
inbox 177
inch 310
incisor 50
incubator 53
index finger 15
India 318
Indian Ocean 312
indigo 274
Indonesia 319
induce labour v 53
industrial park 299
infection 44
infertile 20
infield 228
inflatable dinghy 215
inflatable ring 265
information 261
information screen 213
in-goal area 221
inhaler 44, 109
injection 48
injury 46
ink 275
ink pad 173
inlet 61
inline skating 249
inner core 282
inner tube 207
inning 228
innocent 181

english

english

english

english

english

english

благодарности blagodarnosti • acknowledgments

DORLING KINDERSLEY would like to thank Christine Lacey for design assistance, Georgina Garner for editorial and administrative help, Kopal Agarwal, Polly Boyd, Sonia Gavira, Cathy Meeus, Antara Raghavan, and Priyanka Sharma for editorial help, Claire Bowers for compiling the DK picture credits, Nishwan Rasool for picture research, and Suruchi Bhatia, Miguel Cunha, Mohit Sharma, and Alex Valizadeh for app development and creation.

The publisher would like to thank the following for their kind permission to reproduce their photographs:
Abbreviations key: a-above; b-below/bottom; c-center; f-far; l-left; r-right; t-top)

123RF.com: Andriy Popov 34tl; Brad Wynnyk 172bc; Daniel Ernst 179tc; Hongqi Zhang 24cla, 175cr; Ingvar Bjork 60c; Kobby Dagan 259c; leonardo255 269c; Liubov Vadimovna (Luba) Nel 39cla; Ljupco Smokovski 75crb; Oleksandr Marynchenko 60bl; Olga Popova 33c; oneblink 49bc; Robert Churchill 94c; Roman Gorielov 33bc; Ruslan Kudrin 35bc, 35br; Subbotina 39cra; Sutichak Yachaingkham 39tc; Tarzhanova 37tc; Vitaly Valua 39tl; Wavebreak Media Ltd 188bl; Wilawan Khasawong 75cb; **Action Plus:** 224bc; **Alamy Images:** 154t; A.T. Willett 287bcl; Alex Segre 105ca, 195cl; Ambrophoto 24cra; Blend Images 168cr; Cultura RM 33r; Doug Houghton 107fbr; Hugh Threlfall 35tl; 176tr; Ian Allenden 48br; Ian Dagnall 270t; Levgen Chepil 250bc; Imagebroker 199tl, 249c; Keith Morris 178c; Martyn Evans 210b; MBI 175tl; Michael Burrell 213cra; Michael Foyle 184bl; Oleksiy Maksymenko 105tc; Paul Weston 168br; Prisma Bildagentur AG 246b; Radharc Images 197tr; RBtravel 112tl; Ruslan Kudrin 176tl; Sasa Huzjak 258t; Sergey Kravchenko 37ca; Sergio Azenha 270bc; Stanca Sanda (iPad is a trademark of Apple Inc., registered in the U.S. and other countries) 176bc; Stock Connection 287bcr; tarczas 35cr; Vitaly Suprun 176cl; Wavebreak Media ltd 39cl, 174b, 175tr; **Allsport/Getty Images:** 238cl; **Alvey and Towers:** 209 acr, 215bcl, 215bcr, 241cr; **Peter Anderson:** 188cbr, 271br. **Anthony Blake Photo Library:** Charlie Stebbings 114cl; John Sims 114tcl; **Andyalte:** 98tl; **Arcaid:** John Edward Linden 301tl; Martine Hamilton Knight, Architects: Chapman Taylor Partners, 213cl; Richard Bryant 301br; **Argos:** 41tcl, 66cbl, 66cl, 66br, 66bcl, 69cl, 70bcl, 71t, 77tl, 269tc, 270tl; **Axiom:** Eitan Simanor 105bcr; Ian Cumming 104t; Vicki Couchman 148cr; **Beken Of Cowes Ltd:** 215cbc; **Bosch:** 76tcr, 76tc, 76tcl; **Camera Press:** 38tr, 256tr, 257cr; Barry J. Holmes 148tr; Jane Hanger 159cr; Mary Germanou 259bc; **Corbis:** 78b; Anna Clopet 247tr; Ariel Skelley / Blend Images 52l; Bettmann 181tl, 181tr; Blue Jean Images 48bl; Bo Zauders 156t; Bob Rowan 152bl; Bob Winsett 247cbl; Brian Bailey 247br; Chris Rainer 247ctl; Craig Aurness 215bl; David H.Wells 249cbr; Dennis Marsico 274bl;

Dimitri Lundt 236bc; Duomo 211tl; Gail Mooney 277ccr; George Lepp 248c; Gerald Nowak 239b; Gunter Marx 248cr; Jack Hollingsworth 231bl; Jacqui Hurst 277cbr; James L. Amos 247bl, 191ctr, 220bcr; Jan Butchofsky 277cbc; Johnathan Blair 243cr; Jose F. Poblete 191br; Jose Luis Pelaez.Inc 153tc; Karl Weatherly 220bl, 247tcr; Kelly Mooney Photography 259tl; Kevin Fleming 249bc; Kevin R. Morris 105tr, 243tl, 243tc; Kim Sayer 249tcr; Lynn Goldsmith 258t; Macduff Everton 231bcl; Mark Gibson 249bl; Mark L. Stephenson 249tcl; Michael Pole 115tr; Michael S. Yamashita 247cticl; Mike King 247cbl; Neil Rabinowitz 214br; Pablo Corral 115bc; Paul A. Sounders 169br, 249ctcl; Paul J. Sutton 224c, 224br; Phil Schermeister 227b, 248tr; R. W Jones 309; Richard Morrell 189bc; Rick Doyle 241cr; Robert Holmes 97br, 277ctc; Roger Ressmeyer 169tr; Russ Schleipman 229; The Purcell Team 211ctr; Vince Streano 194t; Wally McNamee 220br, 220bcl, 224bl; Wavebreak Media LTD 191bc; Yann Arhus-Bertrand 249tl; **Demetrio Carrasco / Dorling Kindersley (c) Herge / Les Editions Casterman:** 124bl; **Dorling Kindersley:** Banbury Museum 35c; Five Napkin Burger 152t; **Dixons:** 270cl, 270cr, 270bl, 270bcl, 270bcr, 270ccr; **Dreamstime.com:** Alexander Podshivalov 179tr, 191cr; Alexxl66 268tl; Andersastphoto 176tc; Andrey Popov 191bl; Arne9001 190tl; Chaoss 26c; Designsstock 269cl; Monkey Business Images 26clb; Paul Michael Hughes 162tr; Serghei Starus 190bc; Isselee 292fcrb; Zerbor 296tr; **Education Photos:** John Walmsley 26tl; **Empics Ltd:** Adam Day 236br; Andy Heading 243c; Steve White 249cbc; **Getty Images:** 48bcl, 94tr, 100t, 114bcr, 154bl, 287tr; David Leahy 162tl; Don Farrall / Digital Vision 176c; Ethan Miller 270bl; Inti St Clair 179bl; Liam Norris 188br; Sean Justice / Digital Vision 24br; **Dennis Gilbert:** 106tc; **Hulsta:** 70t; **Ideal Standard Ltd:** 72r; **The Image Bank/Getty Images:** 58; **Impact Photos:** Eliza Armstrong 115tr; Philip Achache 246t; **The Interior Archive:** Henry Wilson, Alfie's Market 114bl; Luke White, Architect: David Mikhail, 59tl; Simon Upton, Architect: Phillippe Starck, St Martins Lane Hotel 100bc; **iStockphoto.com:** asterix0597 163tl; EdStock 190br; RichLegg 26bc; SorinVidis 27cr; **Jason Hawkes Aerial Photography:** 216t; **Dan Johnson:** 35r; **Kos Pictures Source:** 215cbl, 240tc, 240tr; David Williams 216b; **Lebrecht Collection:** Kate Mount 169bc; **MP Visual.com:** Mark Swallow 202t; **NASA:** 280cr, 280ccl, 281tl; **P&O Princess Cruises:** 214bl; **P A Photos:** 181br; **The Photographers' Library:** 186bl, 186bc, 186t; **Plain and Simple Kitchens:** 66t; **Powerstock Photolibrary:** 169tl, 256t, 287tc; **PunchStock:** Image Source 195tr; **Rail Images:** 208c, 208 cbl, 209br; **Red Consultancy:** Odeon cinemas 257br; **Redferns:** 259br; Nigel Crane 259c;

Rex Features: 106br, 259tc, 259tr, 259bl, 280b; Charles Ommaney 114tcr; J.F.F Whitehead 243cl; Patrick Barth 101tl; Patrick Frilet 189cbl; Scott Wiseman 287bl; **Royalty Free Images:** Getty Images/Eyewire 154bl; **Science & Society Picture Library:** Science Museum 202b; **Science Photo Library:** IBM Research 190cla; NASA 281cr; **SuperStock:** Ingram Publishing 62; Juanma Aparicio / age fotostock 172t; Nordic Photos 269tl; **Skyscan:** 168t, 182c, 298; Quick UK Ltd 212; **Sony:** 268bc; **Robert Streeter:** 154br; **Neil Sutherland:** 82tr, 83tl, 90t, 118, 188ctr, 196tl, 196tr, 299cl, 299bl; **The Travel Library:** Stuart Black 264t; **Travelex:** 97cl; **Vauxhall:** Technik 198t, 199tl, 199tr, 199cl, 199cr, 199cctcl, 199cctcr, 199tcl, 199tccr, 200; **View Pictures:** Dennis Gilbert, Architects: ACDP Consulting, 106t; Dennis Gilbert, Chris Wilkinson Architects, 209tr; Peter Cook, Architects: Nicholas Crimshaw and partners, 208t; **Betty Walton:** 185br; **Colin Walton:** 2, 4, 7, 9, 10, 28, 40l, 42, 56, 92, 95c, 99tl, 99tcl, 102, 116, 120t, 138t, 146, 150t, 160, 170, 191ctcl, 192, 218, 252, 260br, 260l, 261tr, 261c, 261cr, 271cbl, 271cbr, 271ctl, 278, 287br, 302.

DK PICTURE LIBRARY:
Akhil Bahkshi; Patrick Baldwin; Geoff Brightling; British Museum; John Bulmer; Andrew Butler; Joe Cornish; Brian Cosgrove; Andy Crawford and Kit Hougton; Philip Dowell; Alistair Duncan; Gables; Bob Gathany; Norman Hollands; Kew Gardens; Peter James Kindersley; Vladimir Kozlik; Sam Lloyd; London Northern Bus Company Ltd; Tracy Morgan; David Murray and Jules Selmes; Musée Vivant du Cheval, France; Museum of Broadcast Communications; Museum of Natural History; NASA; National History Museum; Norfolk Rural Life Museum; Stephen Oliver; RNLI; Royal Ballet School; Guy Ryecart; Science Museum; Neil Setchfield; Ross Simms and the Winchcombe Folk Police Museum; Singapore Symphony Orchestra; Smart Museum of Art; Tony Souter; Erik Svensson and Jeppe Wikstrom; Sam Tree of Keygrove Marketing Ltd; Barrie Watts; Alan Williams; Jerry Young.

Additional photography by Colin Walton.

Colin Walton would like to thank:
A&A News, Uckfield; Abbey Music, Tunbridge Wells; Arena Mens Clothing, Tunbridge Wells; Burrells of Tunbridge Wells; Gary at Di Marco's; Jeremy's Home Store, Tunbridge Wells; Noakes of Tunbridge Wells; Ottakar's, Tunbridge Wells; Selby's of Uckfield; Sevenoaks Sound and Vision; Westfield, Royal Victoria Place, Tunbridge Wells.

All other images © Dorling Kindersley
For further information see: www.dkimages.com